John Wesley Hill

Twin city Methodism

Being a history of the Methodist Episcopal church in Minneapolis and St. Paul

John Wesley Hill

Twin city Methodism
Being a history of the Methodist Episcopal church in Minneapolis and St. Paul

ISBN/EAN: 9783337111618

Printed in Europe, USA, Canada, Australia, Japan

Cover: Foto ©Andreas Hilbeck / pixelio.de

More available books at **www.hansebooks.com**

TWIN CITY METHODISM

— A HISTORY OF THE —

Methodist Episcopal Church

— IN —

MINNEAPOLIS AND ST. PAUL, MINN.

WITH

Illustrated Biographical Department Containing
Pen Pictures of Preachers and People.

BY REV. J. WESLEY HILL, D. D.

MINNEAPOLIS:
PRICE BROS. PUBLISHING CO.
JANUARY 6, 1895

TO OUR POSTERITY

WHO HAVE DONE MUCH FOR US

IN AWAKENING US TO MAKE OUR PART

OF THE WORLD READY FOR

THEIR COMING

AND WHO WILL WISH TO KNOW

WHAT MANNER OF

ANCESTORS THEY HAD, THIS BOOK IS

AFFECTIONATELY DEDICATED

Index

Business

Preface

Twin City Methodism is the first work of the kind that has as yet been published in the history of the Methodist Episcopal Church. It does not claim the cyclopedia style, for it is limited to the interests of local Methodism, and has not dealt with these facts in an elaborate manner. It is a plain, simple presentation to the friends of the church and to the general reader, of the chief events of Twin City Methodism, as gleaned from history and biography.

The size of the book is no measure of the available material, for at times the editor has been overwhelmed by the very wealth of information which he has been compelled to condense.

Twin City Methodism makes no pretension of original investigation, nor is it weighted down with wearying discussions. Its aim is to be a hand book of Methodist information, some of which has been scattered through various publications, while much has never been placed in book form.

It briefly traces the Wesleyan stream from its beginnings in these cities, down to its present majestic flow. This current of Methodist history is well typed by the "Father of Waters" which connects the Twin Cities. Its head waters arise noiselessly and unseen, steadily gathering breadth and volume, until the roar of St. Anthony tells the story of its cumulated power. And so from these early streams of influence Twin City Methodism has enlarged into a mighty river of Christian life and power, bearing upon its bosom the treasures of civilization, and the destiny of the great cities which it has enriched with the commerce of the skies.

Not only is the gradual growth and development of this history followed through all the important events and emergencies that constitute it, but much attention has been given to Twin City Methodism in its relation to the individual man; for after all, Methodist history is but the story of her people. It is not the account of the sublime faith and heroism of the few, but rather the picture of the many, in all their relations, peculiarities and identities, struggling together to establish the Church of Christ.

We are thus brought to see the motive principle of personalities, and to be inspired by pondering their achievements and measuring their influence for good upon the world.

As portraiture is the demand of the times and contributes so much to the understanding of biography, it has been made a prominent feature of this work to have every sketch. as far as possible, embellished with a photo engraving.

Pictures of home surroundings add so much to biography that it has been deemed desirable to insert views of residences, which give to the work a new feature, the portrayal of dwelling places which in the future will become the ancestral homes of Twin City Methodists. Scattered through this book will be found brief business sketches of leading Methodists and citizens, which will not only give some faint conception of the vast commercial strides of the Twin Cities but will be of inestimable value to young men, showing the essential conditions of business success, and illustrating the theories of commercial colleges in the achievements of living men. Thus, covering the entire field of Methodist life and activity, this book will prove not only valuable to the Methodist reader, but to the general public, for in it will be found much that pertains to the public life and prosperity.

The editor takes pleasure in referring to the assistance which he has received in the preparation of this work from Rev. J. F. Chaffee, D. D.; Rev. William McKinley, D. D., and Rev. Chauncey Hobart. He also returns thanks to many of his brethren in the ministry and membership for important facts furnished.

The enterprising publishers, Price Bros. Publishing Co., have done themselves great credit by the style and mechanical execution of the work. Bramblett and Beygeh have done all the art work, the choice character of which should convince the most fastidious that it is not necessary to send away from home for first-class work in this line. We are under obligations to Leslie & McAfee, the popular paper house, for the fine quality of paper furnished by them for this book. Doubtless some mistakes will soon come to light, but having been corrected we trust that Twin City Methodism will prove interesting and profitable to the present generation, and furnish at least some important material for the future historian.

J. WESLEY HILL.

Introduction

Cities have been called "storm centers." They have also been long held as civilizers. Metalic balls are sometimes polished by being tied in a bag together and knocked about. Men in a city knock against each other, knock off the rough corners, polish up the surfaces, enkindle each other's thought, fire up their genius, and reach elevations in intellectual activity and noble endeavor not otherwise attainable. Cities are centers of power. They are social forts. They send out the styles and fashions for the country, and draw into themselves like great maelstroms, and consume in themselves all the best and greatest and strongest of the land. The best cattle, best horses, best grain, best fruit, best products, also the best workmen, best tradesmen, best artists, best lawyers, best preachers, best of social beauty and life—all drift on the invisible and resistless current that moves steadily and forever toward the cities, the centers of human want and power. They epitomize the nations. They are microcosms of the races. They make destiny. Great as are the cities, great enough to be the luminous points and peaks, piercing the horizon as one looks over the ages, yet they are only accumulated masses of individuals. As the sun cannot light up and guild the broad front of the mountain except as it lights up and guilds each particle of sand and soil in all that front; sends some individual ray of light down on to each tiniest point of exposure, so the sweep and history making power of a great city must come from the reflections of the deeds and purposes of each of the unnumbered individuals that live and love and act and die in its swarming thousands. The histories of these individuals, and incipient institutions, and solitary churches become the store-house of knowledge from which the historian finally brings forth the wonderful bulk and cumulative greatness of the story of the people. Without these histories there could be no antiquity, no manifest national growth and social evolution. A nation without these histories would be a man without a memory.

Time was when there was but one man in a nation, and that was the king. All worthy events emanated from him and gravitated about him and his doings. The great libraries of past histories are filled with the accounts of what he did. History was his story. But those times are gone. No longer is the brain of a nation on one seat, and its thinking done by one brain. Now thinking is distributed. Events have popular parentage. Everybody is interested in everybody. Thus it happens that the great Historian is the man who writes the history of the People. Green, in his great History of the English People, tells of the growth of ideas, of the maturing of liberties, of the multiplication and enlargement of industries: in short he discovers in history the *individual man*. The battles of kings and the fate of empires are incidental matters, side lights exhibiting the common man.

This unique, unpretentious volume, called "TWIN CITY METHODISM" comes out of the spirit of our times and enters into a field of industry and investigation that is barely rising on the horizon, and whose continental treasures stretch away in uncounted leagues. The individual grains in this new continent may seem insignificant, but their aggregate is unmeasured. Some of these biographies may appear to be of the merest local interest, yet they will make up the record of a great church and of a conquering people. We are not always wisest judges concerning those nearest us. Even a prophet was said to be without honor in his own country. Aristides the Just, standing by the box on the square where men were blackballed and thus driven into exile, was asked by an ignorant Athenian who did not recognize him, if he could write. He replied, "Yes." "Then," said he: "write on this shell the name of Aristides." "Why? What harm hath he done the state?" asked the statesman. "None that I know of," said the man, "but I am tired of hearing him called 'Aristides, the Just'." The old hero wrote his own name on the shell, saw it dropped into the box and went into voluntary banishment. The man next to him in the public

square sent him into exile, but even wandering there he carried
with him the glory of Athens and by his simple greatness helps
to carry that same glory through many centuries. It may be that
the brief and unpretentious biographies, so quietly dropped into
these pages, with so little appreciation of what they are, may yet
prove helps by which the glory of our fair cities may be floated in
the memory of men.

There is in this volume an omen of good to our Methodism.
We are *bound together*. We may also see a fair degree of connec-
tionalism. We are members of one family. We are illustrating the
old law of strength in union. Contributions of life and spirit in
this book are parts of that great concentration of purpose that cannot be resisted. The old fable of the bundle of sticks which the
dying chief gave to his sons and which they could not break,
taught the value of union. He separated the sticks and they broke
them easily. This emphasized the weakness of separation. This
book may help us as a people to stay in the bundle.

The great nations are not those that grow by conquest and
piracy, but those that grow by colonization, that save their increase.
The problem of Methodism is this, to save her increase. Converts
at Methodist altars have kept the great orthodox churches from
death. If she could reclaim her own, she would be more than a
match to all other social and religious forces. The movement inspiring this book looks to the arrest of emigrations, and the awakening of proper immigration, and the careful housing of all our off-
spring. It also hopes to enkindle a resistless *esprit de corps*.

In Westminster Abbey one walks among the buried kings of
England. But in Smithfield one walks over the ashes of the living
kings of mankind. These were the men that made the world
tolerable as a residence. In Methodist history and experience one
sees the heroes of the race. These are the men that turned the
world upside down. Magnificent ancestry and richest inheritance.
It remains for us to so combine and handle our forces that we shall
have both Westminster Abbey and Smithfield.

Centuries before these Twin Cities are as old as London, men
shall marvel at the millions of their citizens, wonder where in the
unbroken blocks of trade the old lines between the cities were

drawn, and shall search their ancient records to learn the stories of the youth of these great municipalities. As scholars read with delight to-day the stories concerning Romulus and his first wall, of Numa and his first laws: of the creeping of the populations upon the seven hills. so in the life of these Twin Cities men shall find inspiration to search out their early foundations, and study our guiding principles, and follow our growing dominion. This book may yet glimmer like a taper directing the researches of patient scholars of the coming future to correct knowledge concerning institutions and men of our time. The Church that has called it into being shall shine like a Divine torch illumining a pathway beyond the stars.

C. H. FOWLER.

Minneapolis Methodism

In July, 1849, Rev. Matthew Sorin, a "supernumerary" preacher belonging to the Philadelphia Conference, while visiting at the Falls of St. Anthony, organized the few Methodists living there into a class, with John Draper for a leader. This was the first step for the establishment of a Methodist church. Minnesota became a territory March 3d, 1849. The first church of St. Anthony was organized four months later, July 7th. The whole population of the territory was 4,680, and that of St. Anthony, now Minneapolis, about 300. The village was about two years old, and was little more than a company of settlers living in small, unpainted cabins scattered along the river bank. A ferry boat made irregular trips across the river not far from the present Central avenue bridge. A small log, schoolhouse on Third street, now University avenue, between Second and Third avenues southeast, served the various Protestant churches for religious services.

In 1849, the Minnesota District of the Wisconsin Conference was formed, with Rev. C. Hobart as Presiding Elder. The first stationed preacher, Rev. Enos Stevens, was appointed by the Wisconsin Conference of 1849, as a missionary to St. Anthony Falls. He was a typical Methodist pioneer missionary, such as most of the circuit riders of early Methodism were. His circuit included St Anthony, Fort Snelling, Red Rock, Cottage Grove, Point Douglass and Bissel's Mound. The next preacher was Rev. C. A. Newcomb, who remained two years. Rev. E. W. Merrill, a local preacher, served the church in 1851-2. Rev. Eli C. Jones was appointed to this mission in 1852 and remained two years. During his pastorate, a frame building for church purposes was erected, at a cost of $1,000. Rev. S. T. Creighton took charge of the church in 1854, and was followed the next year by Rev. Andrew J. Nelson. Rev. Sias Bolles became pastor in 1856. A parsonage was built for him. The church building was enlarged during this pastorate. The financial troubles of 1857 threw the struggling church into serious straights, but through the good management of Rev. J. F. Chaffee, the society was able to hold its own. During his two years of service, large additions were made to the membership. His pastorate was blessed with

FIRST CHURCH

one of the most remarkable revivals ever known in the history of Northwest Methodism. A year and a half of peace and quietude followed under the pastorate of Rev. Cyrus Brooks. He was followed by Rev. Thomas Day. After him came Rev. E. R. Lathrop, who served a year and a half in 1861-2. He was appointed chaplain in the Tenth Regiment of Minnesota Volunteers, and his second year was finished by Rev. Wm. McKinley, who remained until 1864, through the dark years of the civil war. The pastors who followed were, C. F. Wright; F. W. Berry, who after six months of service, died, February 19th, 1866: Harvey Webb, who remained three years; J. W. Shank; D. Cobb; W. W. Satterlee; J. R. Creighton; S. G. Gale; Harvey Webb; J. W. Martin; T. McClary; Robert Forbes; A. C. Williams; John Stafford; C. A. VanAnda; W. C. Rice; J. F. Stout; Thomas McClary; and Willian Fielder, the present pastor.

The old church building was sold for $200 and was moved across the street. The new edifice was built on the same lots and cost about $7,000. The basement and lecture room were finished so as to be dedicated in December, 1872. Rev. Samuel Fallows, now Bishop of the Reformed Episcopal Church, preached the dedication sermon. During the pastorate of Rev. S. G. Gale, 1874-5, the main audience room was completed and dedicated. It had seats for 500. The building, with parsonage, was valued at $20,000. This property was sold in 1890 and the same year the church obtained possession of the house of worship previously occupied by the Olivet Baptist Church, on the corner of Fifth street and Ninth avenue southeast, where its services are now held. The church property is valued at $35,000; the membership is about 350; the Sunday School numbers over 200 and prosperity characterizes all the departments of church work.

WESLEY CHURCH

A Methodist class was organized on the west side of the river in 1852 by Rev. A. C. Godfrey, a brother of Ard Godfrey, who was at that time superintendent of the saw mills on the East side. The class was composed of Rev. Godfrey and wife, Sister Tuttle and her mother, and Mrs. Steele, the mother of Franklin Steele. At this time there were but few houses on the west side and most of them were rough shanties. In November, 1852, the first quarterly meeting of the circuit, of which Minneapolis was a part, was held at the home of Brother Godfrey. In 1853, E. C. Jones, of St. Anthony, was asked to take the class on the west side, and soon after this the Sunday school was started. The first regular place of meeting was in the land office which was then situated about where the corner of Eighth. avenue south and Washington avenue is now located. A short time afterwards the place of meeting was changed to a hall in a building which was situated on the property now occupied by the St. James Hotel. Here the little class and Sunday school worked on without a preacher until the annual conference of 1856. when Rev. R. McDonald was assigned to that charge. He, however, left the work. and Rev. William H. St. Claire was appointed. The people began to think of a church, but it was not untill 1857, under the pastorate of Rev. J. D. Rich, that the little white church on Third avenue south, between Fourth and Fifth streets, was built and dedicated. Rev. J. F. Chaffee, then pastor of St. Anthony, and now Presiding Elder of the Minneapolis District, assisted in the dedication. In 1858 T. M. Gossard was appointed pastor. In 1859 Rev. J. O. Rich took charge of the church. During this year there was a good revival. In 1860 Rev. J. F. Chaffee was appointed, and at the end of two years he reported to the Conference 159 members and 30 probationers.

In 1860, the Minneapolis District was organized, and Rev. D. Brooks was made Presiding Elder. . In 1862 Dr. Chaffee was made Presiding Elder and Rev. Daniel Cobb became pastor at Minneapolis. In his second year he was elected chaplain of the Sixth, Minnesota and went to the war, and Dr. John Quigley followed him as pastor. The church had been increasing rapidly, and again the members realized the necessity of a new building. Suiting action to the thought. two lots were bought on the corner of Seventh street and First avenue south, and a church started in 1866. They had thought of calling the new edifice the Seventh Street M. E. Church, but 1866 being the centennial of Methodism it was decided to name it "Centenary". In 1867 Dr. Chaffee became pastor. and in 1868 the new church was formally dedicated. With the new location and elegant equipments Centenary Church forged ahead. During two years there were nearly 300 conversions. Rev. J. W. McGregor was appointed pastor in 1870 and Rev. G. C. Wells in 1871-2. Brother Wells died in May, 1873, and his year was filled out by Rev. J. L. Fasig. Rev. A. Hollington became pastor in 1873 and officiated for one year. Rev. S. McChesney followed in 1874-5. In 1876-7 Rev. Daniel Cobb was again appointed. From 1878 to 1879 Rev. Mr. Loyd was pastor. In 1879 Rev. C. A. VanAnda took charge of Centenary and remained the full term of three years.

During previous years several churches had been organized on the west side of the river in addition to Centenary, and each

WESLEY CHURCH

one of them drew members from the mother church. In 1870 what is now Thirteeth Avenue Church was organized. In 1872 Foss Church was added, and in 1875 Hennepin Avenue Church. Franklin Avenue followed. Rev. Mr. Wagner became pastor in 1882 and he, too, remained the full term of three years. Dr. Van Anda then came back for another three years, and he was followed by Dr. Miller. All these years were marked by steady growth and again the church quarters seemed to be cramped. Already the idea of a new edifice was slowly revolving in the minds of the faithful and the thought would occasionally creep out. In 1889 Rev. H. H. French, a young man from the East, was appointed pastor. The congregations increased and the new church idea took quicker motion. Centenary energy could not be supressed. and finally, in 1891. ground was broken on the corner of Grant street and First avenue south for the new church. Again suiting the name of the church to the sequence of Methodist events, the year being the anniversary of the death of John Wesley, the new church was called "Wesley".

In this sketch of Wesley Church we have necessarily used the pastors as way-marks and guides in considering its growth. But the lives of many of its parishioners are also entitled to special mention. The three Harrison brothers were in the fore-front of the pioneers. Dr. Goodrich also was a hard worker, and the church records all through the years have been enriched by such names as Bryant, Hamor, Lillibridge. Moses, Calkins, Galpin and Stanton. The women were not in the rear. If one could see them trudging the rounds collecting the weekly subscriptions to the fund which was to buy the lots for the Centenary Church to stand upon, he could hardly repress his admiration for the faithfulness and energy of the gentler sex. Mrs. Geo. Galpin, Mrs. Annie Goheen, Mrs. H. F. Lillibridge. Mrs. William Harrison and many others are entitled to great credit for the part they have taken in the growth and development of Centenary.

When the plan for the new church was first outlined everything was ready except the cash. Where could the money come from? The growth of Minneapolis had been rapid and had made Centenary Church property valuable. But what was its value to the members of the church if they could not realize that value from it? Here, Horatio F. Lillibridge, now in heaven. came forward and shouldered the burden. His credit was good and he could get all the necessary funds. He purchased the church property at a valuation $25,000 higher than the property is worth to-day, but lest some cavilling critic should think he took it as a speculation he gave the church a contract that if they could get more for the property at any time within two years he would gladly allow them to take the larger sum. Mr. Lillibridge mortgaged his best property to procure funds for pushing the work.

So Wesley was built. A beautiful stone structure, magnificient in its architecture and beautiful and complete in all its appointments. The cost of the little white church on Third avenue south was a few hundred. The cost of Centenary Church was $42,000. And now comes Wesley Church costing in round numbers $150,000. These figures indicate in some measure the growth and prosperity of the Mother of Methodism in Minneapolis on the west side of the river. She still has on her rolls a few members who were with her in her infancy. These have witnessed the early struggles, the steady and marvelous growth and then the final crowning triumph.

SIMPSON

In 1882 J. G. Teter was appointed to Twenty-Fourth street and Simpson. Under the direction of J. F. Chaffee, who was that fall appointed to the Minneapolis District, two lots were purchased at the corner of Twenty-Fourth street and Twenty-Third avenue south, and an old church was purchased of the Swedish Methodists which was moved onto these lots. At the same time, two lots were purchased on the corner of First avenue south and Twenty-eighth street, and a chapel which is now the lecture room of Simpson Church, was built. This church has had a most prosperous career. It is in the midst of a large, thrifty, American population and has, beyond doubt, a growing outlook. The present edifice was built during the pastorate of Rev. J. M. Bull, at a cost of $17,000. It will seat five hundred. It was a great undertaking for the society at the time and some debt was incurred, but happily during the present pastorate of Peter Clare, this indebtness has been removed. This is a well organized, well worked society and no church in the city has the promise of greater out-come. The following have been the pastors: 1882-5, J. G. Teter; 1885-8, J M. Bull; 1888-91, W. K. Marshall; 1891-4, Peter Clare. Present membership, 400.

HENNEPIN AVENUE

In the early part of the winter of 1875, about ninety members went out from Centenary Church and were organized, under the direction of Bishop Merrill, as the Hennepin Avenue Church. It is not necessary to discuss the merits of the cause which led to this separation. But the people who went out, were, in a large degree, the builders of the church home which they left. They built

HENNEPIN AVENUE

however, cheerfully and heroically, in mid-winter, a wooden structure —they called it a tabernacle. It was built on the corner of Eighth street and First avenue north, and was dedicated by Dr. Chaffee. The society called as their pastor, A. Hollington, who had served two years previously, for one year, as pastor of Centenary. At the end of one year, he was succeeded by C. M. Heard who served the full term of three years. During this time, T. A. Harrison purchased the present magnificient site where the church stands, corner of Hennepin avenue and Tenth street north. The tabernacle was moved onto the back part of the lot where the parsonage building now stands. At the close of Dr. Heard's term the membership had increased to 125. He was succeeded by Dr. Chaffee, during whose term of three years the presenth Curch was built and paid for at a cost of about $65,000, and the membership was doubled. The parsonage building, a double tenement, was erected later, half of which makes a commodious home for the pastor and his family, the other half

INTERIOR VIEW OF HENNEPIN AVENUE

being rented. This church has stood foremost, not only in the city, but in the conference, as a liberal supporter of all our Methodist work, having taken a leading part not only in City Missions and Church Extension work, but in all our benevolent causes, especially giving liberally to foreign missions and to Hamline University. Even if others have done according to their ability, it is fitting that this church should receive this meed of praise. The pastorate has been as follows: 1875-6, A. Hollington; 1876-9. C. M. Heard; 1879-82, J. F. Chaffee; 1882-4, A. C. Williams; 1884-7, J. L. Pitner; 1887-9, R. M. McKaig; 1889-91, O. H. Tiffany, who died in this city, October 24th 1891. After Dr. Tiffany's decease, F. O. Holman, who had been previously appointed assistant pastor, succeeded to the pastorate. After three years of the most brilliant success, Dr. Holman's health was so imperilled that he was compelled to seek the benefits of a more congenial climate. Rev. J. Wesley Hill, pastor of Fowler Church, succeeded to the pulpit from May until the conference in October, when Rev. E. L. Watson was transferred from the Baltimore Conference and appointed pastor. His pastorate is opening most auspiciously, and prophesies are heard on all sides of great success. The church is valued at $116,000 and the parsonage at $28,000. The membership is over 600.

TRINITY

TRINITY

In 1884 F. I. Fisher was appointed to Taylor Street. The work was feeble then and gave little promise of future greatness. The succeeding pastors have been: 1885-6, B. F. Kerfoot; 1886-9, James Door: 1889-92, C. M. Heard: 1893, W. K. Marshall.

During Dr. Marshall's first year the house of worship was greatly enlarged and his pastorate from the first proved a great success. The name of the church has been changed to Trinity. The Epworth League of that church is flourishing, and the Junior League is quite phenominal, having a membership of nearly 200. This charge is in the northeast part of the city, and is surrounded by a large and growing community, and will doubtless become one of our most important churches. The church is valued at $6,000, and the membership is over 200.

FOREST HEIGHTS

FOREST HEIGHTS

The Forest Heights M. E. Church, located at 2022 James avenue north, is one of the younger and most promising societies in the city. It origniated as a mission in the spring of 1885, the Rev. Mr. Campbell acting as pastor for several months. To him belongs the credit of establishing the work. Nathaniel McCarthy, of the Hennepin Avenue Church, acted as superintendent until the mission became an independent chapel. C. E. Olmstead organized the class and was appointed leader and has continued to fill that office most acceptably until the present time. In the fall of 1885, Rev. J. B. Freeman was appointed to the mission and labored successfully for several months. He was followed by Rev. E. S. Pilling, under whose administration the little band undertook to build a church. It was a great undertaking, but the practical sympathy and help of the Hennepin Avenue Church made success possible, and in the beginning of 1886 the present church building was erected. The Rev. J. B. Higgins was appointed to the charge in the fall of 1887. During his brief but helpful pastorate, the parsonage was built on the lot adjoining the church. At the close of a successful year of service, he was followed by Rev. C. A. Cressy, appointed in 1888. In 1889 Rev. C. N. Stowers entered upon the duties of this pastorate. He spent two prosperous years and entered upon the third year of service with greatly impaired health. He was compelled to resign his charge in the following January. The Rev. Wm. Hanson was appointed to the work in February, 1892. He was succeeded in 1894 by Brother Clemens, who is making an excellent start. The membership numbers 150. The Sunday School has about 200 pupils enrolled. An Epworth League numbering about 40 members, and the Junior Epworth League with about 80 members, are important factors in the life and work of the church, and they hold large promise for its future power and prosperity.

WESTERN AVENUE

In 1883 David Tice was appointed to the City Mission. Out of this, under his labors, grew the Western Avenue Church. He began his work on Western avenue in one of his own buildings, and as a fruit of his labor the church was organized by the Presiding Elder, J. F. Chaffee, under the name of Western Avenue M. E. Church to which Brother Tice was appointed pastor from 1884 to 1886. During that time he built the present structure which was dedicated in the fall of 1886 by J. F. Chaffee. That was work in which from the beginning the pastor largely made "brick without straw." The church has made a good record, but it has been the result of a hard struggle; among other things it has been embarrassed by a heavy indebtedness, but under the faithful labors of Rev. R. R. Atchison and backed by the indomitable will of Bishop Fowler and the liberal people, the whole debt has been provided

WESTERN AVENUE

for. This provision was not a farce for the debt has been paid and the mortgage burned in the presence of a delighted audience, December 31st, 1893. The pastorate has been: 1883-6, David Tice; 1886-9, J. W. Martin; 1889-91, R. M. Carter; 1891-2, J. J. Crist; 1892-3, R. R. Atchison. The present pastor is Thomas Mc-Clary. The church is valued at $10,000. The membership is about 225.

TWENTY-FOURTH STREET

In 1883 David Morgan was appointed to Twenty-fourth Street and Taylor Street, during which year a house of worship was built at Taylor street and dedicated by Bishops Foss and Warren. After that year brother Morgan was pastor at the Twenty-fourth Street until the fall of 1886, when he was succeeded by R. R. Atchison, who held the charge for one year. The other pastors have been: 1887-9. H. J. Van Fossen; 1889-91, J. C. Gullet; 1891-3, A. F. Thompson.

This church has not altogether fulfilled its early promise. This is in part, at least, owing to the fact that the population about

TWENTY-FOURTH STREET

it has become mostly foreign. But this ought not to prevent its success, and must not. The church is not large nor elegant, but it is comfortable; far better than the beginnings of many of our stronger churches, and the parsonage is comfortable though small. The debt on it has been removed through the willingness of the people, the persistence of the pastor and the helpfulness of Presiding Elder Stafford and Bishop Fowler. The church should take courage and make for itself a name. It has a membership of 115, with property valued at $4,000.

In 1882 Broadway appears in the list of conference appointments with J. A. Wright, pastor. During the year previous, under the pastorate of Rev. R. Forbes at First Church, and through his determined lead, a chapel was reclaimed from others not rightfully in possession, as he believed, and moved onto the lot where it now stands, on Broadway. Its history has been one of severe struggle from the first and the end is not yet. But it is a little Methodist

BROADWAY

Church in the right place and success will surely come. About two years ago, under the pastorate of J. E. Henderson, it enlarged its house of worship, and now has an inviting, commodious church building. The following have been the pastors: 1882-6, J. A. Wright; 1886-9, C. B. Brecount: 1889-90, James Castles; 1890-1, R. A. Sadlier: 1891-2, J. E. Henderson: 1892-3, W. L. Langvell: 1893, J. A. Wright, who has inspired the church with larger faith and heroism and greatly increased the membership and congregation.

FOSS

In 1871-2 Thos. McClary had charge of Seventh Street and North Mission. During the year a little house of worship was built on Third avenue north near Washington avenue, and was called the Washington Avenue Church. Here the little society worked and worshipped with varying success, until the pastorate of J. R. Berry, which extended from 1880 to 1882, during which time the Foss Church was built and dedicated. J. B. Hingeley is the

FOSS

present pastor. The church has been very much improved during the year at a cost of $1200; value of the property, $12,000; membership, about 200 The pastorate has been as follows: 1871-2, Thos. McClary; 1872-4, John Stafford; 1874-5, J. T. Latton; 1875-8, L. Hall: 1878-80, N. M. Learned: 1880-2, J. R. Berry; 1882-3, H. J. Crist: 1883-5, J. M. Bull: 1885-8, F. O. Holman; 1888-9, S. B. Warner; 1889-90, D. R. Gray; 1890-3, B. Longley; 1893-4, J. B. Hingeley.

FRANKLIN AVENUE

In 1871 a little Church called Hobart Chapel was built on a leased lot. It was moved under the pastorate of N. M. Learned the same year, to the corner of Franklin avenue and Fifth avenue south, where the Franklin Avenue Church now stands. But Franklin Avenue first appears in the list of appointments as a part of the Seventh Street charge in 1876, J. W. Martin, pastor. In 1877, however, it appears as a distinct charge, to be supplied by C. Snyder. The Sunday school was organized in 1871 by Hon.

FRANKLIN AVENUE

J. T. Wyman. The present church edifice was built in 1881, under the pastorate of N. M. Learned, Joseph Dean, since deceased, having been a liberal contributor to the building fund. During the past few years it has secured and paid for an exceedingly eligible site for a new church on the corner of Portland avenue and Twenty-second street. It has had a fairly prosperous career, is in the midst of one of the finest communities in the city, and should, and doubtless will, have a great future. Its pastorate has been: 1877-8, C. Snyder, supply; 1878-80. John Pemberton; 1880-2, N. M. Learned; 1882-5, C. A. Van Anda; 1885-6, F. G. Wagner; 1886-8, N. W. Jordan; 1888-9, C. N. Stowers; 1889-3, R. N. McKaig; 1893, F. D. Newhouse; 1894, Frank Doran. Its church property is valued at $25,000 and the membership stands at about 300. This church only needs to "go forward" and build a house of worship that shall be in character with that part of the city, in order to make sure for itself a great destiny.

THIRTEENTH AVENUE

THIRTEENTH AVENUE

The Seventh Street Methodist Church, now Thirteeth avenue, was organized by J. F. Chaffee in 1870-1 while he was in charge of the City Mission. A house of worship was erected at a cost of about $7,000, on Seventh street and Twelfth avenue south, and was dedicated July, 1871, free of debt. This church is now owned and occupied by the Swedish Methodists. During the pastorate of J. B. Starkey, 1882-5, the church, under the Presiding Eldership of

J. F. Chaffee, was organized and incorporated as the Thirteenth
Avenue Church and the present house of worship was dedicated
free of debt by Bishop C. B. Foss. The building of these two
churches, the Seventh Street and Thirteeth Avenue, was made
possible by the great liberality of T. A. and H. G. Harrison, and
their sister, Mrs. A. H. Goheen. The present church property is
valued at $13,000, and the membership is about three hundred.
The present pastor is F. M. Rule, under whose earnest pastorate
the church is in a flourishing condition.. The following pastors
have served this church: 1870-1, J. F. Chaffee: 1871-4, Thomas
McClary; 1874-7, J. W. Martin; 1877-8, J. R. Akers; 1878-80, J.
R. Creighton; 1880-2, W. W. Satterlee; 1882-5, J. B. Starkey;
1885-8, W. K. Marshall; 1888-91. Thos. McClary; 1891-3, J. B.
Hingeley; 1893-4, F. M. Rule.

PARK AVENUE

During the summer of 1893, inspired by Dr. Stafford and
Bishop Fowler, the City Mission and Church Extension authorities
determined to inaugurate a new church enterprise, which they
finally did by the purchase of two lots on the corner of Park avenue
and Thirty-fourth street which is an exceedingly eligible site, in
the midst of a fine, large and almost churchless community. The
lots cost $3,000 and only $150 was paid on them because of the
hard times. The chapel was also built in the same way; namely,
on credit. It was dedicated, however, free of debt, November 5th,
by Bishop Fowler; Bishop Warren preaching, and Dr. Chaffee
begging. Since then. taxes. accrued interest and the balance of
the first thousand dollars on the lots have been paid. It has been
a hard pull, with the pull still on because a small part of this has
been advanced by the treasurer of the City Missionary and
Church Extension Society. The amount advanced, will doubtless
soon be paid by the churches whose collections have not been
taken. T. W. Stout is the young and vigorous pastor of this
promising church. Already it has a membership of something
more than 50, and the time is not far distant when the Park
Avenue Church will stand among the foremost churches of Minneapolis Methodism.

CAMDEN PLACE

In 1886 the North Church, Lake street and Bloomington Avenue, all appear in the list of appointments for the first time, but the work at the North Church, which is now called Camden Place, is much older than that. It was formerly called Shingle Creek appointment, and was for several years the "trailer" on the Brooklyn Center Charge. It has a prosperous membership, a neat

CAMDEN PLACE

brick church, a comfortable parsonage, and about all the conditions necessary to success. The pastorate of Geo. R. Hair has been signalized by unusual prosperity. Under his earnest preaching, a wide-spread revival occurred last spring and the membership was greatly increased and strengthened. Its pastorate has been: 1886-7, H. J. Van Fossen; 1887-9, R. R. Atchison; 1889-90, J. W. Martin; 1890-5, H. W. Knowles; 1893, Geo. R. Hair; 1894, C. F. Sharpe. The church is valued at $4000; parsonage, $1200; membership, above 100.

LAKE STREET

Lake Street Church is located at one of the most important points in the city. For some time before its organization, the Rev. David Tice had discovered the necessity and opportunity for its existence, and with characteristic zeal and determination, he continued to work until the new organization and church location were effected. The present church property was purchased during the

LAKE STREET

pastorate of D. H. Higgins, which began in 1886. It was purchased by Joseph Dean. The purchase was made on credit, and the price, though thought to be reasonable at the time, proved later to be large. It handicapped the society for several years with an almost crushing burden, but through the persevering efforts of the pastor, H. J. Van Fossen, the liberality of the members of the church, and the helping hands of many sympathizing friends on the outside, the debt has been wholly provided for and despite a little shrinkage will be fully paid. The church has hardly grown as rapidly as was at first hoped, but this has largely been because the early promise of growth in that part of the city has not been up to expectation. The time is near at hand, however, when the population of that community will greatly increase. Then the mission of Lake Street Church will be fully realized. The pastorate has been as follows: 1886-8, D. J. Higgins; 1888-91, T. F. Allen; 1891-2, J. W. Davids; 1892-3, H. J. Van Fossen. The church is valued at $7000; membership, 120.

MINNEHAHA

Work was begun at Minnehaha by C. H. Brace in 1889, whose pastorate lasted to 1891. The church had been built, however, under the directions of the Presiding Elder John Stafford and Brother Brace as pastor, prior to the fall of 1889, and appears in the minutes of the Conference as having cost $4000. Ours is the only church at Minnehaha, and when business revives again, and people begin to push out to the suburbs, it will have a great field of usefulness. The membership is small but plucky and needs the sympathy and help of the larger churches in the city. In addition to Brother Brace, the pastors have been: 1891-2, E. N. Nicholson; 1892-3, H. L. St. Clair. Value of church property, $4500; membership, 15.

ST. LOUIS PARK

St. Louis Park is not in the corporate limits of Minneapolis, but is generally regarded as a part of the city and so the name appears in the minutes in the list of city appointments. Our work was inaugurated here by David Tice, under whose labors, supplemented by those of Dr. Stafford, then Presiding Elder, the present house of worship was built at a cost of about $4000. The depression last fall made quite a change in the outlook, but the future of that community is assured, as is also that of the church.

In 1892 S. F. Kerfoot was appointed to succeed Brother Tice. The church property is valued at $5,000, and the membership is about 40.

BLOOMINGTON AVENUE

The Bloomington Society was organized by J. F. Chaffee and the entire work of soliciting and collecting the money for the building was done by him. The church was dedicated during the summer of 1886. J. L. Pitner preached the sermon. During the pastorate of J. G. Teter, a comfortable parsonage was built, leaving,

BLOOMINGTON AVENUE

however, the too frequent legacy of debt: but under the wise administration of the present pastor, Elijah Haley, the debt is being provided for. The community about this church is growing, the condition of the church is healthful, and its prospects encouraging. Its pastoral line is a short one: 1886-7, George West: 1887-90, J. G. Teter: 1890-4, Elijah Haley, who is doing a good work. The church is valued at $4000: parsonage, $1600: present membership, 100.

FOWLER

In the Conference minutes of 1892, appears in the list of city appointments, "Dupont Avenue, David Tice." In 1893 Dupont Avenue gives place to Fowler Church, David Tice appointed pastor. Its location is both sightly and central and in the midst of the largest territory unoccupied by the Methodist Church in Minneapolis and surrounded by a community which for wealth and intelligence is surpassed by none in the city. It is the high ground between the business section and the lakes. People not anchored in other parts of the city will be likely to live in this region as soon as circumstances will permit. It will be a family section. God pays especial attention to families. He founded his church in the family. He uses the family as the unit of moral power. Its sanctity is hedged about with all the power of His Divinity. The family is the fort in which He entrenches Himself in the race. From this stronghold He goes down for the rescue of the wayward and for the conquest of the world. As soon as he rescues the first He places the desolate in families and as rapidly as He conquers the latter He hallows and blesses it by the benign presence of His Church. In this generation Fowler Church will be a Family Church. In the later generations it will be crowded by marts of trade and become an Institutional Church.

The demand for this church is emphasized by the fact that the field is open. People feel that they ought to have church privileges within walking distance. Some favorite preacher or old social ties may draw them to greater distances, but as a rule they do not long continue to attend churches so far away that their children cannot walk to Sunday School and Young Peoples' meetings. Half a mile is about as far as they are likely to walk and send their little ones. This makes it expedient for a great denomination that feels its responsibilities for the religious culture of the people of the city to provide suitable places of worship within at least one mile from each other. The city, in its business experience, makes such or better provision for the school accommodation of its children. Wherever a large public school is planted, there is proof that not far away *a church may find a good site*. The noble

school edifice near the Fowler Church answers the question o
need. Methodism is called of God to care for all classes. She
can take up in her great arms all sections of society. She has
made a glorious record by her care for the poor. She has long

FOWLER

felt that the church that preaches to the most poor of this generation will preach to the most rich of the next. Making her people
prosperous she has no right to abandon them as soon as her lessons
in virtue, in good habits, in economy, in industry, have brought
forth their legitimate fruit of prosperity. She must minister to all

classes. She must be present on Lowry Hill with appropriate and
efficient agencies for the shepherding of that growing and important community. This and similar considerations induced the
authorities of the Methodist Church to buy the very desirable lots
on the corner of Franklin and Dupont avenues.

In the early spring of 1894. Rev. J. Wesley Hill, D. D., was
transferred from Helena, Montana, and undertook this work.

CHAPEL OF FOWLER

There was no society, no membership, no money, no church edifice,
no parsonage, only a lot unpaid for and a Board of Trustees deeply
engaged elsewhere, but determined to erect a suitable building.
The accompanying cuts represent the church as it will be when
completed and the chapel which is now under process of erection.
This building on Dupont avenue is rapidly advancing and will
be occupied not long after these lines are printed. It will seat
1140 people and has all the best and most elegant appointments

for efficient work. including parlors, Epworth, Young People's, social, dining, serving and toilet-rooms. It is not expected to involve this enterprise in serious financial embarassment at any time. It is hoped to reach the auditorium in the not remote future. But with elegant appointments, perhaps the best west of Pittsburgh for a large congregation, the Society can afford not to hazzard the enterprise by haste, or make it less than the best by inattention.

The name Fowler Church was given to it by the Board of Trustees out of respect for the resident Bishop, C. H. Fowler, and it has been retained in spite of his most earnest request, as he felt embarrassed in working for the enterprise by its name.

The purpose of the Trustees and friends of this church is to produce a church that will glorify God, help forward his kingdom among men, honor the great denomination whose appliances it augments and commend itself to the judgment and taste of the people in the midst of whom it is planted.

In spirit and name it is to be a Methodist Church, which means that it is to be the best possible for its environment and work. Its catholicity will offer a home to all who seek communion with God. In the language of the first great Methodist—"Whom God accepts we need not reject." It is confidently expected that at the altars of this church multitudes will find pardon and from its service many will graduate into heaven.

EPISCOPAL RESIDENCE

In 1881 the coming of Bishop Foss as Resident Bishop of Minneapolis was signalized by the purchase of an Episcopal residence. Mrs. A. H. Goheen offered her residence and beautiful grounds on Nicollet avenue between Eleventh and Twelfth streets on such favorable terms that the property was purchased for about $13.000, a considerable portion of which she gave herself. It is true to history to say that the movement to secure an Episcopal residence was inaugurated by J. F. Chaffee and the money made and provided for, was solicited by him and. of which, except about $1,000. was contributed by the members of the Hennepin Avenue Church.

ASBURY HOSPITAL AND REBECCA DEACONESS HOME

In 1887 the first experiment was made in this state in our denomination with the deaconess movement by the organization of the Northwestern Deaconess Home, at No. 2745 Second avenue south. Good work was done here, but after a short existence, some complications arose and the project was abandoned.

ASBURY HOSPITAL AND REBECCA DEACONESS HOME

On the 17th day of August, 1891, the Rebecca M. Harrison Deconess Home was organized in memory of the wife of T. A. Harrison and was largely supported by the donations of Mrs. Sarah H. Knight. As many as six deaconesses were connected with the Home at a time, and were sent to all parts of Minneapolis, usually under the auspices of some Methodist church, to visit and care for the sick and poor, and spiritually comfort and advise with all classes in need.

A WARD IN ASBURY HOSPITAL

A PRIVATE ROOM IN ASBURY HOSPITAL

Its work has proved a great blessing to many homes as well as to a multitude of the homeless.

Its Board of Managers consists of Sarah H. Knight, Anna H. Goheen, Rev. J. F. Chaffee, S. C. Robinson, Caroline E. Thorpe, Mary H. Robinson, J. Force, Sarah F. Force, John Stafford, Harriet R. Stafford and H. N. Farnam.

The Home was merged into the corporation known as Asbury Hospital and Rebecca Deaconess Home, which was organized on

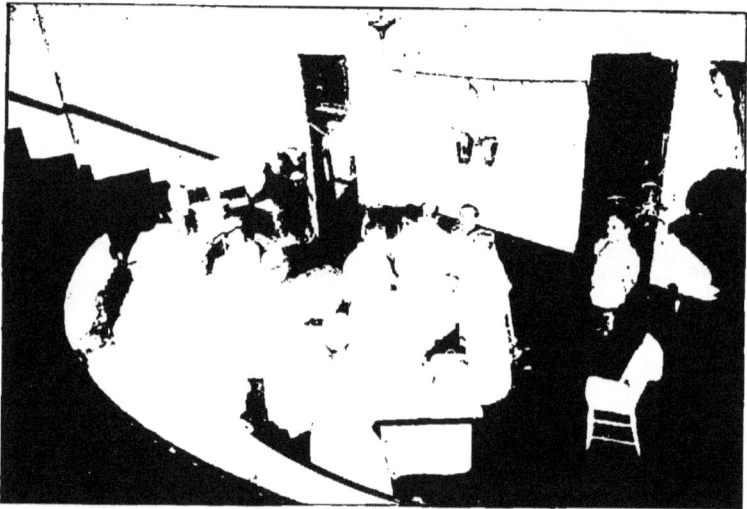

OPERATING ROOM IN ASBURY HOSPITAL

the 26th day of April, 1893, in memory of Thomas Asbury Hari-son and wife. Its general purposes are to "establish, maintain, and conduct hospitals and deaconess homes in Minnesota." All persons, without regard to religious belief or nationality, can be treated surgically or medically and cared for in the hospital, excepting such persons as are suffering from an infectious or contagious disease; and all properly educated physicians, duly licensed by the state, may treat their patients therein. The Hospital has a large staff of able physicians and surgeons who treat all charity patients free of charge.

As to the Home, it gives necessary instruction, maintenance and assistence to women engaged in deaconess work or preparing therefor and, as far as practicable, develops and maintains them in the various forms of Christian work. Their consecration is to "minister to the poor, visit the sick, pray with the dying, care for the orphan, seek the wanderer, comfort the sorrowing, and save the sinning." Truly this is "pure religion and undefiled," and yet how many are giving it the warm support, which its merits demand?

ASBURY HOSPITAL AMBULANCE

Under the law passed by the Legislature in 1893, the corporation closely resembles Hamline University. There is no stock issued or to be issued. A carefully selected board of persons perpetuates itself, in part; but three classes of three each are selected in alternation by the Minnesota Annual Conference. The resident Bishop is ex-officio a member of the Board.

The present hospital building and site were purchased by Mrs. Sarah H. Knight and donated to the corporation. Its value is estimated at $30.000.

Its support is derived from pay patients, contributions from churches and individuals, of real property, personal articles and money. For the year ending August 31, 1893, the sum of $3,700 in money was contributed by 155 Methodist churches, Sunday schools, Leagues and Endeavor societies in Minnesota.

From February 16, 1893 to August 31, 1893, (date of published report) 1148 persons were treated in the Free Dispensary.

In its report there were represented eighteen nationalites, twelve creeds and sixty-three occupations. They came from eighty-one points in Minnesota; sixteen in Wisconsin; ten in North Dakota; eight in South Dakota; two each in Illinois, Iowa and Montanna; and one each in Michigan, Missouri and Ohio.

In the annual statement published September 1, 1894, the superintendent's report closes as follows:

"WHAT WE WANT

"1. To pay off our debt of nearly $12,000. The property is estimated to be worth $35,000.

"2. More room—in the hospital for patients; in the Free Dispensary, for the better handling of that branch; in the Deaconess Home, to meet the enlarged growth of that work; in fact, for all departments, for we are crowded to the utmost capacity, with as many as four persons of the working force sleeping in a fair sized room. This means one or more new buildings. With more rooms for pay patients, and more wards, the income would be correspondingly increased, and without materially increasing the running expenses.

"Can this be done? There is one way in which this debt can be paid and the necessary buildings erected this year, that is, by each of the 30,000 members of Minnesota Methodism sending the Treasurer $1.00." This plan should receive a hearty response from every church in the conference."

RESIDENT BISHOPS

Minneapolis Methodism has been favored with an Episcopacy as genuine and genuinely apostolic as the church has ever had. Bishop Merrill came to St. Paul in 1872 and exercised a careful oversight of Minneapolis Methodism. Cyrus D. Foss was elected

Bishop in 1880 and at once chose Minneapolis as his place of residence. Eloquent in the pulpit and on the platform and catholic in his feeling toward other churches, he was highly appreciated. In 1888 Bishop J. N. Fitzgerald, recently elected, came in his place. He is a man of solid parts, and endeared himself to many people during his residence of four years in this city. The affliction which came upon his son Ray in the partial loss of sight, while here, created profound sympathy.

In 1892 came Bishop Charles H. Fowler, being still present with us. It takes him but a short time to leap into the saddle, and in the presence of a great emergency he can command his forces in a grand charge, or change front without the flutter of a pulse. Scholarly, alert, bold and persistent, he is invaluable whether in the lead or behind pushing. With but few, if any, equals in the American pulpit, and no superiors on the platform, he is the pride of our local Methodism and the delight of our citizens without respect to creed or party.

The above is but an outline of the history of Minneapolis Methodism, hastily written, not wholly accurate perhaps, in some respects, but the best that could be done under all the circumstances. Not including the German, Swedish and Norwegian departments of our work, we have nineteen churches, valued at $520,-900; four parsonages, valued at $33,200, and a membership of about 4000, including probationers, with nearly 4000 members of our Sunday Schools. If we add to this our Episcopal residence, our Methodist Hospital and Deaconess Home work, the large amounts given to Hamline University, besides all our contributions to the benevolent work of the church, we may well exclaim, "Behold, what hath God wrought." We may not indeed have whereof to glory, but the results are not contemptible, and will not be surpassed in the next thirty-seven years except by strenuous and consecrated effort.

St. Paul Methodism

It is a question of very little importance whether First Church, so called, is really entitled to that name, or whether the title more properly belongs to what is now known as Central Park Church Yet it has been discussed with no little feeling.

The first building erected by the St. Paul Methodists for church purposes was a small frame structure on Jackson street, in 1847-8, but which was never finished and was finally relinquished to the owner of the ground on which it stood. In 1849 a small brick church was erected on Market street, fronting on what is now known as Rice's Park. This church was soon outgrown, and in 1856 a much larger house was finished, on the corner of Ninth and Jackson streets. The entire membership united in this enterprise, and it is claimed that the understanding was, that when the house was ready for occupancy the membership was to move into it, and leave the Market street house unoccupied.

For some reason, not generally understood, when the time for removal came a few families refused to leave the old church. A sharp controversy followed. The bell was taken away and the Sunday school library, but the few kept possession of the house. At the ensuing session of the Conference, August 7th, 1856, they were recognized as an independent charge under the name "St. Paul West," John Penman, pastor. The Jackson Street Church was set down as "St. Paul East," E. J. Kinney, pastor. The latter was in St. Paul District, D. Brooks, Presiding Elder; the former in Minnesota District, John Kerns, Presiding Elder.

In 1857 the two churches were by special arrangement united in one pastorate; Cyrus Brooks, a transfer from the Cincinnati conference, had charge assisted by a talented young man from Baltimore Conference, Wm. S. Edwards. At the conference in the spring of 1858 the churches were separated and made independent charges; with C. Brooks at Jackson Street, and W. S. Edwards at Market Street. This name was retained by the latter church until 1873 when it removed to its present location and assumed the name of

FIRST CHURCH.

Jackson Street Church has also changed its location and its name and now both churches claim to be the mother of Methodism in St. Paul. But as we know not how else to speak of them, it must not be considered an offense, when, in this sketch, we call them by the names which they now bear.

When in April, 1858, the two churches were made independent charges the second time, Market Street Church, as it was then called, numbered about 40 members. Its growth was slow, yet eight years later the number had about doubled. Then, in consequence of deaths and removals, there was a falling off; so that in 1870 there were reported but 44 members. After that there was a pretty steady growth, until the exodus under Dr. Smith, in the beginning of 1888.

When in 1873 the church took possession of its new home, under its new name, it found itself burdened with rather a formidable debt; and this, with the lamented death of Hon. John Nicols, on the 30th of July of that year, a leader and liberal contributor in every church enterprise, caused a feeling of discouragement very unfavorable to progress. In the summer of 1878 Bishop Foster visited St. Paul, and under the inspiration of his stirring words, responsible parties assumed the indebtedness and relieved the corporation.

In 1879 Dr. Samuel G. Smith was transferred from Iowa and stationed at First Church. Under his ministry the church prospered and at the close of his three years term of service, he was appointed Presiding Elder of the St. Paul District. In 1882 Emory Miller, D. D., another transfer from Iowa, succeeded Dr. Smith at First Church. At the end of two years he returned to Iowa, leaving the church about as he found it.

In the meantime Dr. Smith's health had proved insufficient for the Presiding Eldership: he had given up his district, had visited Europe, and returned in time to succeed Dr. Miller at First Church. As he had left that charge only two years before, after a three years' pastorate, there was a Disciplinary barrier in the way of his appointment. The charge was left to be supplied. Dr. Smith received a merely nominal appointment to a little ephemeral

FIRST CHURCH

mission across the river, and served as the supply for First Church. He was appointed to the charge next year, 1885, and reappointed in 1886 and 1887.

He had long been dissatisfied with the "time limit" in our itineracy, by which, as it was then, a preacher was not allowed to serve "the same appointment more than three years in six." As he was very outspoken on the subject, he had a number of sympathizers among the more wealthy members of his congregation. Besides, he had other reasons which prompted him to take the step which resulted in the organization of "The People's Church." Arrangements were all completed— he had notified the resident Bishop of his intentions, and on Sabbath, the first day of January, 1888, he preached for the last time as a minister of the Methodist Episcopal Church. This was not "a happy new year" for First Church, for its members were strongly attached to Dr. Smith, and the final severance of such ties could not be otherwise than painful.

The very next Sabbath after the pulpit was vacated it was most satisfactorily supplied. Dr. F. O. Holman was taken from Foss Church, Minneapolis and placed in charge of First Church, St. Paul. Thus there was no break in pulpit ministration or pastoral oversight.

A number of excellent members, and the larger share of the wealth of the church went with Dr. Smith. It can be no reflection upon any others to say, that among those who left, the loss of none was quite so deeply felt as that of the family of the late Hon. John Nicols. He in his lifetime was a loyal Methodist, and with his excellent wife had stood firmly by First Church through its most trying vicissitudes. Indeed, there were times when but for their support, moral and financial, it must have proved a failure.

But all were missed and mourned, and though the number who left was not so great as had been expected, yet the departure of these was very depressing. One cannot but admire the quiet and dignified determination with which those who remained took up the added burden which they were thus called to bear. There was no bluster, no sign of faintheartedness; but under the new leadership things moved right on, and so they have continued.

Dr. Holman was appointed to the charge the following year, but before its close was compelled, by failing health, to give it up, much to the regret of his people. Rev. J. B. Starkey was employed to fill out the year.

In 1889 Dr. Coultas was transferred to this conference and appointed to First Church.

He was followed by the present pastor, C. B. Wilcox, D. D., now in the fifth year of his pastorate. He is modest and unassuming, but does not feel called upon to apologize for his position. His ministry has been successful from the first; and now, at the beginning of his fifth year, the church has a membership of over 300. The church is at peace, is in good working condition, and more than satisfied with its present pastor, whose term of service must close at the end of this Conference year.

CENTRAL PARK

As Central Park Church and First Church have a common history until their separation and recognition as Jackson Street Church and Market Street Church, and as that history is included in the sketch of First Church, it need not be repeated here.

After the separation of the Jackson and Market Street Churches at the conference in 1858, Rev. Cyrus Brooks remained in the pastorate of Jackson Street. W. S. Edwards was appointed pastor of Market Street Church. Rev. J. F. Chaffee succeeded him and continued two years. After him the following pastors served in succession: J. S. Peregrim, 1861; B. F. Crary, 1862. In the latter part of the year he was appointed army chaplain and Edward Eggleston took his place as pastor until May, 1863, when on account of failing health, he resigned and A. J. Nelson supplied the remainder of the year. At the Conference of 1863, B. F. Crary, having returned from the army, was re-appointed and served until May following when he was elected editor of the Central Christian Advocate and J. N. Martin supplied until the Conference of 1864. when Cyrus Brooks was returned to Jackson Street. From 1865 to 1868 Daniel Cobb was pastor: 1868-9, E. S. Gillette: 1869-72. William McKinley: 1872-4, J. W. McGregor: 1874-6. Charles Griswold; 1876-7, O. Williams: 1877-8, John Stafford: 1878-9. J. F. Chaffee: 1879-81. S. M. Davis: 1881-4, W. K. Marshall: 1884-7, Robert Forbes: 1887-91, J. E. Smith, the last half year supplied by W. W. Satterlee: 1891 4, Frank Doran. William McKinley is now pastor, having been appointed at the Duluth Conference, October 9. 1894.

CENTRAL PARK

There was a debt of $5,000 on Jackson Street Church when it was opened in 1857 and this, being followed by the financial crash of that year, continued to accumulate until in 1860 it amounted to $9,000. That year it was reduced to $5,500 and continued to grow for eight years more. During the pastorate of Daniel Cobb the debt was paid, the church improved and a gracious revival of religion enjoyed.

In January, 1888, the congregation removed from Jackson Street to the new church, corner of Twelfth street and Minnesota, and the name changed to Central Park Church. This church, including lot and furnishing, cost $86,000. On it was a debt of $56-000 which, during the past year, has, by sale of the old parsonage property on Robert street and by a donation of $6000 from the Church Extension Board, been reduced to $30,000.

The number of church members at present is 338; of Sunday School scholars, 250, with Gen. Geo. C. Smith as Superintendent. The central location of this church in the capitol city of the state has made it an important factor in the history of Minnesota Methodism. The changing character of the population around it, while it has hindered the numerical growth of the church, has enlarged the sphere of its influence by bringing to it and sending from it to every part of the northwest thousands of workers whose lives and labors will be felt for good far and wide forever. Among them are men and women eminent and honored in every profession and position in life. Some of the fathers and founders of this church were also among the fathers and founders of St. Paul and their names are imperishably associated with the history of the city as well as of the church. Benjamin F. Hoyt, Nathaniel McClean, Ira Bidwell, Parker Paine, A. F. Parker, John H. Reaney, Alexander Wilson, C. D. Strong and Dr. John H. Murphy will long be remembered among the laymen whose work of faith and labor of love have helped to make Central Park and the city of St. Paul what they are.

CLINTON AVENUE

The first recorded effort to establish Methodism in the section of the city of St. Paul now occupied by the Clinton Avenue Church was made by the Rev. Silas Bolles, in 1856 or 1857; but the flood of 1857 swept away whatever beginnings were made, and the field was unoccupied for some years. About the end of July, 1869, Robert Withey established a Sunday School; and following this a meeting was held to consider the organization of a church, at which were present Methodists, Baptists, Presbyterians, Episcopalians and Disciples, and as the Methodists were the only people who could promise regular preaching without much pay it was decided to make the union Sunday school a Methodist school and to organize a Methodist Episcopal Church. The society for some time was connected with the "Pine Bend circuit," and at the Conference held in Owatonna, September, 1870, Rev. F. A. Scott became pastor; but he failed in health and died before the close of the year. The field has since then been served in order and with varying success by the following pastors: C. H. Savidge, G. W. Richardson, W. Kerr, S. F. Tuttle, H. P. Satchwell, John Stafford, N. M. Learned, David Tice, J. G. Teter, David Morgan, W. S. Mathew, A. W. Edwards, J. F. Stout, W. C. Rice, W. S. Cochrane and J. C. Hull. A church was built and, in September, 1873, dedicated by Bishop Merrill. In the conference minutes of 1875 the name of Clinton Avenue appears for the first time. The church, through all its early history, occupied a hard field, but made a heroic struggle, and, with the great activity and inflation of real estate, undertook the erection of a splendid church and parsonage. This was done during the pastorate of Rev. J. F. Stout, the fine church building being erected in 1888, on the crest of the boom period. The cost of the building was about $50,000, and the parsonage is reckoned at $5000 additional. At the time of dedication the indebtedness was subscribed, and if the good times had continued all might have gone well with the society; but as things turned out, a great burden of debt was left, which has, until recently, hung over the church like the "Old Man of the Sea." Under its crushing weight, many have become discouraged and have gone to other churches. After the collapse of real estate values, there was left little hope of collecting the subscriptions and liquidating the debt of Clinton Avenue Church; and it was only by the good financial management of Pastor Rice that the society was prevented from going on the rocks. He, with the valuable help of some energetic laymen of the church, reduced the debt very materially during the two years of his pastorate: and a loan of $20,000 was secured, which for a time afforded delay of the

CLINTON AVENUE

impending distress. It was hoped that times might improve, so that some way would appear to save the property: but instead of improvement, there was continual and increased depression, so that as a last resort Bro. Rice appealed to his old friend, Mr. John D. Blake, of Minneapolis, who generously offered eighteen lots in Lincoln Street Supplement to Minneapolis, provided it would clear the Clinton Avenue Church from debt.

Two years elapsed after the offer of the property by Brother Blake and the mortgage had accumulated interest until it amounted to $23,000, of course due from non-payment of interest. At the Conference session held in Wesley Church, Minneapolis, in the fall of 1893, it was currently reported that Clinton Auenue would have to go to the wall. No one seemed willing to undertake its rescue and the case was generally regarded hopeless. This conference passed a resolution asking the Board of Church Extension to grant help to both Central Park and Clinton Avenue, St. Paul. Few had any hope that churches which had been built at so great cost would receive such aid. It is well known that help in such exceptional cases can be given only on recommendation of the annual meeting of the Board of Church Extension. By the good favor of Providence, which thoughtless men would call a coincidence, the annual Board meeting was fixed for St. Paul.

The new pastor, Rev. J. C. Hull, at once set about the rescue of the church property. The plans formed and the proposition presented were entirely his own and were submitted to no one until presented by him before the special committee at the Church Extension Board meeting. The special committee to which the cases of Central Park and of Clinton Avenue had been referred, and of which Bishop Fowler was chairman, recommended the granting of the request for Clinton Avenue; but when the proposition came before the Board for action, the Senior Corresponding Secretary neatly defeated it by moving that the request be referred to the Executive Board at Philadelphia, stating that the Executive Board had power to do that without the recommendation of the annual meeting. But its author, while not a member of the Board, quietly said: "They shall never cover up my proposition in that grave. They must adopt or defeat the recommendation of the special committee to whom it was referred." With this determination he labored faithfully all the afternoon and evening until the time of the next morning's session, preparing the way for a reconsideration, which was secured by a motion of Dr Chaffee. The report of the special committee, recommending that the request of Clinton Avenue be granted, was passed with but one negative vote. The proposition provided for the granting of $17,000, and the acceptance of the 18 lots offered by Mr. Blake, as collateral for the money. Rev. Mr. Hull then set about getting the mortgage reduced from $23,000 to $17,000, which he succeeded in doing, and in addition obtained $350 to pay the taxes which had accumulated on the Minneapolis property during the two years in which it had been held for the church. With these additional leverages, and with most valuable assistance from Bishop Fowler, he continued to follow up the recommendation of relief through the Board of Church Extension; and after five months of anxiety and uncertainty, the whole matter was carried successfully through. The lots were deeded directly to the Board of Church Extension and the mortgage purchased by the Board, with the agreement that five years of time should be allowed in which to dispose of the Minneapolis property. The local management of the business of the church has been no less successfully managed by the pastor, who had volunteered to carry everything until the church should be on a substantial footing. He has secured the release of judgments against the society, and so managed the current expenses that no new debts have been allowed to accumulate; he has also paid off various obligations which had for some time rested against the church. Clinton Avenue Church has thus been put upon a substantial footing, under the inspiration of which the congregation is growing, and every department of the church is making advance. The church is still in an unfinished condition, not having the gallery built in the audience room, and the steam-heating plant not yet in; but for the present the galleries are not needed, and the church is heated by three large furnaces. There are large and commodious engine rooms, the stairways for the galleries are completed, and abundant space for a large pipe-organ, so that in time the church may be thoroughly equipped. It has excellent basement room, including a well furnished kitchen, with gas cooking range. The ladies of the society are noted for their capability in furnishing a good church dinner. Clinton Avenue Church stands in the midst of a population of 30,000 people, and in the very nature of things must have a great future.

OLIVET

Under the direction of Dr. Robert Forbes, of Jackson Street Church, a Sunday school was organized July 11, 1886, with Mrs.

A. L. Morrison in charge. in a hall near the corner of West Seventh and Bay streets. The Sunday School was removed to the chapel on Juno street, which was dedicated October 3, 1886, at 3 p. m., by Dr. Robert Forbes. At the first quarterly conference held on the premises, with S. B. Warner, Presiding Elder, in the chair, and B. F. Kephart pastor, it was decided that the name of the edifice should be "The Olivet M. E. Church." This church has the unique distinction of being out of debt. The property is valued at $3000. Growth in membership has been small as the surrounding population is largely foreign. A flourishing Sunday School, a good Epworth League, a thoroughly active Ladies' Aid Society and delightful harmony are branches that assure us that there is vitality in the vine. The following is the roll of pastors: B. F. Kephart, one year: Edward Gill. one year; A. F. Thompson, one year; George W. Empey, one year; J. D. Deets, one year; and James Castles, who is now in his third year.

ST. ANTHONY PARK

St Anthony Park Church was organized in the summer of 1889. C. M. Heard was the pastor at that time. Since then it has had a fluctuating experience. At present it has a membership of 30, and a Sunday School with an enrollment of 80. The present Pastor is J. W. Fryckberg. The house of worship was opened for public service January 1, 1891. The site was purchased at a cost of $1500, and the building was erected at a cost of $3000. The property is valued at $5500, and the present indebtedness $2000.

KING STREET

A Sunday School was organized January 15, 1882, at the residence of Mr. J. A. McConkey, 404 Morton street. In the fall of the same year the church society was organized with F. O. Holman, pastor of Bates Avenue, in charge. After six months the work was turned over to Hamline students who filled out the remainder of the year. Besides Bro. Holman, the following is the roll of pastors: John Pemberton, three years; King Street having

Riverside as an out-appointment: David Morgan, five years: John W. Powell, one year: and James Castles, who is now serving his third year. In 1883 a chapel was erected on King Street, and dedicated by S. G. Smith, Presiding Elder. In 1888 the Clinton Avenue people donated their church edifice to the King Street society, and in the same year a parsonage was erected next door to the church. The church property which is splendidly located is valued at $6000 on which there is a mortgage of $950. The membership is 60, with a flourshing Sunday School. Every department of the church is in a healthy condition.

GRACE

On September 6, 1868, Grace Church was formally organized by Rev. D. Cobb, pastor of Jackson Street Church. In 1869 a comfortable chapel was erected. The following summer it was dedicated by William McKinley, pastor of Jackson Street Church. In the fall of 1878 it was thought best to organize the society into a church. The conference sent Rev. T. L. Tuttle to take charge of the work. He brought the people together and the church was known as the Third Methodist Church of St. Paul. Afterwards the name was changed to Grace Church.

In the fall of 1874 Rev. John Stafford was sent as pastor. It soon seemed necessary to build a new structure. How to accomplish this was a serious question. Mr. Stafford wrote: "For in addition to our own poverty, the city, and especially our church in the city, was passing through the worst financial struggle it had encountered since 1857." The undertaking at last seemed possible. The lot on Hopkins street was bought for $1,400. $400 paid down and the balance in five years. The cash payment was made in March, 1875. The contract for building was let for $2000 and the church was ready for dedication June 13th. The indebtedness was $1500. Bishop Merrill preached the dedication sermon and then presented the financial situation to the people. Finally, by the generosity of the Bishop and Mr. J. H. Davidson, and also of friends in the First Church, the entire indebtedness was removed. Rev. J. H. Crist was appointed to the pastorate in 1877. He served the church two years and was followed by H. C. Jennings, who also served two years. These were years of great prosperity. A mission was started on Dayton Bluff, which is now the Bates Avenue Church. In October, 1881, Rev. C. E. Cline was appointed pastor. In 1882 Rev. S. B. Warner was appointed. In 1884 Dr. Stafford was returned. Rev. J. H. Dewart followed him. It was during this time that the present chapel was built. It was

GRACE

dedicated in 1886. Bishop Foss preached the sermon. The people were asked to pledge $8000. The entire amount was promised but for some reason many of the subscriptions failed to materialize in cash. **Rev. N. W. Jordan** became pastor of the church in 1888. Rev. Aaron Turner succeeded him. He was followed by Rev. Robert Craig. Rev. E. Pilling succeeded him. In 1892 Rev. S. B. Warner was returned. Everything seemed promising, when, in the midst of his pastorate, he had an opportunity to go to Colorado which he accepted. In 1893 Rev. Mr. Handy was brought to the pastorate. He remained a few months and then, deciding to prepare for the medical profession, resigned his relation. A few weeks later Rev. Milton G. Shuman, then a local preacher in Helena, Montana, was appointed as the supply. Under his pastorate, many embarrassed interests found well nigh immediate relief. At the last Quarterly Conference of the year he was unanimously invited to remain for another year and at the Conference in October, 1894, he was re-appointed.

HAMLINE

The first sermon at Hamline was preached by Rev. C. F. Bradley, September 12, 1880. A class was formed and a Sunday School organized at once. Prof. Bradley was pastor for two years, during which time the foundation was well laid for a model church. Prof. G. S. Innis was appointed pastor and served for one year. S. G. Gale was then made pastor and served the school for three years. P. Innis succeeded him to the close of the conference year. In 1886 Rev. Wm. McKinley was appointed pastor and held this position until 1891 when he was made Presiding Elder. Prof. Innis served again as supply for the rest of the year. In 1891 Rev. W. H. Daniel was transferred from the Indiana Conference and stationed at Hamline. He was succeeded in 1892 by Rev. Frank B. Cowgill who still continues in the pastorate.

The church has grown steadily from the beginning. The Sunday School is in a prosperous condition and there are two Epworth Leagues with a membership aggregating 150 and a flourishing Junior League. The church has a membership, including probationers, of more than 400. Unusual intelligence and efficiency characterize the church. The congregation is liberal in all its contributions to the local and connectional interests of Methodism.

BATES AVENUE

The Bates Avenue Church grew out of a Sunday School which was started in 1866. The place of meeting was an old school house at the corner of Mariah avenue and Cherry street.

These young people were encouraged and greatly helped in their work by Mr. James Yandes, a wealthy man who lived on Mound street. In 1867 the school passed into the hands of the Y. M. C. A. of St Paul, which continued the supervision of it until 1875, when the Grace Methodist Episcopal Church bought the house and grounds and organized a Methodist Sunday School.

During the year the present site was purchased. The old school house and grounds were then sold and the present building was paid for with the proceeds plus the subscription raised on dedication day.

In the spring of 1876 the corner stone was laid by Rev. Cyrus Brooks, and in the early fall the church was dedicated by Bishop Cyrus D. Foss, without a membership or organization, the trustees of Grace Methodist Church presenting the house for dedication.

A list of members was enrolled October 24, 1882, an organization effected November 6, following, and the Bates Avenue Methodist Episcopal Church started on her career as a Mission Church, with Rev. F. O. Holman as her first pastor. In 1882 Bates Avenue and King Street were united as one charge. But such was the energy and push of the people of Bates Avenue and the zeal of their pastor, that the Presiding Elder, Dr. S. G. Smith, was enabled to say in his report to the Conference of 1893, "Bates Avenue has become a self-supporting charge." The church has been served by the following pastors: F. O. Holman, who took charge in 1882; F. I. Fisher in 1885; John Pemberton in 1886; Robert Forbes in 1887; J. H. Dewart in 1888: Thomas McClary in 1891, and William S. Cochrane in 1893. Her present membership is 176. She has now a property valuation of $5000 with an indebtedness of $860, and a fair prospect of usefulness.

TRINITY

Trinity M. E. Church, Merriam Park, is a smaller, but otherwise a facsimile, of the Forest Heights M. E. Church of Minneapolis. In the summer of 1885 Major J. A. Sabin, of old Jackson Street Church, who had already done very generous things for

St. Paul Methodism, placed $1000 in the hands of his pastor, Dr.
Robert Forbes, saying, "Use this for the good of the church, ac-
cording to your own judgment." Dr. Forbes at once visited Merriam
Park and consulted with O. P. Shepherdson, W. B. Martin, H. B.
Clark, A. J. Douglas, Dr. J. H. Nichols, Geo. H. Tiffany, W. O.
Hillman and a few others, and proposed that if $1000 could be
raised in the Park, he would give the thousand dollars in his hands
to the Merriam Park people to build a Methodist Episcopal Church.

TRINITY

The proposal was accepted. Dr. S. B. Warner, Presiding Elder,
co-operated and officially organized the church, and appointed Dr.
Forbes pastor. When the subscriptions reached $700 the pastor
secured the remaining $300 among his personal friends in the
cities, and in September the building was commenced. Meanwhile services were held in Woodruff's Hall, Sunday afternoons,
by Dr. J. H. Dewart, S. G. Smith, Robert Forbes and others. At
the conference of 1886 Rev. George H. Way was appointed as-

sistant pastor of Jackson Street, Dr. Forbes being pastor. Brother Way resided at Merriam Park, it being understood that he should preach there every Sunday morning and give the evenings to the missions under the care of Jackson Street Church Wesley, Epworth and Olivet. Dr. Forbes dedicated the church in the following July, after a sermon by Dr. F. O. Holman. At the dedication subscriptions were taken to cover the entire cost of building. The church has had eminent pastoral service, among them being Revs. Stowers, Doran, Heard, McAdoo, Pilling and Sutton. The present pastor is Rev. John Pemberton.

EPWORTH

This church was organized in 1884 under the direction of Rev. Robert Forbes while he was pastor of the old Jackson Street Church. It began in a Sunday School conducted in the home of Mr. and Mrs. Thomas Wren, 557 Rice street. The building of a chapel followed. It was located on Marine street one block west of Rice. This location proved to be unwise and the church was re-located at the corner of Aurora and Makubin street. Owing to the foreign population about it, its work is mostly of a missionary character. Revs. J. H. Sutton and J. C. Gullett have been among the successful pastors. Rev. E. L. Ferris is in charge.

OXFORD CHURCH

On the evening of March 29, 1887, a meeting was held at the residence of S. B. Johnson, and plans were adopted for the completion of the organization of the Oxford Church. There were present at this meeting Rev. S. G. Smith, George N. Hillman, G. J. Kirkland and others. On Sunday afternoon, April 3, the Sunday school was organized. In the mean time prayer meetings were held for several months in the Calvary Reformed Episcopal Church. On Thursday evening, March 26, the church was formally organized, with 19 charter members. At the close of the

Conference year there were 34 members.   The church was dedicated by Bishop Foss.   The property is valued at $10,000, and
the present membership is about 60.   This church has experienced
many reverses, but the membership is courageous, and under the
pastorate of Brother Jamison the skies are brightening.   Much
credit is due George N. Hillman, whose energy, loyalty and
princely giving, have preserved the church in the presence of great
peril.

OXFORD

HAMLINE UNIVERSITY

In January 1854, a Methodist district clergyman of Wisconsin,
presented to Hon. W. P. Murray, then a member of the Minnesota
Territorial Legislature, a draft of a bill to incorporate the Minnesota Seminary, an institution to be under the control of the Wisconsin Conference of the Methodist Episcopal Church.   The bill was
handed over to Gen. Isaac Van Etten, who introduced it into the
Territorial Council.   It was referred to a committee of which
Mr. Murray was chairman, which agreed to a bill incorporating a
university to be located "on the Mississippi river between St. Paul
and Lake Pepin."   Mr. Murray, insisted that the name of the new

institution should be "Hamline," in honor of Bishop Hamline. The committee agreed upon the name "Hamline University of Minnesota," which is the incorporate name. On the fourth day of March, 1854, the bill passed both houses, and was approved by the Governor, W. A. Gorman, on the third of April. At the head of the list of incorporators, many of whom are well known in Minnesota pioneer life, is Alexander Ramsey. On the following sixteenth of May, the Trustees of Hamline University met in the "Methodist Church of St Paul."

The work was carried rapidly on. Red Wing offered the best inducements in the way of land, etc., and the university was located there. Bishop Hamline donated real estate in New York and Chicago. The New York property, which to-day is worth $500,000, was immediately put upon the market and sold for $6000. The preparatory department was opened November 16th, 1854, under the leadership of Rev. Jabez Brooks. Dr. Brooks resigned his position in 1857 on account of failing health, and the presidency was taken by Rev. B. F. Crary, D. D. He resigned in 1861 to take the position of Superintendent of Public Instruction, and Dr. Brooks was elected president, the course havin the meantime been changed to a collegiate grade.

The University continued in successful operation until 1869, furnishing a place for the higher education of the young men and women of the northwest. Over 2000 students were enrolled during that time. But the financial condition of the institution had been growing worse, owing to the financial panic of the years following 1857, and in 1869 the work of the school was suspended and the property in Red Wing sold to pay the debts. A change of location had been decided upon, which caused a delay of two years. The board of trustees had scarcely commenced the new building in St. Paul, when the crisis of 1873 greatly crippled their efforts, and finally caused operations to be entirely suspended.

At the Rochester Conference in 1878 it was decided to renew the work, and Rev. John Stafford was appointed agent. By his indefatigable labors the new building was completed and ready for use, September 22. 1880, when, after eleven gloomy years, the long-looked for day arrived when the doors of the Hamline Uni-

Apparatus Room

Ladies' Parlor

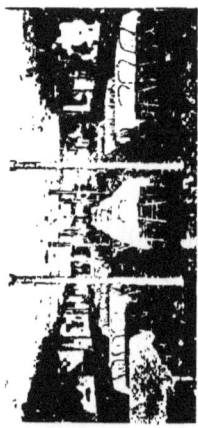

Young Hall

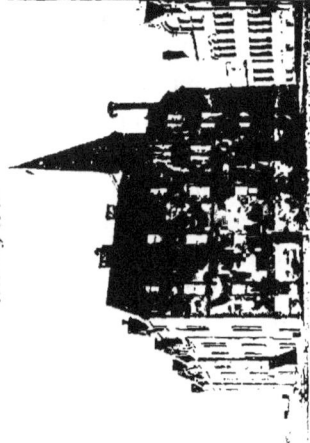

Ladies Hall

History Classroom

Chemical Laboratory

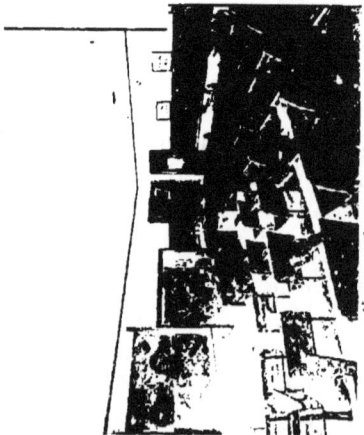

Science Lecture Room

versity were again thrown open to the students of the Northwest under the presidency of Dr. John.

During the first year at Hamline there were 113 students enrolled. The attendance has increased with each succeeding year, until the total enrollment is now about 2,500, with a yearly average of 300.

The building first erected was destroyed by fire in 1883. The work of rebuilding was begun at once, and on the thirtieth of January, 1884, the new university hall, a more commodious and beautiful building than its predecessor, was dedicated. This was the first year of Dr. Bridgeman's administration. The school has had a period of marked prosperity during the last few years. The courses of study have been broadened from time to time, until they now include all the higher studies found in the best colleges of the country.

In all my poor historical investigations it has been, and always is, one of the most primary wants to procure a bodily likeness of the personage inquired after; a good portrait, if such exists; failing that, even an indifferent, if sincere one. In short, *any* representation, made by a faithful human creature, of that face and figure which *he* saw with his eyes, and which I can never see with mine, is now valuable to me, and much better than none at all. This, which is my own deep experience, I believe to be, in a deeper or less deep degree, the universal one; and that every student and reader of history, who strives earnestly to conceive for himself what manner of fact and *man* this or the other vague historical *name* can have been, will, as the first and directest indication of all, search eagerly for a portrait, for all the reasonable portraits there are; and never rest till he have made out, if possible, what the man's natural face was like. *Often I have found a portrait superior in real instruction to half-a-dozen written "Biographies," as biographies are written; or rather, let me say, I have found that the portrait was as a small lighted candle by which the biographies could for the first time be read, and some human interpretation be made of them.*

Thomas Carlyle.

Biographical Department

BISHOP C. H. FOWLER

Biographies

BISHOP C. H. FOWLER, D. D., LL. D.

Charles Henry Fowler, Resident Bishop in Minneapolis, was born in Burford, Ontario, Canada, August 11, 1837. His father, Horatio Fowler, was born in Troy, N. Y., of English-Scotch ancestry, traceable to an old chief of the eighth century. His mother, Harriet Ryan, was born in Vermont, daughter of Henry Ryan, a man of great intellectual powers and phenomenal physical strength, who for thirty years was Presiding Elder and planted Methodism in Vermont and in the wilds of Canada. He married a Miss Patterson, a cousin of Noah Webster. Elder Ryan enjoyed the friendship of Ethan Allen, who, in spite of his skepticism, believed in this heroic itinerant. Ryan mortgaged his farm for all it would carry, and with the money built the first Methodist church in Toronto.

Young Fowler, having the metal of hisgr and father, made his way with little aid through both college and a theological school, living part of the time on but a few cents a week, walking across the country carrying his valise on his back to save stage fare, and, during the summer vacations, working as a farm hand. He wrote speeches and orations for some of the wealthy young men who were willing to win distinction in such a way. One Fourth of July oration paid his bills for a year. During the vacations in his theological course he taught school. He was twice graduated in the same suit of clothes. At the end of eight years hard study, he was but thirteen dollars in debt.

He was an accomplished swimmer, and, while a student at the Garrett Biblical Institute, performed heroic feats in rescuing the passengers from the wreck of the Lady Elgin. As a student, he was especially able as a mathematician and orator. In his post-graduate course he was distinguished in Greek, and was recognized as the best authority in the institution in the use of the particles in the New Testament Greek. In 1859 he was graduated as vale-dictorian from the Genesee College, now Syracuse University, and in 1861 from the Garrett Biblical Institute. The latter institution conferred upon him the degree of D. D., the first that it had ever

EPISCOPAL RESIDENCE

conferred upon anyone. He subsequently received the degree of LL. D., from Syracuse University, and also from the Wesleyan University.

In 1859 he commenced the study of law in Chicago, but before being admitted to the bar he yielded to the convictions of his early years and gave himself to the ministry. His pastorate was in Chicago, where he spent in all eleven years in the service of the principal churches there, during which period occurred the most extensive and most thorough revival ever witnessed in the city.

Having the largest auditorium in the city, except Bryan Hall, he had vast congregations. From 1872 to 1876 he was president of the Northwestern University. During his wise and vigorous administration the number of students in all departments very. greatly advanced and the University received distinction and public favor. In 1872 he was sent to the General Conference, and also in 1876, 1880 and 1884, leading the delegation twice.

In 1874 he was sent to the General Conference of the M. E. Church South as a fraternal delegate. The commission was composed of A. S. Hunt, C. H. Fowler and C. B. Fisk. As this was the first delegation ever sent to the Church South, much public interest was excited. During the week succeeding the great Chicago fire, he put through the Rock River Conference the plan that pooled the interests of all the burned churches and arranged to have these represented upon the following Sabbath in every principal city of the United States. He himself visited Philadelphia and secured for the demolished churches over $40,000, the gifts including watch chains, finger rings and jewels. In 1876 he was appointed by the Govenor of Illinois to deliver the oration on that state at the Centennial in Philadelphia. In the same year the General Conference elected him to the editorship of the New York "Christian Advocate," the most important periodical of the church. In this capacity his sagacity, courage and eloquence as a thinker and writer were conspicuous, and soon brought the circulation of this journal to the highest figure of its history.

In 1880 when the declining interests of the missionary cause demanded the most effective ability in the church, Dr. Fowler was elected General Missionary Secretary. During the several years preceding his election to this office, the receipts of the treasury had declined from $690,576 in 1872. to $559,371 in 1879, although the church was steadily advancing in membership from 1,458,041 in 1872, to 1,699,426 in 1879. But under Dr. Fowler's adminstration this decline was arrested, and the advance was from $559,371 in 1879, to $831,028 in 1884. During all these years he was almost constantly on the platform or in the pulpit pleading for missions and giving missionary information.

In May, 1884, he was elected Bishop by the General Conference in Phildelphia. He was consecrated and ordained Bishop by Bishop Simpson, this being the last official act of that eminent divine. The new Bishop resided eight years on the Pacific coast. In 1885 he sailed from New York for South America. During that voyage he applied unremittingly to the study of the Spanish language and, the Sunday after landing in Montevideo, assisted in

SECTION OF LIBRARY

a funeral service in Spanish and made a speech in a Spanish Sunday School. He was the first Protestant Bishop to visit Paraguay, where he planted a mission with church and school. He established other missions at the foot of the Andes, also in the lower provinces of Brazil and also down on the border of Patagonia. His many articles on the products, resources, and social conditions of South America, appearing in the secular and religious press, were widely read and highly commended. The South America mission which has had a struggling existence for many years, through his prophetic insight and persistent advocacy, soon became an assured success, and Bishop Fowler won the title of the "Apostle of South America."

Upon his return to the United States, in 1886, he resumed his work in the far west. In July, 1888, he sailed for Japan, Corea, China, and a tour of visitations to the missions around the world. His visit to Japan changed the entire character of the work of the missions there. At Pekin he organized the Pekin University, and in Central China, the Nankin University. He appointed the faculty, and authorized the chancellor to purchase land in the city of Nankin for a site, promising to see that the funds were forthcoming. Soon the university had nine acres of ground within the walls of the city and erected four beautiful university buildings. The Fowler College of Theology in this group is named in recognition of his services. So earnestly had he advocated the interests of China that politicians in California called him "Mr. Ah Fowler," but the church in many places calls him the "Apostle of China." He also visited the Methodist missions in Europe and planted the mission in Hammerfest, in the Artic Circle, the most northerly city of the globe.

At St. Petersburg, Russia, in his private room in the hotel d'Angleterre, with his wife, son, the preacher to be appointed pastor, and the Presiding Elder of Finland, he organized the first Methodist Episcopal Church of St. Petersburg. By his prudence and knowledge of Russian treaties, he avoided conflict with the Russian police and secured their protection under the law.

In California and the Pacific coast, Bishop Fowler was for eight years identified with nearly every church enterprise. Through his guidance, the church facilities in San Francisco, especially, were improved, though there is hardly a principal city in the country that has not felt the vigor and wisdom of his administration. He established the Maclay College of Theology in Southern California and secured an endowment of $150,000. The case was presented at his first interview with Senator Maclay, and in half an hour the Bishop had the securities for the endowment in his

pocket. He consolidated the schools in Nebraska, and founded
the Wesleyan University of that state in Lincoln.

He transferred the educational work of Methodism in Italy from
Florence to Rome, and there ordained a Methodist Institute. His
administration as a Bishop has been conspicuous for its vigor,
thoroughness and gentleness. For catholic scholarship and untir-

VIEW OF PARLOR

ing industry he has won much renown. His work on the "Falla-
cies of Colenso," wrought out in the first year of his ministry, was
exceedingly timely and gave him a marked standing for scholarship, logic, and courage. It demonstrated that another man was
ready to grapple with the solid questions and great controversies.

As a preacher of the Gospel he is perhaps most remarkable.
His words are simple and direct, being of Saxon origin. He
handles the greatest themes and speaks out of conviction; is full

of illustrations enriching with historic examples and with facts from
science and nature. Under his preaching entire congregations
have risen to their feet. At the close of one of his university
lectures, while president of the Northwestern University, lecturing
on evidences of Christianity, on the theme "What a man must believe who refuses to believe the Bible," it was said that every un-
converted person present, over 100 in all, went forward to the altar
as a seeker.

The corner stone of Christ Church, in Pittsburgh, and Calvary,
in Alleghany City, were laid by him in one day. He published
memorial addresses upon Bishop Ames, of Baltimore, and upon the
life and character of Bishop Gilbert Haven, of Boston, Mass. His
funeral oration in Chicago on the day of Mr. Lincoln's burial, and
his oration on Grant, delivered at the request of the city authorities
of San Francisco, and his oration on the character of Rev. Edmund
S. Janes, in New York city, will long be remembered. He made
the prayer at the dedication of the World's Fair buildings, Chicago,
in 1893.

In 1892 Bishop Fowler established his home in Minneapolis,
Minn., to whose entire citizenship he has endeared himself through
his powerful precepts and example. He has imparted fresh inspiration to Twin City Methodism and has devised and executed the
plan by which a number of the churches have been saved from
financial ruin.

His habits are simple. He is always cheerful. He is sympathetic in feeling, generous in nature and easily accessible. He is
known as the "great commoner." His home is always open. It is the
center of hospitality and of all the graces of Christian character and
culture. In 1868 he was married to Myra A., daughter of the Rev.
Dr. Luke Hitchcock, one of the most eminent men of the church.
Being of rare grace, culture and common sense, she has proven
herself a helpmeet in the largest sense, and no small factor in the
present proud position of her husband. He has one son known by
his writings as "Carl Fowler." He was recently elected President
of the Senior Class in the classical course, of the State University.

CYRUS DAVID FOSS, D. D., LL. D.

Cyrus David Foss, Bishop in the Methodist Episcopal Church, son of Rev. Cyrus and Jane Campbell Foss, was born in Kingston, New York, January 17, 1834. His father was an itinerant Methodist preacher. His mother was a woman of strong sense and deep piety; her great ambition was to train her five sons in the footsteps of their father.

In his boyhood he attended school during the winter months and assisted his father, who was then broken in health, on a little farm. After a thorough preparatory course of study in Amenia Seminary, N. Y., he was admitted to the Wesleyan University. In 1854, at the age of twenty, he graduated at the head of his class. He was at once employed as teacher of mathematics in Amenia Seminary, which position he held for three years, and during the last years was its principal.

He entered the Traveling Ministry in the New York Conference in the spring of 1857, and was stationed a Chester, Orange Co., N. Y., during 1857 and 1858. For the next sixteen years he was pastor of six of the most prominent churches in the cities of Brooklyn and New York.

In 1875 he was elected president of the Wesleyan University. His earnest desire was to remain in the pastorate, for which his love was deep and strong, and in which his labors had been crowned with success. But so general was the conviction throughout the church that he ought to heed this call, and so emphatically was that conviction expressed, that he yielded his preference and accepted the place. For five years he discharged the duties of his office in a masterly manner, and the friends of the institution rejoiced that it was under such a leader.

He was chosen by the New York Conference, at the head of its delegation, to represent it at the General Conference in 1872, 1876 and 1880. In 1878 he visited the General Conference of the M. E. Church South, as a delegate to present the fraternal salutations of the M. E. Church; and in 1886 he visited the British Wesleyan Conference at its session in John Wesley's historic church, "City Road Chapel," London, on a like errand. At the

General Conference of 1880 he was elected and consecrated as Bishop.

In 1870 Mr Foss received the degree of D. D. from his Alma Mater, and that of LL. D. from Cornell College, Iowa, in 1879, and again from the University of Pennsylvania in 1889.

CYRUS DAVID FOSS, D. D , LL. D.

He has been a frequent contributor to the religious papers of his own church and to the Independent: and has gained a wide reputation as an able and brilliant writer. Articles from his pen have also appeared in the Sunday School Times, the North American Review, and other periodicals. He has also published many sermons and addresses for special occasions. In 1881 he delivered an address at his Alma Mater at the semi-centennial of the University.

He is a man of well-rounded character, possessing the great qualities of preacher, administrator, and leader of men. At times eloquent, he is always simple, direct, and convincing and commands the attention of his audience by forceful and earnest presentation of truth.

BISHOP JOHN H. VINCENT, D. D., LL. D.

John Heyl Vincent, M. E. Bishop, born in Tuscaloosa, Ala., Feburary 23, 1832. He was educated at academies in Milton and Lewisburg, Pa., began to preach at the age of eighteen, completed his training for the ministry at Wesleyan Institute, Newark, N. J., and in the four years' theological course of the New Jersey Conference, into which he was received in 1853. He was ordained deacon in 1855 and elder in 1857, when he was transferred to the Rock River conference, serving as pastor in Galena, Chicago, and elsewhere until 1865. In that year he established the "Northwest Sunday School Quarterly," and in 1866 the "Sunday School Teacher." He was appointed general agent of the Methodist Episcopal Sunday School Union, and in 1868 was elected by the General Conference corresponding secretary both of the union and of the Tract Society, in which posts he was continued till 1884. He was the editor of the Sunday School publications of the church, conducting the "Sunday School Journal," published in New York City, with such success that its circulation rose from 16,500 to 160,000, while that of his lesson-books has been nearly 2,500,000 copies. In 1873, with Lewis Miller, of Akron, Ohio, he projected a Sunday School teachers' institute for the purpose of preparing teachers for their work by means of lectures and drills. The institute first met at Chautauqua, N. Y., in August, 1874, and has since assembled each year in the same place. It has extended beyond the limits of its original design, and given rise to allied institutions, which, as well as the Sunday School assemblies and the international lessons, extend their benefits to members of all Christian bodies. The Chautauqua Literary and Scientific Circle, which prescribes courses of reading for all classes of people, was founded in

1878, and within a few years had 100,000 students on its rolls. In connection with this the Chautauqua University was established, a summer school in which lectures on most of the arts and sciences are given, and of which Bishop Vincent, who received the degree of D. D. from Ohio Wesleyan University in 1870, and that of LL. D.

JOHN H. VINCENT, D. D., LL. D.

from Washington and Jefferson in 1885, has been chancellor from the beginning. At the general Conference of 1888 he was elected a Bishop. Among his published works are "Little Footprints in Bible Lands" (New York, 1861); "The Chautauqua Movement" (1886); "The Home Book" (1886); "The Modern Sunday School" (1887); and "Better Not."

GOVERNOR KNUTE NELSON

Knute Nelson, of Alexandria, Minnesota, was born in the parish of Voss, near the City of Bergen, Norway, on the 2d day of

GOVERNOR KNUTE NELSON

February, A. D., 1843. When three years of age he lost his father. He came to the United States with his mother in July 1849, living in Chicago, Ill., till the fall of 1850, when he moved to

the State of Wisconsin, where he resided till August, 1871, when
he moved to Alexandria, Minn., which has ever since been his home.
In boyhood he attended a Methodist Sunday School and at one
time taught a Bible class.

He is a graduate of Albion Wisconsin Academy. He served
in the War of the Rebellion as a private and non-commissioned
officer in Company B, Fourth Wisconsin Regiment, from May, 1861,
until July, 1864: was wounded and taken prisoner on the 14th day
of June, 1863, in the seige of Port Hudson, La. He was admitted
to the bar of the Circuit Court for Dane County, Wisconsin, in the
spring of 1867; was a member of the Assembly in the Wisconsin
Legislature in 1868 and 1869: was County Attorney for Douglass
County, Minnesota, in 1872, 1873 and 1874; was State Senator in
the Minnesota Legislature in 1875, 1876, 1877 and 1878; was Presidential Elector on the Republican ticket in 1880; was a member
of the Board of Regents of the State University from February 1st,
1882, to January, 1893; was a member of the Forty-eighth Congress from the then Fifth District of Minnesota, elected by a plu-
rality of 4,500 over Kindred, Independent Republican, and Barnum,
Democrat; was a member of the Forty-ninth Congress from the
ame District, elected by a majority of 12,500 over Baxter, Democrat: and was a member of the Fiftieth Congress from the same
District, elected by a majority of 41,698 over Long, Prohibitionist.

He was nominated unanimously by acclamation as candidate
for Governor, by the Republican State Convention on July 29th,
1892, and was elected Governor on November 8th, 1892, by a plu-
rality of 14,620 votes over Lawler, Democrat: Donnelly, People's
Party; and Dean, Prohibitionist. After filling this exalted position,
with great credit to himself and the state, for one term, he was
again nominated by his party and re-elected by an overwhelming
majority at the last election.

GEORGE N. HILLMAN

The subject of this sketch was born at Greenwich, Washington County, N. Y., July 14, 1852, of Methodist parentage: united
with the M. E. Church when about thirteen. Attended common
school, village academy and Fort Edward Collegiate Institute.

When about eighteen, he taught the large district school, winter term, at Battenville; afterwards two winter terms at Center Falls, sometimes humorously known as "Hard-scrabble."

When about thirteen, he became an earnest student of Graham's Standard of American Phonography; at seventeen did his first public reporting, and three years later became the official reporter of the

GEORGE N. HILLMAN

Washington County Court. About this time he was married to Miss Mary Emma Cutter, also of Methodist parentage.

Coming to Minnesota in the spring of 1874, he was soon appointed official reporter of the District Court of Hennepin County, residing at Minneapolis a little more than a year. He then resigned to accept the position of official reporter of the District Court of the second judicial district, at St. Paul, which difficult and important position he has held ever since.

He is one of the most accurate and rapid stenographers in the United States, and as a law reporter has had a remarkable career. As early as 1875 he received a flattering testimonial from Henry Ward Beecher upon the report of a sermon delivered at the opera house in St. Paul, who spoke of it as "the best report he had ever

RESIDENCE OF GEORGE N. HILLMAN

received outside of the city of New York." He was employed to report two important impeachment trials at the State Capitol, and made daily transcripts of the testimony for the use of the members of the court, each trial comprising several large volumes; has also reported several legislative investigations, proceedings of conventions, important legal arguments, political meetings, sermons, lectures, etc. In making daily transcripts of court proceedings, his shorthand notes are sometimes dictated by assistants skilled in the art, even in technical cases.

He has ever manifested marked and active interest in religious matters, in charitable institutions in general, in the denomination of his choice in particular, and has contributed materially to the founding and maintenance of Oxford M. E. Church. He has taken an active part in all the various departments of church work and has been particularly helpful in church music, vocal and instrumental.

In his business he is painstaking, careful and industrious, and, while noted for his liberality, has acquired a reasonable competence.

OFFICIAL STENOGRAPHER'S ROOM

Of modest and unassuming manner, of kindly disposition, he has secured the confidence and esteem of a large circle of acquaintances and friends.

He has three sons and three daughters, all young Methodists, musically inclined, who still reside with their parents at their comfortable home in St. Paul, corner of Dale street and Lincoln avenue.

SOMERS C. ROBINSON

Somers C. Robinson, manufacturer, was born at West Creek, Cumberland county, N. C., March 21, 1831, son of Morris and Mary Robinson. His early education was acquired in the district school. When fifteen years of age he left the farm and

SOMERS C. ROBINSON

was apprenticed to the village carpenter with whom he served three years. In the meantime, much against the will of his employer, he joined the Methodist church. This caused him severe persecution and to avoid it he ran away and went to sea. While absent, his employer repented his harshness and asked him to return. This led to a reconciliation, and on his return he completed his term of apprenticeship, and, at the age of twenty-one, he received his first wages as a carpenter. The next year he married Maria H., daughter of Hon. Levi Dare, a prominent citizen of Cumberland county. He continued his occupation of carpenter until he was twenty-six years old when he took up the business of contractor and builder.

RESIDENCE OF SOMERS C. ROBINSON

In 1857 he went to Leavenworth, Kansas, where he found profitable employment at his trade for nine months. Upon his return to New Jersey for his family, the opposition offered by his wife's father to her settling in so wild a place as Kansas then was, determined him to locate in some other section of the west, and in 1858 he took his family to Minnesota and located at St. Anthony, where he built a house and made for them an humble but comfortable home.

After eight years of success as a contractor and builder in St. Anthony, he removed to the new and growing city of Minneapolis, where he continued to thrive. Here he formed a partnership, and entered into the manufacture of building material on a large scale. The business resulted in the Bardwell-Robinson Company, the largest manfacturers of building supplies in the state. His son, Charles N. Robinson, became a member of the concern in 1884. Mr. Robinson is an ardent Republican in politics and an earnest member of the Hennepin Avenue Church. He is also treasurer of the Board of Trustees of the Fowler Church. His charities to churches and schools are large but unostentatious.

REV. WILLIAM KENNEDY MARSHALL, D. D.

William Kennedy Marshall, was born at Steubenville, Ohio, being the son of Abner and Sarah Marshall. His father was of English descent and his mother of Scotch. He was reared and educated in Fayette County, Pennsylvania. In 1857 he established and edited the Brownsville Times, at Brownsville, Pennsylvania. In 1858, he was united in marriage to Miss Sally Gosline of Brownsville. In September of the same year he united with the Methodist Episcopal Church at Brownsville under the pastorate of the late Rev. Ezra Hingeley, D. D. In March, 1860, he was admitted on trial in the Pittsburgh Conference and appointed to Mt. Morris Circuit. Following this, he served two years on the Red Stone Circuit, two years at Ballair, Ohio, and one year at St. Clairsville, Ohio.

In the spring of 1866, he was transferred to Kansas Conference and stationed at Atchison two years, at First Church Leavenworth city, two years, Presiding Elder of Leavenworth District, two years, and Lawrence Station, three years. In 1872 he was chairman of the Kansas Delegation in the General Conference at Brooklyn. In 1875 he was transferred to the St. Louis Conference and stationed at Warrensburg, Missouri. His next appointment was Presiding Elder of the Sedalia District, but failing health made it necessary to give up this work at the end of the year. He then took charge of the Sedalia Station for two years after which he

was stationed at Central Church, St. Louis. Thence he was
transferred, in 1881, to the Minnesota Conference and stationed at
Jackson Street Church. At the close of three years he was assigned to Rochester, then to Thirteenth Avenue, Minneapolis,
then to Trinity and at the last Conference was appointed Presiding Elder of the St. Paul District.

REV. W. K. MARSHALL, D. D.

The honorary degree of Doctor of Divinity was conferred
upon him in 1879 by Centenary College, Indianola, Iowa. He has
been a writer for most of our periodicals from the Advocates up to
the Methodist Review. He has traveled through England, Ireland, Scotland and France. He has gained much notoriety as a

lecturer. He preaches the gospel without apology and always makes immediate application of the truths he preaches to the hearts of the people, expecting instantaneous results.

H. R. BRILL

H. R. Brill was born in the Province of Quebec in 1846. His ancestors were Holland Dutch who settled on the Hudson in

H. R. BRILL

New York. His maternal grandfather and grandmother were named Adam and Eve (Sager). He came to Minnesota with his parents when thirteen years of age. He lived on a farm until he was twenty-one working and attending school winters and sometimes teaching. He attended Hamline at Red Wing off and on for four years and spent one year at Michigan University. He moved to St. Paul in 1867 where he has since lived. He studied law and was admitted to the bar in 1869. He was elected Probate Judge and held that office in 1873-4. In 1875 he was appointed District Judge which position he still holds, having been elected three times since. Although a republican in principle, he has taken no part in politics since his elevation to the bench He has been trustee of Hamline University for many years and was president of the board for some time. His father and mother and grand parents on both sides were active and honorable Methodists. His father's house was known far and wide as a stopping place for Methodist ministers where they were always royally entertained. Mr. Brill has always taken an active part in church affairs. He has served as Sunday School teacher, librarian, and superintendent frequently. He has served as steward, district steward, trustee, Member of Lay Electoral Conference several times. He is chairman of the Board of Trustees of the First Church, St. Paul, of which church he has been an influential member ever since he located in St. Paul. He was received into the church at Red Wing while a student there, by Dr. Cyrus Brooks. He was a member of the last General Conference and chairman of the Judiciary Committee, writing all the reports.

REV. R. R. ATCHISON

Rev. R. R. Atchison was born at Elizabeth city, New Jersey, September 14, 1844. He was converted in early life and began in the ministry as a local preacher in 1871. As such he preached for eight years in Boston, Massachusetts, and seven years in Chicago, Illinois. He joined the Minnesota Conference in October, 1886 and was first appointed pastor of the Twenty-fourth Street Church, Minneapolis. During the year the indebtedness on the church was paid, the church was remodeled and the people were blessed with a gracious revival in which many were converted. At the following Conference he was appointed to North Church, at Camden Place, and enjoyed two prosperous and happy years in this pastorate which were blessed with two successful revivals, after which the church building was enlarged and paid for.

REV. R. R. ATCHISON

At the Conference in 1889 he was appointed to the First Church, St. Cloud. This church had been without a settled pastor for nine months. Religious interest was at low ebb and the church building sadly out of repair. Before the close of the year, 50 persons professed conversion, 36 of whom united with the church. The church was remodeled at a cost of $1,219, all of which was raised and paid as soon as the work was completed. At the Conference in 1891, he was appointed to the Western Avenue M. E. Church, Minneapolis. He found a loyal and liberal society struggling under a weight of $3,200 debt. Brother Atchison took an immediate hold of the situation and did not relinquish his grasp until the debt was paid. Two successful revival seasons crowned his ministry, in which over 100 were converted. 87 of whom have united with the church.

After such an unbroken record of pastoral success, characterized by spiritual triumph and rare executive ability, it is not strange that, at the recent Conference, he was appointed Presiding Elder of Willmar District of the Northern Minnesota Conference.

WARREN HOWARD HAYES

The subject of this sketch was born at Prattsburgh, N. Y., August 22, 1847, of good New England stock. His ancestors emigrated from Scotland to Derbyshire, England, thence to Windsor, Conn., in 1680, where descendants of the family still live, having given many honored names to professional, municipal, state and federal positions, the most prominent having been President R. B. Hayes.

The early years of his life were amidst the country scenes of the large and successful farm of his father. George Goundry Hayes, in central N. Y. At five commencing school life at "the little red

school-house:" at twelve entering a private school in Italy, thence
two years at Watkins Academy, here, in 1865, joining on probation the First M. E. Church, (whose present fine edifice erected in
later years, was from his first church design) two years 1867 and
1868 at Genesee Wesleyan Seminary at Seima, N. Y.   In the fall

WARREN HOWARD HAYES

of 1868 entering Cornell University on Oct. 8th, inaugural day, having passed the first year class examinations and after three years
successful work in the courses of Civil Engineering and Architecture, graduating with his class June 21, 1871, having taken two
President White first prizes for proficiency.

The next ten years were given to the practice of his chosen
profession, Architecture, offices in Elmira, N. Y., where he was
married in 1881 to Miss M. F. Beardsley.

Church Architecture from the first was made a special study
and practice.

The growing fame of the Twin Cities later attracted his attention as affording a center for wider practice and an office was
opened in Minneapolis, thirteen years since, and where in 1886 he
was married to Mrs. Lillie Cook VanNorman of Hamilton, Ont.,
his first wife having died four years previous. Mr. Hayes' services
as a church Architect, are in demand east and west, some of his
home work being familiar with the Twin Cities, he having designed
nineteen of their better churches, as well as many of the prominent
business and school buildings, among the latter are those of Hamline
University and the House of The Good Shepherd Convent in St.
Paul.

HENRY BEEMER

Henry Beemer was born in Ontario, Nov. 5, 1836, of Methodist
parentage. His father Joseph, and his mother Elizabeth Beemer,
were fully consecrated to the great work of the church and their
home was always open to ministers and missionaries. This was a
typical, Christian home, free from all selfishness, bitterness and
cynical treatment of others. Its atmosphere was laden with
Christian love and its altar continually burned with the fires of true
devotion. It is not strange that the son, Henry, is so strong in his
devotion to Christ and allegiance to the church.

He was educated in the public schools. In 1860 he moved to
Michigan, thence to Illinois in 1865 and to Iowa in 1866, where
nineteen years of his life were spent. For twenty years he was
engaged in the monument business and for the past twelve years
has been engaged in life insurance. In both lines he has been
signally successful. His sterling integrity, indomitable energy :
rare social qualities. great heartedness, and warm sympathy for all
in need of help have been the elements entering into his successful
career.

He came to Minneapolis in 1885. He had been converted in 1883 at Marshalltown, Iowa, where he united with the church. He was a Methodist when he reached Minneapolis and at once united with Simpson Church. He afterwards united with the Lake Street Church which he helped to organize. He is now a prominent and influential member of Wesley Church. He was elected a delegate to the General Conference at Omaha in 1892.

HENRY BEEMER

He was married in 1857 to Nancy Averill. Four children have been born of this union. The two eldest are dead: one son and one daughter are living.

Mr. Beemer is one of the progressive citizens of Minneapolis. His name stands for the moral as well as material interests of the city. There is no question mark over his attitude upon any great public question. He has been one of the liberal supporters of our church and is always ready to help the helpless and to contribute to deserving enterprises.

W. C. RICE

W. C. RICE

W. C. Rice was born in Will County, Illinois, August 3, 1840, and came to Minnesota and settled at Rochester in 1856. He was converted and joined the Methodist Episcopal Church when nineteen. He was educated at Hamline University. In 1863 he was married to Miss Emma Eberman. He united with the Minnesota Conference in 1865. On account of failing health he located in 1881, but in 1889 he was re-admitted to the effective rank. He has filled the following appointments: St. Charles, Plainview, Wabasha, Rochester. Presiding Elder of Rochester District, Red Wing, First Church, Minneapolis, Clinton Church, St. Paul, and Zumbrota. While located he supplied the Presbyterian church in Red Wing one year, and the Congregational church in Zumbrota six years, during which time he edited the Rochester Post one year and was the first State Dairy Commissioner for two years. He has secured the building of three parsonages, the building or purchasing of three churches, and has led the churches in paying $60,000 indebtedness. He has received 558 persons into the churches on probation and has baptized more than 350.

As a preacher he is precise and logical never failing to interest and edify his large congregations. He is thoroughly consecrated to the work and prizes above all things the privilege of preaching the gospel.

ELIJAH HALEY

Elijah Haley was born near the city of Oxford, England, April 7, 1836. He was educated in the National School under the care

ELIJAH HALEY

of the State Church. At the age of fourteen, he carelessly wandered into a primitive Methodist chapel. He here became convinced that he needed a change of heart and under the burning exhortation he immediately surrendered to God and received that great blessing. Life took on a new form to him. He at once felt that it was fraught with great responsibility. He heard the voice of God calling him in to his vineyard and he responded, —"Here am I, send me."

At the age of nineteen he was given a license to preach as a primitive Methodist local preacher, and served as such until 1871 when he entered the regular ministry, on the Barrsley circuit, Yorkshire. After having traveled four years he was refused admission into the conference, being over twenty-five years of age,—which was the iron-clad limit of the church. On a pressing invitation from a friend, he brought his family to America. In 1876 he was admitted into the Illinois Conference, Bishop Wiley presiding. In this Conference he served the following charges: Dawson, two years; Chesterfield, one year; Raymond, three years. While at the latter place he was transferred to the Minnesota Conference where he served High Forest, three years; Kasson, two years; Eyota, two years; Bloomington Avenue, four years, the present year completing the five years' term. His work at the Bloomington Avenue Church has been very successful. Under his indefatigable labors, the indebtedness has been removed and the church has been brought into a state of peace and prosperity.

JOSEPH C. PIERSON, JR.

Joseph C. Pierson was born May 1, 1857, at Newark, New Jersey. His ancestors were the founders of Newark: he is a descendant of Rev. Abraham Pierson, the first Presbyterian minister of Newark, whose son was the first president of Yale College. His great, great grandfather settled near Springfield, N. J., and during the Revolutionary battle of Springfield his house was used for the wounded colonial soldiers, it being still in possession of the Pierson family.

JOSEPH C. PIERSON, Jr.

Mr. Pierson was educated at the Newark Academy and the Pingry Institute, of Elizabeth, N. J. At the age of seventeen he entered the hardware store of Hart, Bliven & Mead, New York City. The following year he went into the office of James Clark Wilson & Co. where he was employed in several positions until the firm failed.

In 1877 he went to San Francisco. Although especially skilled in the hardware business, his energy and tact were sufficient for any employment and upon arriving in California he soon received a position in a stationery house as entry clerk. He remained there until he became salesman in the large and well known hardware house of Huntington, Hopkins & Co., which position he occupied to his credit until his failing health compelled him to move to Nevada where he remained for a year. He then returned east and occupied several responsible positions until October, 1882, when

PIERSON HARDWARE CO.'S STORE

he started in manfacturing hardware in Newark, N. J. In 1884 his business was consolidated with the old and reputable wholesale and commission house of Flagler, Forsythe & Bradly, to which firm his name was added.

On December 21, 1883, he was united in marriage to the youngest daughter of Abraham Baker, whose father was one of the Knickerbocker families of New York City.

Mr. Pierson was for some time a member of the Unitarian Society, in which he was an active and influential worker, but in 1890 he came to recognize Christ as more than a mere man, as the

"Son of the living God" and the Savior of the world. He at once united with the Methodist Church of Plainfield and became active in its movements as well as a zealous worker in the Y. M. C. A. Upon coming to Minneapolis, he incorporated the Pierson Hardware Co., which business, under his management, has grown in prosperity until it ranks among the strongest houses in the Northwest.

He is an official member of the Fowler Church and a tireless worker in the Y. M. C. A. He is genial and pleasant, always affable to his customers and hospitable in his beautiful home. Although absorbed in business, the success of which is a testimony to his rare ability he is nowhere as happy or contented as at his own fireside, where his wife and children are the constant objects of his tender care and love.

F. A. DUNSMOOR, M. D.

Dr. F. A. Dunsmoor was born May 28th, 1853, at the little settlement of Harmony, now included within the city limits of Minneapolis. His father, Jas. A. Dunsmoor, came to St. Anthony in 1842, from Farmington, Me., where he had been a man of prominence, representing his district in the legislature and discharging other offices of trust and honor.

Fredrick Alanson received his education at the public schools of Richfield and Minneapolis, and later, at the State University. At the age of sixteen he taught school for one term: then, following the strong bent of his own inclinations, he began to read medicine in the office of Drs. Goodrich and Kimball, going later to New York, where he took the full course of the Bellevue Hospital Medical College, of the three years 1873, 1874, 1875, taking his degree of M. D. in March, 1875. During these years he also received private instruction in surgery from Dr. Frank H. Hamilton: in diseases of the chest, from Drs. Loomis and Flint; in pathology, from Dr. E. G. Janeway, and in chemistry, from Dr. R. Ogden Doremus. After graduation he entered into a partnership with Dr. H. H. Kimball, which was disolved in 1877.

In 1876 he was married to Elizabeth Emma Billings Turner, daughter of the late Surgeon Geo. F. Turner, U. S. A. Mrs. Dunsmoor comes of good pioneer blood. Her father, Surgeon Turner, a lineal descendant of the famous Puritan, Capt. Miles Standish, was stationed at Ft. Snelling in 1846, when all this region

DR. F. A. DUNSMOOR, M. D.

was a vast "happy hunting ground," and was the contemporary and beloved friend of such pioneers as Gov. H. H. Sibley, Gen. R. W. Johnson, Franklin Steel, Father Geer, Rev. Dr. Williamson, and others. Seven children have been born to them, of whom but three are living, Marjorie Allport, Elizabeth Turner, and one son, Fredrick Laton.

In surgery he ranks deservedly high. It has been his master passion from boyhood.

As an operator he is bold, rapid and skillful, with firmness and precision of touch, which seems intuitive to him. His enthusiastic love for his profession keeps him abreast of every advance, both in the practice of surgery, and in the invention and improvement of instruments and appliances. Flying visits to the great medical centers keep him in touch with the leading surgeons of the day, and he is well known and highly rated outside of the limits of his own field, being summoned to attend cases in Chicago, New York, Montana, Washington, California, and so far south as the city of Mexico.

A warm-hearted, companionable man, he loves to meet with men in every walk and does not restrict his affiliations to the medical profession. He is a Mason, a Druid, a Good Templar, etc., and an active member of the Hennepin Avenue Methodist Church where he has served for many years on the official board. In habits he has always been a total abstainer from the use of liquor and tobacco, and in his manner of life, thoroughly domestic, being never happier than when he can gather a congenial group of friends about him in his elegant, hospitable home on Tenth street and devote a few half hours to social intercourse and music.

HORATIO FRANCIS LILLIBRIDGE

Horatio Francis Lillibridge was in every sense the world's idea of a self-made man. His father was a school teacher, and he the youngest of a family of seven children. Salaries of pedagogues were small in those days and consequently the father had little means above the family necessities. The youngest son was born May 26, 1836, at Staffordville, Connecticut. When he was only six months old his father, the only support of the family, was taken away and thus the mother was left with her seven children. The older children had scattered, even then, and it was decided that the mother and Horatio should live with his grandmother. There was in her that which afterwards became so characteristic of her son, indomitable perseverance, indefatigable industry, and the highest sense of honor.

At the age of nine years Horatio commenced work in one of the cotton mills, so numerous in Connecticut, at a meagre salary; but his faithfulness to his work never wavered. He was employed in various ways until the age of fourteen when he became a clerk in a general store. At seventeen he commenced work for a bank and here he gained valuable knowledge in book-keeping and accounts. Even at this time his ambition was large and he looked westward for its gratification. His money had all been spent in helping the family but his mother and sister had saved a little. He borrowed $100 of them and came to Minneapolis at the age of nineteen. Remaining here but a month, he pushed on to Monticello, and there invested his $100 in town sites between that place and Forest City. As it was only boom property his money was sunk beyond recall. This experience, coming so early in his western career, was invaluable to him as it taught him that careful conservatism and excellent judgment which he afterwards manifested in so great a degree.

His conversion was a matter of early development. His grandfather was a Baptist preacher and the grandson leaned towards that denomination, but on January 2, 1859, he married Cynthia A. Jenks, whose family were staunch Methodists and a short time before his marriage he, too, united with the Methodist Church.

His life at Monticello was the commencement of his remarkable business career. First a clerk, then a partner. After nine years he returned to Minneapolis. He had some capital and first went into the lumber business but sold out and commenced work as book-keeper in the Pacific Mill. Again he became a partner, and was interested there until he went into the bakery business. Here he met his highest success and by honesty, industry and economy built up his magnificent business and fortune.

About ten years ago he began thinking of a new edifice for Centenary Methodist Church. The question was thoroughly agitated, but it was not until four years ago that the way seemed clear. Mr. Lillibridge was a deep thinker and in all his undertakings prayer was his great stronghold. After thinking and praying about the building of the new church for a long time he decided to render the necessary assistance. Here the character of the man and his consecrated purpose shone forth in greatest splendor. In order to obtain the necessary funds he mortgaged his best real estate. Not only did he furnish money but he gave his time and labor. His ability as a financier was needed in the building of the church and he looked after every detail with careful consideration and unquestioned success.

About six years before his death his health had become impaired by his close confinement to business and he travelled extensively, but despite everything else he took time to look after the church.

He died June 3, 1894. His friends said that no ordinary funeral sermon could do for him, and so it was arranged that the service should be an open one—for testimony, not for eulogy. Several friends spoke from the fullness of their hearts. Judge Vanderburgh, Rev. C. A. VanAnda, D. D., Rev. Jabez Brooks, D. D., Mr. J. E. Bell, Rev. R. M. Carter, Rev. George Galpin and Rev. H. H. French, all contributed their testimonies. The church—his church, was filled with mourners. Nearly 100 of the employees of the American Biscuit Company were there in a body as a token of their love and respect. Then he was laid away in Lakewood Cemetery.

In life he gave liberally of time, labor and money, and although he has gone, he has provided $15,000 more for different branches of church work. His wife and two daughters survive him, who have his spirit of loyalty and consecration to the church.

WILLIAM McKINLEY, D. D.

William McKinley was born in Glasgow, Scotland, March 24, 1834, son of George and Margaret McDonald McKinley. His paternal grandfather, John McKinley, lived in the north of Ireland, but moved to Scotland during the political troubles of 1793. His maternal grandfather, Angus McDonald, was a Scotch highlander and British soldier in the wars of the French revolution. In 1841 young McKinley emigrated with his parents to the United States,

settling in Baltimore Co., Md., and in 1849 he accompanied an
uncle to Illinois where he spent the next six years in teaching
and attending school and private studies. He was chiefly educated
at private schools in Maryland, and at Rock River Seminary,
Mount Morris, Ill., supplemented with a brief period at Beloit

WM. McKINLEY, D. D.

College, Wis., left the latter institution on account of ill health,
and in 1855 came to Minnesota. He was licensed to preach in the
same year, and in 1856 was admitted on trial in the Minnesota
Annual Conference of the Methodist Episcopal church: received
into full membership in 1858, an ordained elder in 1859. During
the last named year he was married to Amy A. Sumner, who died
in 1871. He was again married in 1876 to Alice B. Hayward.

Dr. McKinley served successively as pastor in the following charges: Northfield, Minn., Trempealeau, Wis., Hokah, Minn., one year each: Taylor's Falls four years. He was for one year chaplain in the army. Other pastorates held by him were at First Church, Minneapolis, two years: First Church, Winona, three terms, nine years; Jackson Street, St. Paul, three years: First Church, Duluth, two years: Knoxville, Tenn., one year; Church of Christian Endeavor, Brooklyn, N. Y., one year; Red Wing, three years; Hamline, St. Paul, five years: Presiding Elder of Winona district, two years, and of St. Paul district three years. He is now pastor of Central Park Church, St. Paul. He was elected delegate to the General Conference of the Methodist Episcopal Church in 1876, 1880, and 1892. The degree of D. D. was conferred on him by Hamline University in 1884.

CHARLES W. DAVIES

Charles W. Davies was born in 1854 at Whitesboro, N. Y. His parents were Welch, and sturdy members of the Congregational Church. Their son Charles was a precocious youth. He was always quick, wide awake, ready to answer any question and of an inquisitive turn of mind.

He completed the course of public schools and entered as a student into the Whitesboro Seminary. Here he continued to take elective studies until he was twenty years of age. Upon leaving school, he went to Utica and served as an apprentice in a large jewelry store. He felt a natural inclination toward engraving and after working under one of the engravers of that city long enough to acquire a thorough knowledge of the art he formed a partnership with his employer which continued for two years. He then went to Syracuse and started into business for himself. But no sooner had he gained a foot-hold than he was burned out, thus being reduced to a state of most embarrassing poverty; yet possessed of unflinching courage he faced the world determined not to surrender. At this time he was drawn toward the West and started for Minneapolis. He stopped at Grand Rapids where he worked a while at his trade and again at Chicago finally reaching his destination. Without friends, standing or resources in this new city, he began business in his own name. He was determined to succeed. He converted a store box into a table and with a few tools and plenty of pluck he began as the pioneer engraver of Minneapolis. How well he has succeeded needs no statement, for his business, under his tireless and persistent care, has grown until its

CHARLES W. DAVIES

patrons are not only of his own city but throughout the entire Northwest. He has won a reputation for rare ability in his art and does work for those of the most delicate taste and refined style. His place of business, at 610 Nicollet Avenue, is neat and commodious and always supplied with the latest and best materials in the line.

He was married in 1885 to Miss Clara S. Getz, of Delaware, Ohio. She was reared in a Methodist home and is a lady of strong Christian character. Their home, 916 Girard avenue, is always open to their friends and is filled with books, music and rare works of art.

HERBERT W. SEAGER

Herbert W. Seager was born August 16, 1864, at Red Wing, where his parents were leading members of the Methodist Church. His grandfather was a Presiding Elder in the Western New York Conference for several years and was known as a man of great power in the ministry. His parents moved to Minnesota in 1857 and settled at Red Wing, but subsequently moved to St. Paul where Herbert was educated in the public schools. In 1880 he was employed as a clerk in a large wholesale fruit and confectionery store. He continued in this position for one year and then went to work for an agricultural implement firm. This firm failed in 1884 and he then went into the office of Nichols & Dean, in St. Paul, as book-keeper and remained until he moved to Minneapolis and began as cashier of the Minneapolis Iron Store Company. Having been reared under Methodist influence he had always felt it his duty to be a Christian but did not reach a decision to accept Christ until 1890 when he was thoroughly converted at his own home.

He was married September 10, 1885, to Miss Harriet H. Barston, of St. Paul. After his conversion, himself and wife united with Grace Church, St. Paul. Upon coming to Minneapolis they identified themselves with the First Church, during which membership Mr. Seager has served in various official capacities. He has taken a special interest in the Epworth work of the church and become so thoroughly identified with the movement that his influence won recognition among the young people of the sister churches. As a result, he was elected at the last convention at Red Wing as State President of the Epworth League and confirmed by the late Annual Conference. This gives him a broader field for his unusual ability as an organizer. It places him in the leadership of 321 leagues and at least 14,000 leaguers. It is believed that under his administration the work of the league in Minnesota will receive a great impetus.

JOHN D. ENGLE

John D. Engle was born November 6, 1860, in Maryland. His parents were members of the Methodist Church. He attended the public schools in his boyhood and subsequently was a student in Hamline University. He was converted at the age of twelve and united with the Methodist Church with which he has been connected ever since. He is at present an official member of the Merriam Park Church in St. Paul.

He was married in 1886 to Miss Eunice Dowling and is the father of three children.

He is the popular agent of the Globe Furnishing Company and is well known among the church people of the Twin Cities.

CHARLES CURTISS COFFEE

Charles Curtiss Coffee was born at Alliance, Ohio, June 1, 1862, of Methodist parentage. After graduating from the High School at Alliance in 1879 he attended Mt. Union College.

His father was a dentist and the son decided to follow the same profession. He entered his father's office in 1880 where he received his initial training, but he realized the necessity of the most thorough preparation and after pursuing a course in dental surgery in the Pennsylvania College, he graduated in 1884. After practicing with his father for two years he took a pleasure trip into the West and spent some time at Lake Minnetonka. During this trip he became so impressed with Minneapolis that he decided to make

it his home.   He returned East and closing out his interests
there came to Minneapolis in 1886, where he has since prosecuted
his profession.

He was married to Miss Alma V. Welt, September 19, 1888,
at Alliance, Ohio.   They are members of the Hennepin Avenue
Church, having united with it soon after coming to Minneapolis.

CHARLES CURTISS COFFEE

Dr. Coffee was a very active member of the church at Alliance
and was especially effective in the musical department.   As a dentist he has forged his way to the head of the profession.   His motto
has always been "first class work" and upon this basis he has become well and favorably known among the people of Minneapolis.

He is thoroughly conversant with the latest methods and facilities of his profession and in his attractive offices in the Century Building he has a complete equipment for meeting all the demands of his large practice.

GEORGE M. LANGUM

GEORGE M. LANGUM

George M. Langum was born in 1867 at Spring Valley, Minnesota. His parents were members of the Lutheran Church. He attended the public schools until he was thirteen years old. After this he attended the High School at Castle, South Dakota; the college at Brookings, South Dakota, for two years; the State Normal School, at Madison, S. D., for over a year, and the Business College at La Crosse, Wisconsin, from which he graduated in the commercial and shorthand department. While in Dakota he devoted some of his time as a teacher in the public schools. He also taught while a student at the La Crosse Institution.

Upon graduation, he was placed in charge of the Actual Business department. After serving in this capacity for a season he attended the Northern Normal School at Dixon, Ill., graduating from its pen and art department. While at Dixon, he also assisted in teaching.

He then came to Minneapolis where he is serving at present as principal of the commercial department of the University of Commerce and Finance.

Mr. Langum is bright and capable as a teacher. He is a member of the Fowler Church.

SILAS D. HILLMAN.

The second son of George W. and Chloe A. Hillman was born upon a farm in the town of Greenwich, Washington County, New York, September 23. 1845. His parents were earnest and loyal members of the M. E. Church. An elder brother, Rev. John H.

SILAS D. HILLMAN

Hillman, a graduate of Garrett Biblical Institute, at Concord, was for many years an efficient and leading member of the New Hampshire Conference. The subject of this sketch united with the church when thirteen years of age; attended common schools and Greenwich Academy until eighteen years of age when he engaged his first school, teaching two terms in his native state and five terms afterwards in Minnesota, coming to 'he latter state in the fall of 1867. In June, 1870, he married Miss M. J. Somerville, the amiable and accomplished daughter of Hon. Wm. Somerville, of Olmsted County. In the winter of 1874 he prepared and secured the passage of a general act by the legislature authorizing the employment of stenographic reporters in the courts of this state. He was appointed official reporter of the third judicial district and occupied that position for some sixteen years, being also employed from time to time in other portions of the state and in Wisconsin. In the spring of 1874 he purchased an interest in the Rochester Record and Union and was for some six years associate editor and publisher of that periodical. In the spring of 1882 he removed to Minneapolis where he has since resided. In 1885 he was elected secretary of the State Horticultural Society, which position he continued to occupy for a period of five years. He has devoted himself chiefly for the last twenty years to the work of his profession, performing his first court work as a stenographer in an important trial at Rochester, in the fall of 1873. He is at present one of the official reporters of the district court of the fourth judicial district which embraces the county of Hennepin and three other counties. In church work he has taken an active interest; he was for some two years a member of Simpson M. E. Church and superintendent of the Sunday School. Himself, wife, a daughter, Miss Ada B., a graduate of the city High School and now a student at the State University, and Loyd, his eldest son, are now members of Hennepin Avenue M. E. Church. He has contributed to the erection and support of numerous sister churches and is interested in the success of the Fowler Church and especially in "Twin City Methodism."

FRANKLIN MARSHALL RULE

Franklin Marshall Rule was born in Lewisburgh, Va., April 20, 1845. He went with his parents to Indiana, in 1859, and came to Minnesota in 1883. His education began under special teachers at home, there being no public schools in Virginia at that time. He attended the public schools of Indiana, received an academic training under Prof.. W. A. Moore, of Earlham College, studied Greek with Prof. Philander Wiley, D. D., of Asbury University, and gave two years to the study of medicine. He taught two years in the public schools of Indiana, and was principal of Transitville Institute two years. He entered the Northwest Indiana

FRANKLIN MARSHALL RULE

Conference in 1868, and has served the following charges: Camden, Rossville, Ninth Street, LaFayette. Michigan City, Rochester, South Bend, Indiana; Northfield, Pipestone, Marshall, and Thirteenth Avenue, Minneapolis, where he is located at the present time. He has been for three years State Secretary of the Chautauqua System of Education. In all his charges he has been very successful. He combines good preaching ability with practical pastoral work. He mingles among the people like a commoner. His sermons have thought enough for the gravest, and spirit enough for the most fervid. He is perfectly at home in the pulpit, and his church is always filled to hear his stirring, instructive and eloquent words.

WILLIS G. CALDERWOOD

WILLIS G. CALDERWOOD

Willis G. Calderwood, the subject of this sketch, is an energetic worker in the field of Christian labor which he has chosen, and since his identification with the church in Minneapolis, in 1892, has made his service as valuable as faithful, concientious attention to duty could.

He first joined the Simpson Church, but was shortly afterward requested to take charge of the Sabbath School in the Minnehaha

Church, in which capacity he served a year, at the end of which time he was compelled by circumstances to resign the work. From Minnehaha he transferred his membership to First Church, where he found opportunity for labor waiting him.

Sabbath school and prohibition work have taken his chief attention and he has been instrumental in the organization and maintenance of several societies which have for their object the destruction of the legalized saloon.

Mr. Calderwood is a native of Wisconsin, born in 1866. His father, John Calderwood, a native of Scotland, is a retired minister of the Wesleyan Methodist Church, and his mother is of 1620 Puritan stock. His wife, Alice, the daughter of Rev. Charles Cox, a Wesleyan Methodist minister, is an earnest, though a retiring woman, of unusual Christian grace, and an efficient co-worker with her husband.

THOMAS ASBURY HARRISON

Thomas Asbury Harrison, son of Thomas and Margaret Harrison, was born near Belleville, Illinois, December 18. 1811. His father was an elder in the M. E. Church, and for many years preached twice a week. The family moved to Belleville in 1803 in order to get away from a part of the country were the only badge of respectability was the ownership of slaves.

Young Harrison's early education was meagre, being chiefly attained at a private school at Belleville. So apt was he, however, and so great were his diligence and application, that during the latter part of his school life he was made the teacher of his classes. Upon reaching his majority he went into the milling business with his father and brothers and built the first Harrison mill in Illinois. This was mainly accomplished by means of borrowed money, and but a short time after it was finished, and while full of wheat and flour, it was consumed by fire, entailing an almost total loss as there was no insurance on either the mill or its contents. Such a catastrophe would have overwhelmed a man of weaker character, but with Mr Harrison it was but a spur to renewed efforts, and the mill was at once rebuilt, Mr. Harrison working as a day laborer in order to save one man's wages. For some years the mills were run at but little above living expenses, and for a time at a positive loss, but the extra quality of the production, and the out-breaking of the Crimean war, eventually changed this state of affairs, and the foundation of the Harrison fortune was laid. The firm prospered

THOMAS ASBURY HARRISON

for a number of years, and only sold out at a time when, in Mr. Harrison's judgment, the business was beginning to wane. That he was right in this opinion was confirmed by the ill-fortune of his successor, whose failure may be partly accounted for, however, from the facts that he was compelled to hire four men to do the work that by Mr. Harrison had been done alone.

In 1860 Mr. Harrison took a permanent residence in Minneapolis, where his brother had established himself some years previously. The severity of the first winter almost persuaded him to return to the South at the first opportunity, but with the approach of spring he determined to remain as first planned. One of Mr. Harrison's first enterprises in Minneapolis was the buying of a piece of neighboring ground for which he had no use, a fence which obstructed his view, and which the owner persisted on maintaining, being his only reason for the purchase. The deal proved to be advantageous, however, for the subsequent rise in the value of that property alone gave him an independent fortune. His first investment of importance in Minnesota was in the First National Bank of St. Paul, and, later, he became a heavy stockholder in, and a director of both the Chicago, Milwaukee & St. Paul, and the St. Paul, Minneapolis & Omaha railroads. In 1862 he and his brothers built Harrison Hall, the first substantial modern structure in Minneapolis, and the beginning of the era of substantial building in that city. In 1863 he and his brothers, H. G. Harrison and Wm. M. Harrison, entered a partnership with Joseph Dean & Co., which for many years was the largest and most important lumber firm in the city, and under whose management the Atlantic & Pacific Mills were built.

When the civil war broke out, Mr. Harrison, who had been a close student of its underlying causes, and who had a strong sympathy for the Union, turned over thousands of dollars to the government, and, at first, without so much as a scrap of paper to show for it. He realized, however, that the government must first be saved or all his earnings of a life time would be useless. It was by accident that Mr. Harrison became connected with the State National Bank of which he was subsequently president, and whose liabilities, though he was under no obligations to do so, he paid out of his own pocket. He had loaned a friend some money, taking as security the stock of this bank, whose affairs he learned later were in a most doubtful shape. After much anxious consideration he decided to part with the fruits of several years of anxious toil and pay off every creditor of the bank. He then organized the Security Bank of which he was made president, and which under his careful management achieved a phenomenal prosperity, being to-day one of the strongest financial institutions in Minneapolis. That is in no small degree due to Mr. Harrison's watchful care and the confidence in which he was held by the people, and the efficient corps of assistants that he gathered around him. He continued as president of this bank until his death.

RESIDENCE OF MRS. SARAH H. KNIGHT

In the year of 1839, at Belleville, Ill., Mr. Harrison was united in marriage to Rebecca Greene, an educated and highly accomplished woman, a loving wife and willing helpmeet. She died February 14, 1884. Five children, two sons and three daughters, were born of this union, of whom W. W. Harrison, Mrs. S. H. Knight and Mrs. Dr. E. B. Zier are now living. Above all else Mr. Harrison was one to whom others would look for guidance and direction. Moreover, though a most enterprising and valuable citizen, he never seemed able to realize his own importance, each token or mark of esteem accorded him being ever a surprise. Of most generous disposition he neglected no public enterprise, while his liberality towards those who applied to him for aid was proverbial. As a member of the Hennepin Avenue Church he was always

MRS. T. A. HARRISON

eager to promote its interests. His donations to all churches and schools were frequent and liberal. For Hamline University his affection was deep and abiding, and many struggling students were, through him, enabled to obtain an education.

His death was directly attributed to the malarial fever, which he contracted in 1885 while traveling in the South. The most

skillful physicians in the country were consulted but the evil was
never entirely eradicated and he was contemplating a winter in
California when the end came, October 27. 1887. Mr. Harrison's
most conspicuous traits were unflinching integrity in all relations
of life, a sound judgment and an indomitable will. Added to these,
however, were kindness of heart, a cheerful spirit. and a ready
sympathy. His character compelled at once the respect and love
of all, and his memory will be long and gratefully cherished by the
city whose good fortune is so largely due to him.

REV. WILLIAM EDWARD HILL. A. M.

Rev. William Edward Hill was born October 12, 1858, in Vanwert,
Ohio. He comes from Methodist stock. his father and grandfather
having been ministers of the gospel. He was converted at the age
of eleven, and at this time was impressed that he should enter the
ministry. He attempted to shake off this early impression but
could not free himself from the hand of God which firmly held him.
His early education was acquired in the public schools. He subsequently pursued a course in the Ohio State Normal University.
In his attempt to silence "the still small voice" that summoned him
to the work of the Master he learned a trade, but not satisfied, followed the profession of school teaching. He then became a clerk,
book-keeper, and traveling agent, but in all these vocations, the
Divine call seemed more and more imperative. In 1884 he surrendered fully to God and gave himself up to the ministry of Christ.

Providence seemed to lead him into the West and in the spring
of 1885 he found himself upon a large and unpromising circuit in
Washington Territory. but his zeal, courage and rare executive
ability were equal to the emergency and he soon built up order out of
chaos. Under his preaching, a revival wave swept over his charge
and at every point the membership was greatly increased and the
church strengthened. At the principal point where the members
worshipped in a Presbyterian church, the congregation and membership so greatly increased that within a few months after his
appointment to the charge a new church was built. While in
Washington Territory he was appointed principal of the Normal

WILLIAM E. HILL

department of the Lewiston College, also Superintendent of schools of the Nez Perces Indian Agency, at the same time serving the church as pastor at Lewiston, Idaho.

He was transferred by Bishop Foster to the Central Ohio Conference in 1887. After serving as pastor one year he felt the need of fuller preparations for his life work and spent three years at the Ohio Wesleyan University. Since then he has served important charges in his Conference, and is at present pastor at Elmore, Ohio. He is known among his brethren as a revivalist. His whole ministry has been signally owned and honored of God. Although but a young man, hundreds have been converted under his ministry. He is especially able as a preacher of the Word which he handles with the skill of a specialist. He stands squarely for the "faith once delivered to the saints" and has never allowed himself to drift on the tide of a popular or so called "progressive theology." He is flat footed and square toed in his orthodoxy and preaches the truths of the Gospel without cant or caviling.

In 1887 he was married to Miss Alice Dukes, of Findlay, Ohio, a lady whose consecration, tact, and general accomplishments particularly qualify her for the great work with which she is identified.

REUBEN RAYNER LANGRELL

Reuben Rayner Langrell was born in Ottowa, Canada. He was converted when a boy and united with the church at the age of fifteen. His early education was acquired in the public schools, where by rare diligence he qualified himself for the activities of subsequent life. In the spring of 1888 he moved to St. Paul. Upon reaching this city, he identified himself with the Central Park Methodist Church. Upon thus connecting himself, he did not shrink back into a corner and wait to be sought out, complaining of the absence of social life in the church, but went to the front, made himself known, participated in all the public services and identified himself with every line of Christian work. He was soon made director of the choir and chorister of the Sunday school.

REUBEN RAYNER LANGRELL

Epworth League, and prayer meeting. His work in this capacity was greatly appreciated. He came to Minneapolis to live early in August, 1894, where he became identified with the Fowler Church of which he is an earnest and active member. Mr. Langrell is the assistant state manager of the Banker's Alliance which is the leading insurance company on the Pacific coast.

CLINTON E. OLMSTEAD

Clinton E. Olmstead was born May 3, 1849, in LaSalle County Illinois. His parents were native born Americans, thoroughly patriotic and set for the defense of truth and righteousness. His mother was a life-long Methodist and by her consistent example gave herself to the task of developing the son in Christian life. Doubtless the lessons received from her pure lips have been the moulding influence of his eventful career. His early days were spent on the farm where he developed a powerful physical frame and also learned by hard experience the true dignity of labor.

When the war broke out he was all ablaze with love of country. The shot on Sumter pierced his heart and aroused every power of his young manhood in resentment. His parents plead with him in vain to remain at home, for he was a mere boy but sixteen years of age, but so intense was his patrotism that in a moment of great excitement he slipped away and became a volunteer soldier in the Thirty-ninth Regiment of the Illinois Infantry. His burning ambition for the wild excitement of battle was not to be disappointed for he soon found himself at the bloody front. He engaged in fourteen hard battles, was at the seige of Petersburg and distinguished himself for valor and patriotism. After eleven months of field life he returned to his home and resumed work upon the farm.

At the age of twenty he was married to Miss Helen Linsday, the daughter of one of the most prominent lawyers of Marseilles, Illinois. In 1871 he came to Minnesota and took up a homestead where he remained for three years, removing to Minneapolis in 1883.

He at once engaged in the real estate and loan business and although surrounded by the shrewdest business men, he soon became known for his great business ability. He was not long in gaining for himself a place in the rivalries of trade. Others have failed in business or been compelled, by the pressure of the times, to suspend, but his offices in Temple Court are still open and he stands in the front rank of one of the most prosperous and progressive lines of business in the city.

Mr. Olmstead is a strong, robust, honest, straightforward, manly man; he is a sincere Christian and a genuine Methodist. He is all aglow with zeal and love for the Church. He believes that Methodism represents the greatest evangelistic power in the world.

CLINTON E. OLMSTEAD

He has been fully indentified with the church since coming to Minneapolis. He first united with the Foss Church and then when he saw a ray of light shining through an open door on Forest Heights, he at once seized the opportunity and declared it was God's call for a Methodist church.

The first prayer meeting was held in a secluded hall which was lighted with a lamp carried by Mr. Olmstead from his home. Mr. Olmstead was appointed leader as soon as the church was organized and he has occupied this position with great honor to himself and church ever since. When standing before his class he seems like one filled with the spirit of the fathers. He exhorts, reproves, rebukes, strikes at sin, pleads for deeper consecration and urges the people into a richer Christian experience. Although a zealous member of the Forest Heights Church, he believes in Minneapolis Methodism and is all the while working for the enlargement of our common borders.

He was one of the first trustees of Fowler Church and has assisted it by deed as well as word. He has the courage of his convictions in all things and when he once takes a position he stands as immovable as a basaltic rock. He is always cheerful and genial, interested in the success of all who are worthy, and delights in responding to every opportunity to elevate, dignify and ennoble the world in which he lives.

B. F. STAHL

Among the well known men who have gained both prominence and position in the great Northwest, is Mr. B. F. Stahl, manager of Northwestern General Agency of the old Aetna Life Insurance Co. Born in Ohio, September 21, 1838, Mr. Stahl received the benefits of a liberal education, and was afterwards admitted to the bar, and practiced law in Ohio for a number of years. Giving his attention largely to laws governing insurance interests, he became so proficient in that branch of jurisprudence, that his services were sought by a number of old line insurance companies, and he was induced finally, to relinquish his legal practice, and enter the services of the Aetna Life Insurance Company of Hartford, Conn., as general traveling agent of the State of New York. This position was filled so creditably that the company soon made Mr. Stahl, its manager for the Northwest, with headquarters in St. Paul. Coming to St. Paul in December, 1885, the subject of this sketch has managed so successfully, that the territory controlled by him ranks second in the list of the company's general agencies. Conversant with every detail of the business, and thoroughly familiar with legal and general insurance technicalities, he has exhibited splendid abilities as a manager, and is to-day the acknowledged peer of any man in the insurance field. With untiring energy and comprehensive grasp, he seized upon an hitherto undeveloped ter-

B. F. STAHL

ritory, and has made it a very garden spot for the company he represents.

Mr. Stahl's prominence in the insurance world is shown in the fact that in 1890 he was elected to the presidency of the Minnesota Life Underwriters' Association, an office to which he was re-elected at the last annual meeting, without a dissenting vote. At the meeting of the National Association of Life Underwriters, held in

Detroit, Mich., in June, 1891, he was made a member of the executive committee of that association, a compliment as creditable to the Minnesota association as to the worthy recipient.

But it is not in the insurance world alone that Mr. Stahl has achieved prominence: since it is known everywhere that he is one of the most conspicuous figures of the Knights of Pythias fraternity in the entire Northwest. At the seventeenth session of the order, held in St. Paul in September, 1889, he was elected Grand Chancellor, giving to the order the first business administration it had ever known in this grand jurisdiction. Inaugurating needed reforms, and correcting many abuses that had crept into the order, his administration was conducted on a purely business basis, and marked by the most brilliant success throughout. In 1890 Mr. Stahl was appointed a member of Major General Carnahan's staff, with rank of Colonel, a position which he holds to-day.

Although not in active practice, Mr. Stahl is a member of the St. Paul bar, and is honored as a well-read lawyer, thorough practitioner, and sterling business man. Lawyer, knight, gentleman, as he is, Mr. Stahl is held in high esteem by all who know him, and as an insurance man, stands at the head of the list in this State.

Himself and wife are actively identified with the Central Park Church.

REV. CARL A. ANDERSON

Rev. Carl Axel Anderson is a splendid example of what pluck and perseverance can do in securing a liberal education. He was born in Gottenberg, Sweden, August 6, 1859, and emigrated with his parents to America at six years of age. His early life was spent on the farm near Detroit, Michigan, and from a child he was accustomed to severe manual labor. Upon the death of his mother, a noble Christian woman, at the tender age of fourteen he left home to make his own way in the world. The difficulties he encountered would have disheartened a less heroic soul. In the first place, he knew but little English, his education consisting of what he had learned in a six weeks term in a country school. Hard work on the farm had stunted his growth, and his fair complexion

REV. CARL A. ANDERSON

gave him the appearance of a boy ten or eleven years old. His diminutive size made it difficult for him to find employment, but once having found work his faithfulness and energy secured more openings than he could fill.

The one thought that towered above all others in his mind was his desire for an education. The first winter spent away from home he attended a country school for four months. Working on the farm summers, and doing chores for his board winters, he pursued his studies with the zeal of an enthusiast. In two years he mastered the common branches and entered the classical course of the High School in Lapeer, Michigan. This course was completed in Cleveland, O., four years later. In the fall of 1882, Mr. Anderson, matriculated in the Ohio Wesleyan University, Delaware, O., and in three years graduated in the classical course.

After acting as a supply in Michigan during the summer of 1885, Mr. Anderson entered the school of theology, of Boston University in September. From this historic institution he graduated with credit in 1888.

In the summer of 1888 Mr. Anderson married Miss Emeline A. Hornsby, of Cleveland, O., a grandchild in the fourth generation of the immortal John Bunyan. She is the constant and tireless assistant of her husband in all his labors. In the fall of the same year he joined the Ohio Conference. After three years of faithful work, the failure of his health compelled him to seek another climate. Accordingly he came to Minnesota two years ago in search of health. Finding the climate favorable, he transferred in the fall of 1892, to the Minnesota Conference, and was stationed at Moorhead.

Mr. Anderson has been successful from the first; revivals have uniformly attended his ministry. His success in Moorhead, was unusual for such a difficult field. He won the confidence and esteem of all classes. The president of one of the educational institutions of that city said, in speaking of his work: "It is simply wonderful what this young man has done since he came among us. If his most sanguine supporters had prophesied such results as he has achieved, I could not have believed it." A prominent business man of that place said: "Mr. Anderson has done more than any three preachers ever did in Moorhead, in the same length of time."

Mr. Anderson is a magnetic speaker and a faithful pastor. His bearing is easy and his manner of speaking is simple and direct; he has a clear and penetrating voice, and reaches all classes by the breadth of his sympathy. His methods of church work are modern and progressive; he preaches on living topics and his sermons are fresh and original in thought. He gives promise of increasing usefulness. At the last Conference he was appointed pastor at Waseca.

REV. GEORGE ROBSON HAIR, A. M.

George Robson Hair was born in the city of Newcastle-on-Tyne, England, December 6, 1825, of Methodist parents, his ancestry and family being Wesleyan; his father sustained official relations in the church for many years and his grandfather was one of Wesley's class leaders, connected with the "Old Orphan House." Newcastle-on-Tyne, the third preaching place built by Wesley in Great Britain.

He received his education at Bell's Academy in his native city, and studied Theology under Rev. Nathan Rouse, an able polemic divine and preacher, and the author of several theological and controversial works; he received an exhorter's license in 1844, and was licensed as a local preacher in 1845, and as such filled regular Sabbath appointments for several years in his native land.

In 1851 he was married to Miss Elizabeth Selina Davison, his present wife, second daughter of Rev. Edward Davison, deceased. Coming to this country in the spring of 1854 he preached for nine months with the Wesleyan Methodists and was ordained Elder in the city of Albany, N. Y., in 1855. In the spring of 1856 he united with the Wyoming Annual Conference and served the following charges the constitutional term; Lisle and Whitney's Point; Wind-

sor: Lanesboro; Orwell; LeRaysville; Gibson; Kingston; and
Waverly, N. Y.   In 1873 he was appointed presiding elder of the
Wyoming District by Bishop Ames, which he served the disciplinary
four years.   In 1877 he received the honorary degree of A. M.
from LaFayette College, Penn.   He was transferred to the Minnesota Conference in 1879 by Bishop Peck, and his appointments in
this Conference have been as follows: Northfield; presiding elder
of the Red River District, and first Superintendent of the North

GEO. ROBSON HAIR, A. M.

Dakota Mission, and presiding elder of the Fargo District; Owatonna; Mankato; presiding elder of the Mankato District for the
full term of six years; North Church, Minneapolis and Glencoe.

REV. CHARLES H. PAYNE, D. D., LL. D.

Rev. Dr. Charles H. Payne is a native of Taunton, Mass.
When Charles was but a child, his father died and he was therefore obliged to work his way through the world.   His early educa-

tion was in the public schools of Massachusetts, in which schools also he taught for some years; he prepared for college in East Greenwich Academy, R. I., was graduated from the Wesleyan University of Middletown, Conn., and studied theology at the Concord Biblical Institute, now the Boston School of Theology.

CHAS. H. PAYNE, D. D.

Dr. Payne entered the ministry of the Methodist Episcopal Church in the New England Southern Conference in 1857, in which year he was also married. After serving several churches successfully in that Conference, at Sandwich, East Bridgewater, Fall River and Providence, he was transferred to Brooklyn, where he succeeded Dr. C. D. Foss, now Bishop Foss, as pastor of what is now St. John's M. E. Church. This large and strong church was built during Dr. Payne's pastorate and largely through his agency. He was then transferred to Philadelphia, where he served successively the two strongest churches of Methodism in that city, Arch street and Spring Garden street, building the Arch Street Church during his pastorate. Then he became pastor of St. Paul's Church, Cincinnati, which he served until his inauguration as president of the Ohio Wesleyan University in 1876. Remaining president of that institution for twelve years, he was elected to his present office as Secretary of the Board of Education of the Methodist Episcopal Church in 1888. During the twelve years of his presidency of the Ohio Wesleyan University that institution had a wonderful growth, increasing the number of students from 323 to nearly 1000.

During all the years of his pastorate, Dr. Payne was his own evangelist, conducting revival services which always attended his ministry, and thousands were converted in those years of pastoral service. When president of the University he carried the same spirit and efforts into that institution and personally conducted revival services with the students and saw more than 1000 of the noblest young men and women of the country consecrate themselves to Christ under his labors in that institution. These men and women are occupying prominent pulpits and missionary posts the world over to-day.

Dr. Payne has been a wide traveler, having made three trips abroad, in which he visited Europe, Egypt, Syria, Palestine and Greece. He is also an author whose works have wide circulation, not only in this country, but in England and Canada. "Guides and Guards in Character Building," a series of sermon lectures to young men, has had a very wide sale, and abundant evidence has been furnished that large numbers of youth have been led to Christ through its perusal. It was placed in the first reading course adopted by the Epworth League and is still having a large and constant sale.

He is a recognized leader in all forward movements and genuine reforms in Church and State, being an earnest temperance advocate, and an ardent advocate of justice to the colored men and all who are oppressed. In his present position he is preaching and addressing audiences throughout the whole country, and thus reaches hundreds of thousands of people.

THOMAS BARLOW WALKER

Thomas Barlow Walker, manufactuer and philanthropist, was born in Zonia, Greene county, Ohio, February 1, 1840; the second son and third child of Platt Bayliss and Anstis Barlow Walker. The Walkers were of English stock, who settled during the early history of the country in New Jersey, his father leaving that state early in life for New York. The Barlows were also of sturdy parentage, his maternal grandfather being the Hon. Thomas Barlow, of New York, and two of his uncles were for many years judges, Thomas in New York and Moses in Ohio. His father died enroute to California, in 1849, and his mother was left to struggle with adversity with her four young children. From his ninth until his sixteenth year Thomas led the usual careless life of the average, frontier village boy. He was expert with the rifle, shotgun and at the game of checkers.

At sixteen the family removed to Berea, Ohio, where better educational advantages were possible, and where Thomas' boyhood abruptly ended and earnest life began. From sixteen to nineteen his time was divided between work and study. After various business adventures, always attended with hard work, and generally with success, he returned to his books and studies, and the next winter taught a district school in the adjoining township where he had about sixty pupils, among whom were eight school teachers some of them much older then he.

About this time the war broke out, and with his associate students in the Baldwin University he volunteered as a soldier. Having failed to get sent to the front he, after waiting several months and while in search of employment, landed in St. Paul, and the next morning took the train to the city of Minneapolis.

On December 19, 1863, he was married to Harriet G., youngest daughter of the Hon. Fletcher Hulet. Dating from his marriage the history of Mr. Walker is the history of Minneapolis. His first years were years of hardship, self-denial, and patient toil. The summer of 1863 was spent in railroading, after which for some years he gave his whole time to government surveys. In 1868 he began his venture in pine lands. As a consequence of his foresight, Mr. Walker to-day owns more valuable pine lands than any other

THOMAS BARLOW WALKER

man in the northwest. In connection with these surveys and pine land enterprises, Mr. Walker has been, and is yet, extensively engaged throughout various sections of the northwest in the manufacture of lumber.

Mr. Walker is extremely liberal in the use of his wealth for the upbuilding of Minneapolis or for purposes of charity or charit-

able work. Mr. Walker's whole life has been greatly moulded
and influenced by reading the books of public libraries, beginning
with the private library of Father Blake, Catholic priest.   Through
Mr. Walker's influence and efforts the Athenæum Library was
greatly improved. The reading room was enlarged, an assistant
employed and hours lengthened.   The library was also opened on
Sunday and the membership increased by allowing payment by
installments. Mr. Walker purchased several hundred member-

VIEW OF ART GALLERY

ship certificates, which he kept loaned out among his employees
and others.   In the rapid growth of the city he foresaw the
demand for a library that should meet all the wants of our
mixed population, and be free to all.   At the same time it seemed
necessary to maintain two separate libraries and duplicate the
valuable stock of books now in the Athenæum. Mr. Walker
proposed that the, city by taxation, establish a free library upon
condition that the citizens contribute a certain large sum towards
the erection of the building, and that the Athenæum, the Academy
of Science, and the Fine Art Society, be given space in the build-

ing, in consideration of which the books of the Athenæum Library were to circulate upon the same terms as those of the public library, and to be drawn in the same manner. This was agreed to, necessary legislation secured, and Mr. Walker was the first to subscribe to the library fund. When the beautifully designed building was completed, Mr. Walker saw the realization of his desire for many years. The rapid growth of this institution for the five years which have now passed since it was first formally opened, makes its standing in circulation fourth among the public libraries of the country.

The perfect harmony of action between the two boards of the Library and Athenæum, and the pride of the citizens in it, are the best possible witnesses to the wisdom of the board, and liberal policy inaugurated by Mr. Walker. He has been annually elected president of the Library board from its organization in 1885 to the present time, 1894. The liberal provision for art in this building is also due to Mr Walker's interest in, and devotion to it. From its inception he has been a staunch friend and supporter of the art school, which has taken so high a rank among the educational interests of the city, and among the art schools of the country. On the walls of the spacious gallery he has placed samples of nearly all of his own private collection.

The art gallery at his home has been pronounced the choicest collection of art treasures for its size in the United States, and is open to the public on all days but Sunday, a liberality highly esteemed and appreciated both by citizens and strangers. The fame of this gallery has gone throughout the nation, and even to Europe, and many are the expressions of surprise from Eastern connoisseurs over the unlooked-for treasures displayed upon its walls. Mr Walkers home library consists of a large and carefully chosen collection of choice books.

When Mr. Walker constructed his present residence, in 1874, his large lawn was thrown open without a fence. This innovation has now become the custom adopted by a large portion of the citizens of Minneapolis. The benches placed around the lawn under the trees are occupied free by all classes of people during the entire summer. The Minnesota Academy of Natural Science is another institution much indebted to Mr. Walker's interest and patronage for its past support and present fortunate situation, for through his influence, when the library building was designed, the needs and importance of this association were considered and spacious and beautiful apartments were assigned to them. For several years Mr. Walker was a member of the board of managers of the State Reform School, where he made his strong practical business habits felt, and inaugurated many valuable changes, as well as became a great favorite with its inmates.

VIEW OF ART GALLERY

It was especially through the efforts of Mr. Walker that the Minneapolis Business Union was organized, which has been a leading factor in building up the business interests of the city both in the line of manufacturing and wholesale trade. Mr. Walker was elected president of the Union, which is composed of the wealthiest and most influential men of the city, and he has devoted a large part of his time as well as a large amount of money for the benefit of the city.

He is the head of the Minneapolis Land and Investment Company. Mr. Walker was for many years president of the Flour City National Bank. Three years ago he organized a company of which he is president, constructed the central city market, which was probably the finest market building in the United States.

In politics Mr. Walker has always been a radical republican, believing in a sufficient protective tariff to hold our money at home; to build up our manufactories for the employment of our workmen. He is an official member of the Hennepin Avenue Church. Through much doubt and questioning, he has wrought his way up to a clear religious faith, a firm belief in the Bible as the rule of man's conduct, and the only safe foundation on which either men or nations can build. He has also taken pains to ground his growing children in the faith to which he has attained only by tiresome research. He has been the constant director of the education of his eight children, as well as their daily and close companion. From their earliest years they have been supplied with tools and machinery and shops, which have given the manual dexterity and practical knowledge of applied mathematics, for lack of which a large percentage of men are at a disadvantage all their lives. As a result, the boys, while yet in their early years, became expert in the use of tools, and their beautifully outfitted shops form no inconsiderable part of their home. Remembering his own boyhood, Mr. Walker has encouraged the boys in all out of door amusements, especially hunting, which he has shared with them.

MRS. HARRIET GRANGER WALKER

Harriet Granger Walker was born in Brunswick, O., September 10, 1841, youngest daughter of Hon. Fletcher and Fanny Hulet, natives of Berkshire County, Mass. Her grandfather, John Hulet, of Lee, Mass., played a distinguished part in the battle of Bunker Hill, and her great grandfather, also John Hulet, built the first Methodist church in Berkshire county, if not in the state of Massachusetts. When Harriet was six years of age her parents removed to Berea, O., where she attended the Baldwin University. At eleven years of age, she united with the Methodist church, to which her family belonged and with which she has been prominently identified ever since, being a member of Hennepin Avenue Church at present. She early showed marked literary ability, and it was her girlhood ambition to write a book. During her school days she was a regular contributor to several periodicals.

On December 19, 1863, she was married to Thomas B. Walker, her schoolmate and companion since their sixteenth year. They took up a permanent residence in Minneapolis, Minn., where,

MRS. HARRIET GRANGER WALKER

during the first twelve years of their married life, Mrs. Walker devoted herself exclusively to her home and family cares, while her husband laid the foundation of his later business success. Mrs. Walker's work of public philanthrophy began some twenty years ago, and to-day she is actively associated with most of the leading charities of Minneapolis, many of which she has been instrumental in organizing and maintaining with money and hard work. Outside her immediate church work, she, for the past nineteen years, has been the secretary of Bethany Home for the reformation of fallen women. The city authorities make it appropriations from the public funds. The Northwestern Hospital for women and children was organized by her about twelve years ago, and she is its president. It is under the sole management of women directors, and has a training school for nurses with women physicians. It owns one of the finest hospital buildings in the Northwest.

Mrs. Walker brought together from the four leading Christian organizations of the city the Woman's Christian Association, the Sisterhood of Bethany, and the two branches of the Woman's Christian Temperance Union, a joint committee who induced the police commissioners of Minneapolis to create the position of police matron and to allow this committee the nomination of the incumbent by the payment of half her salary. She had visited and investigated the workings of matrons, or the want of matrons, in Boston, New York, Washington, Pittsburgh, Philadelphia, Cincinnati, Cleveland, Chicago and Milwaukee, writing extensively on the subject.

She was one of the first to take up the work of the Woman's Christian Temperance Union. When that organization took up the political issue, however, she was for many years shut out from the work. Upon the division of the Union, she joined the Non-Partisan Woman's Christian Temperance Union and took an active part in temperance again. She now holds the responsible positions of national vice-president and state president of the non-partisan organization, in each of which capacities her genius finds full play. In 1892 Mrs. Walker was elected president of a new organization called the Woman's Council, a delegate representative association of all branches of woman's work in Minneapolis. To her capable leadership is unquestionably due the astonishing growth and prosperity of this body. Seventy associations are represented, covering all departments of thought, study and work in the fields of education, philanthropy, reform, medicine, art, music, the church, literature, history and science. The Woman's Council now publishes a magazine.

The Newsboy's Home is another charity to which Mrs. Walker's active influence has been lent; the Kindergarten Association has had her interest and support, and also the Children's Home, which was an out-growth of Bethany Home.

Mrs. Walker is equally active in her private charities. So much of her time is now required in the giving of advice and help to the unfortunate, that she has been obliged to institute regular office hours and to employ a stenographer to carry on her correspondence. In all her work she enjoys the loving and admiring support of her devoted husband, whose example as well as counsel has been such an inspiration to her work. She is also an earnest advocate of woman's suffrage.

Her lectures written for the Nurses' Training School, Christian Endeavor Society, and temperance work have been published and very widely copied and quoted. Several articles discussing and endorsing the Keeley Cure for inebriety, one of which was read at the World's Temperance Congress in Chicago during the World's Fair have been reprinted and largely circulated. She is a regular contributor to the Trained Nurse's Magazine of New York, and to the Temperance Tribune, of which she is chairman of the publication committee.

Through all her active life however, Mrs. Walker's home duties have always been foremost. Her husband and eight children have been given precedence over every other demand, and when her devotion to her large family, her care of her elegant home with its beautiful art gallery, and the large number of guests who enjoy the hospitality of that home are considered, it seems phenomenal that so large an amount of outside work could have been accomplished. Mrs. Walker has refused to give her time to society; her evenings are given to her family; yet among the women of the city of Minneapolis there is no other one more widely beloved and respected.

JOSEPH DEAN

Joseph Dean was born of Scotch-Irish parentage, January 10 1826, near Enniskillen, Ireland. When Mr. Dean was about six years old, the family emigrated to Canada, settling near Sherbrook,

Province of Quebec. When he was about ten years of age, the
family again moved, and this time the place of their choice was
Belvidere, Ill., some sixty miles from Chicago. Here Mr. Dean
passed his boyhood and attained his majority, attending school,
working on a farm, and learning his trade, that of a carpenter.

JOSEPH DEAN

Soon after he was twenty-one years of age he spent some time in
Chicago, working at his trade.

In the spring of 1850 he was married to Miss Nancy H. Stan-
ley, of Illinois, and almost immediately the young couple moved to
St. Anthony, then an embitious young town whose identity has
long since been lost in that of Minneapolis. Here Mr. Dean was

busy for two years superintending at his trade. In 1852 he took a government claim at what is now Bloomington Ferry, on the Minnesota River, Hennepin county. Here he remained for four years farming, and, with a partner, operating a ferry across the river, and was postmaster and justice of the peace.

In 1856 he returned to Minneapolis, settling on the west side of the river, and resumed his trade, contracting and building. A little later he purchased a planing mill, sash and door factory, located at the falls, which he operated for some time.

Mr. Dean joined the Methodist Church in early life, and to the day of his death he was an active, interested and loyal Methodist in the best sense, and what is even more than that, he was a Christian. In 1856 the Methodists of Minneapolis, that is those living on the west side of the river, decided to build, as they had no church building of their own, but were meeting over a store at the corner of Washington avenue and Second avenue south. The location chosen for the new church was on Oregon street (now Third avenue south) between Fourth and Fifth streets. The church building was erected under Mr. Dean's charge and supervision, he also working with his own hands.

Mr. Dean was superintendent of the Sunday School for nearly ten years, when he was compelled, by pressing business cares and by ill health, to relinquish the work that had been his pride and delight. In 1865 he became associated with T. A., Wm. M. and H. G. Harrison in the lumber business, under the firm name of J. Dean & Co., which firm did a large and active business until 1877.

In January, 1878, The Security Bank of Minnesota opened its doors for business, with T. A. Harrison, president, H. G. Harrison, vice-president, and Joseph Dean, cashier. The organization of this institution took much of Mr. Dean's time and thought, and to the building up of the business of this bank he gave his untiring energy. But his work in this direction, coming at a time when he surely was entitled to rest, told severely upon his health, and in the summer of 1882 he was compelled to sever his active connection with the bank, and seek rest and health in travel. His health he never regained in any large measure. Those who are acquainted with the inside facts, know fully that The Security Bank of Minnesota is indebted in no small degree for the large success it has attained to the wise planning and earnest work of Mr. Dean.

Centenary Church succeeded the little Oregon Street Church referred to above. Mr. Dean remained a member of Centenary Church until 1875 when Hennepin Avenue Church was organized There his membership was held until 1879, when moving to another part of the city, he cast in his lot with Franklin Avenue Methodist Church. His membership was there at the time of his death. In 1874 Mrs. Dean, the devoted wife and mother, was called to a better land. In 1876 Mr. Dean was again married, this time to Miss Elizabeth Stevens, of Illinois. She is still living and is an active member of Franklin Avenue Methodist Church. Mr. Dean died at Eureka Springs, Arkansas, on May 20, 1890. This sketch is necessarily meagre and is intentionally plain. It tells simply of one who started as a young man with the sole capital of a clear head, a strong arm, and a courageous heart, supplemented by a firm and abiding trust in God, and by the companionship, sympathy and loving help of one of the best women who ever lived. He leaves a name in Minneapolis business and church life that his children will ever lovingly cherish.

HOBART O. HAMLIN

Hobart O. Hamlin is remembered as an upright, successful, business man, a loyal and enthusiastic citizen of Minneapolis, and as an unostentatious but active participant in things benevolent and Christian. He was born at Salem, Wayne County, Penn., June 29, 1832, and died in Minneapolis on July 21, 1886. He was the son of Oliver Hamlin, a prosperous merchant. Like many others, he came west partly in consideration of his health.

In 1854 he arrived at the village of St. Anthony, and for a while was engaged in the store of Mr. Stanchfield as a clerk. During the fall of 1856 he formed a partnership with Alphens Rowell and opened a store for the sale of general merchandise.

This proved to be an unfortunate venture, for the new firm had hardly become established before the panic of 1857 swept the country, and they were forced to make an assignment. In the same year he was elected the first auditor of Hennepin county. This position he shortly resigned, but in 1861 he was elected clerk of the district court, and held the office for the full term of four years. This was the extent of Mr. Hamlin's service in public office, but he was always much interested in politics, especially in munici-

HOBART O. HAMLIN

pal affairs, and took an active part as a private citizen in working for the nomination of good men.

When his term as clerk of court expired, Mr. Hamlin became associated with the firm of Gale & Co. This connection continued for eleven years. In 1877 he formed a partnership with Z. E. Brown and engaged in the real estate, loan and insurance business, under

the name of Hamlin & Brown. They were entirely successful and
enjoyed the confidence of the business community, as well as of
many correspondents in the East. This partnership continued
until 1886, when Mr. Brown retired, and the firm became H. O.
Hamlin & Co., with D. W. Jones and James MacMillan as partners.
The business was conducted under this name until Mr. Hamlin's
death.

RESIDENCE OF H. O. HAMLIN

The prosperity which came to Mr. Hamlin in the real estate
business afforded him the complete satisfaction felt in success by a
man who labors faithfully, but who has higher aims in making
money than the mere amassing of wealth. It is suggestive of his
character, that, though he was released by assignment from his
debts at the time of his failure in 1857, every dollar was subsequently paid. In all his business relations he was known as a man
of sterling integrity.

Mr. Hamlin was married in Minneapolis, on September 28, 1862, to Miss Anna C. Rockey. The ceremony was performed by Rev. J. F. Chaffee. Mr. and Mrs. Hamlin began housekeeping in a modest way in a small house on Fourth street, near the court house. Later he bought a cottage on the bluff near Lowry's.

They afterwards lived at the corner of Eighth street and Mary place, where the First Unitarian Church now stands and subsequently in a house on Hennepin avenue on the site of the Lyceum Theatre. They moved to their beautiful home on the corner of Hawthorn avenue and Fifteenth street in 1882. Mr. and Mrs. Hamlin have had seven children: Anna Mary, Grant G., Oliver C., George B., Ernest L., Kate and Hobart O, Jr. Of these Grant, Anna and Hobart are not living.

Mr. Hamlin was one of the organizers of the Hennepin Avenue M. E. Church, and continued an active member and prominent office holder. His attention to church affairs and Christian benevolent work was constant and untiring. He gave himself no rest in these duties. Sunday was one of the busiest days of the week for him. His benevolences were very quietly bestowed. He liked better to have no one know what he was doing in this way, than to have his name appear conspicuously on a subscription list. A gift of $10,000 to the Young Men's Christian Association building fund remained for sometime anonymous. Mr. Hamlin was interested in the Young Men's Christian Association from the beginning. He was one of its early workers, and president of the association for the year 1874-5.

ANNA C. HAMLIN

Anna C. Hamlin, daughter of George and Anna Rockey, was born February 22, 1839, Lancester County, Pennsylvania. She was one of the first Methodists in Minneapolis and perhaps is as familiar with the growth and development of our church in this city as any other member of the connection. She was converted when eleven years of age and united with the church at the age of seventeen.

She came to Minneapolis in 1857 when Minnesota was a territory, and was one of the thirteen members who worshipped in Woodman's Hall, under the pastorate of Rev. Mr. St. Claire. She was married to Hobart O. Hamlin, September 28, 1862. She talks familiarly upon the earliest history of Methodism in Minneapolis. She was present at the opening of the church built in 1858

MRS. ANNA C. HAMLIN

on Third avenue south. She still remembers and is able to recite portions of the sermon preached on that occasion by Dr. Chaffee. For years she has been a member of the Hennepin Avenue Church. She has never faltered in her faithfulness or devotion to the church. Her home is the center of Christian influence and attractiveness.

Her children have all been brought up "In the nurture and
admonitoin of the Lord" and exemplify the careful Christian
training of their mother. We give elsewhere an engraving of her
home which has always been open to Christian people. It was
built during the life time of her husband, with special reference
to the convenience and comfort of his family and the entertainment
of the host of friends who have always deligh'ed in visiting it.

GRANT G. HAMLIN

Grant G. Hamlin, son of H. O. and Anna C. Hamlin, was
born August 12, 1865. and died December 16, 1892. In looking
over his journal we make the following extracts:

"Was converted on the evening of January 7, 1881, at my
home, 718 Hennepin avenue, the present situation of the Lyceum
Theater.

"January 16, 1881, united with the Hennepin Avenue Church
on probation. (In old Tabernacle building.)

"Admitted to full membership December 18, 1881, at new
Hennepin Avenue M. E. Church.

"Read the Bible through when twelve years old.

"Began taking music lessons when twelve years old, and continued for six years.

"Entered High School September 13, age fifteen years. Left
school November, 1884."

In 1885 a cough, which had troubled him at times became
chronic, and for seven years he fought the dread disease, consump-
tion. For five years he was hopeful of recovery but the two remaining years he looked death steadily in the face, with firm faith
and triumphant hope in God.

In writing to his mother he says: "The presence of Jesus lines
with silver every cloud that crosses my life's path. He is a never
failing comfort and support. Without Him I could do nothing."

After his mother had taken the family to Colorado to live on
account of his health, he was very anxious for the welfare of each
one and would frequently say: "I sincerely hope and pray that this

change may prove of great benefit to all of us.   If it should prove
an injury to any, no one would regret the fact more than myself."

In a letter written to his parents while they were away from
home he says: "O, I am so thankful that you so taught and
guided me that I have learned to love the church as dearly as I do.

GRANT G. HAMLIN

It has already been an anchor to my soul in times of darkness, and
I trust will help me through all trying times, that I, with all others
who live this life, must meet.   It is my prayer that this love for
the church, the visible revelation of God to us, may increase continually as the years go by."

About a month before he died he said to his mother: "If it had been God's will to restore me to health, I would finish my education and study theology; as I can not, I trust brother Ernest will be the preacher in our family."

He was always bright and cheerful even when the shadows of death were creeping upon him. He loved to talk upon religious questions and frequently declared that the great mistake of many professing Christians was that they did not accept Christ as a personal Savior and consequently failed to receive the full revelation of God, to them.

His sick chamber was a constant benediction to all. His death was a triumphant entrance into the presence of the Great King.

Although he is gone, the sweet fragrance of his life lingers as heavenly incense in his home, and his words and deeds are still precious to those who knew and learned to love him.

JAMES BALFOUR BRADSHAW

James Balfour Bradshaw was born in Ireland in 1865. He comes of Methodist stock, his parents having been of the primitive type. Their son James was early impressed with his duty to God and through these first impressions was saved from the experience which has characterized so many young men, viz.: sowing wild oats. He acquired his education in the National School of Ireland, during which time he was an earnest student.

Upon leaving school he served an apprenticeship in the grocery business for four years. During this period his natural business tact rapidly developed, winning the admiration of his employer. When his apprenticeship was completed, he stood so well with the proprietor that he was promoted to a salaried position which he occupied with great acceptability for a year and a half. During this incumbency Mr. Bradshaw paid strict attention to business, familiarizing himself with all its departments and phazes, studying human nature as he met it in barter and trade and by every possible way qualifying himself for his subsequent career. He early learned the lesson so often disregarded, that "economy is wealth." He also came to see that "honesty is the best policy" and

that "patience and perseverance conquer all things," and through
the united power of these maxims applied to practical life, he was
able, after remaining with his employer a year and a half to form a
partnership with his brother and launch out into business in his own
name, capital, character and unwearying effort.   The new business

JAMES BALFOUR BRADSHAW

formed was in the grocery line, which he successfully prosecuted
for a year. About this time his attention was attracted to this
country. He had heard of the new world and resolved to see for
himself and to try life under its better, more inspiring, conditions. In 1885 he turned his face toward America, stopping in
Canada where he remained two years, following the grocery

business. In 1887 he closed out his interest in Canada and came to St. Paul, where he served as an employee in a large grocery store for a while, after which he became connected with a whole- sale grocery house as traveling salesman, remaining on the road for three years.

During this time his brother and sister came from Ireland and joined him in his new life. Having acquired fresh experience as traveling agent, he again, in connection with his brother started into business for himself in St. Paul. For nearly four years he re- mained in this business, building it up from almost nothing to one of the largest and most substantial institutions in the entire state. In August, 1894, he sold out his business in St. Paul and purchased the plant of the Great Northern Soap Co., located in Minneapolis, on Nicollet and Twenty-ninth street. In this new enterprise he is associated with his brother, who is one of the most successful young business men in the northwest. The plant has been in operation under this new management long enough to justify expectations and to guarantee the greatest success. It is a manufactory in the fullest sense of the word. All kinds of laundry and toilet soaps are made and with the large market that is open to this line, there is no doubt but what the new venture will steadily grow until it takes rank with the best of its kind in the country. There is no doubt but what this will be the case if honesty, industry, faith, pluck, grit and perseverance cut any figure in the success of life.

Mr. Bradshaw was converted when but a small boy, and at once united with the church. He is a real Methodist. He knows what it is in its simplicity and power. He was reared under the hallowed influence of the Church. His father's house was a favorite place of meeting among the Methodists of that community. Class meetings were held in it as early as seven o'clock Sunday morning and the fires of genuine devotion were never extinguished on the family altar. While in Canada he was connected with the Church and in St. Paul he was a vigorous worker in the Central Park Church. Coming to Minneapolis, together with his brother and sister he united with the Fowler Church in which he has already rendered valuable service. He is a member of the Official Board.

REV. FREDRICK O. HOLMAN, D. D.

Fredrick O. Holman, son of Joshua B. and Sarah Dudley H., was born April 11, 1857, at Canaan, New Hampshire. His father was a Methodist clergyman. When but a child his parents moved to western Massachusetts where he was educated in the public schools. He entered Boston in 1877 and graduated in the class of 1881 with the degree of A. B. In connection with his college studies he preached at Walpole, Massachusetts, during the year of 1879-81 and supplied at Cottage City, Mass., from the fall of 1881 to the fall of 1882. Bright prospects arose before him in the East where prominent and influential friends were interested in his promotion, but on account of lung trouble he was compelled to separate himself from friends and unusual opportunities and move westward. His physician advised him to try the climate of Minnesota. Upon arriving in St. Paul he was appointed to the City Mission, which work comprised Bates Avenue Church and King Street. In 1883 he united with the Minnesota Conference on probation and was appointed to Bates Avenue Church where he preached in 1883-4. In 1885-6-7 he was pastor of Foss Church, Minneapolis, where his labors were crowned with phenominal success, and he became enthroned in the hearts of a loving and grateful people. In January, 1888, he was taken from Foss Church and appointed to the First Church, St. Paul, to meet the emergency arising from the defection of Dr. S. G. Smith. He was returned to the First Church in 1888 but during this year his old trouble coupled with a nervous break-down set in, and at the Conference of 1889 he was compelled to take a supernumerary relation. He rested for two years, part of which time was spent in traveling in Europe and lecturing. Rest brought relief and to the gratification of his many friends he reported to his Conference in 1891 and was appointed to the Hennepin Avenue Church, in conjunction with Dr. O. H. Tiffany who was not able to enter the pulpit after this appointment and died within a few weeks, when Dr. Holman assumed full pastoral charge. From the very start his ministry at Hennepin was of the most successful character. His superb pulpit abilities coupled with his social qualities drew like a magnet and even in the hot summer months the church was frequently too

small to accommodate the multitudes that would throng about his
pulpit to catch the inspiration of his life and words. Soon after
his appointment he delivered a series of sermons on The Evidences of Christianity which have since been published in pamphlet
form and give him high rank as a theological writer. Dr. Holman
is not only a scholar, but a genius. He is one of the few preachers

REV. F. O. HOLMAN

possessed of the ability to preach without the aid of the pen. His
preparation is entirely without notes. He is systematic in his construction, logical in his method and eloquent in his delivery. Many
of his passages are so chaste and finished that one would presume
hours had been devoted to their preparation and yet they burst

from his vast and varied resources, singing like a mountain stream in their rhythmic flow.

On October 4, 1893, he was married to Miss Harriet Hulet Walker, youngest daughter of Thomas B. and Harriet G. Walker, of Minneapolis, a beautiful, cultured lady whose rare attainments and remarkable affability give special strength and adornment to Dr. Holman's success. He received the degree of D. D. from Simpson College, Iowa, in 1889. He was again stricken down with his former trouble in the spring of 1894 and finally compelled to temporarily succumb and remove to Colorado where he still remains. His journey westward was followed by the eyes and hearts of the people of Minneapolis without respect to sect, or creed and they are only comforted in their loss by the good news that the western climate is restoring their friend and brother to his former health and power. The latest news from his western home confirms this report and it is confidently hoped that within a few months or a year at the longest he will again be able to put on the armor and do valiant service in the hosts of the Lord Christ.

REV. HENRY HUGH FRENCH

Henry Hugh French was born October 6, 1858, at Cambridge, Mass. His father, Henry Hugh, was a strict Episcopalian and his mother, Eleanor, was connected with the Congregational Church. The son early displayed a marked ambition to arise to a position of influence and power in the world. He recognized the importance of a thorough education and early began the pursuit of it. He attended the public schools of Boston until he was twelve years of age. Although at this time his school life summarily ended, he did not give up his studious habits, but continued to apply himself to books during several years of severe toil.

In 1875 his hard lot was suddenly changed and a new era in his life was marked by his conversion, at Kingston, N. H., under the pastorate of James Carnes. Immediately after his conversion he felt called to the ministry and began to devote himself to preparation for the great work. He first attended the academy at Kingston, after which he completed a four years' course in the Conference Seminary at Tilton, N. H. He then went to the Boston Theological Seminary and graduated with honor in 1883. During this period he took special studies in the university.

He united with the N. H. Conference on probation in 1881. After graduating at Boston he was appointed to his first charge at Methuen, Mass., remaining there two years. He was then appointed to the pastorate at Great Falls, N. H., after which he served Grace Church at Haverhill, Mass., two years and a half.

REV. HENRY HUGH FRENCH

He was then invited to the old Centenary Church, Minneapolis, of which he was appointed pastor by Bishop Mallalieu. Upon beginning in his new field he encountered many things that would have discouraged a less heroic spirit but "fail" has no place in his dictionary. He has substituted for it the word "strive." Under his strong leadership, the old Centenary Church began to throb with new life. The eloquent preacher soon commanded a hearing and multitudes responded to his trumpet call. The congregations improved at once and the passing months found the membership on the steady increase.

The old purpose to erect the new structure, which had waned to a spark in the hearts of the membership, was soon fanned to a full flame and soon the whole church was illumined with the light of the new enterprise. Nor did this purpose subside until it culminanted in the present magnificent structure. He remained in this pastorate the full term of five years, during which period he received into the church by letter and probation over 300. His pastorate has recently ceased and he has gone to labor elsewhere, but his voice is still heard and his "works do follow him."

His recent change to the Congregational Church was with the greatest love for Methodism and the warmest feeling toward her preachers and people.

He is a man of good physique, makes an excellent appearance on the platform, has a splendid voice, and is a ready and forcible speaker, using no manuscript or notes in a sermon. He is a young man of thorough culture, has a wide range of information and keeps well up with the times. In his preaching he applies the gospel to the questions of the day and is active along all lines of moral reform. He handles his themes with the ease of a skilled musician, calling melodies from his favorite instrument. At times he is fierce and strong, breaking into denunciations of wickedness that strike terror to the heart of the evil doer, and then he is as tender as a sorrowing mother, comforting the broken hearted and poring the oil of gladness into the wounded spirit. His future, measured by the past, must be crowned with glorious success.

CYRUS BROOKS

Cyrus Brooks was born in Westford, Chittenden County, Vt., February 8, 1811. His father was a descendant of the Brooks who became a citizen of Concord, Mass., in 1639. His mother's ancestry is traced back to Samuel Morse, who came from England in 1665, and two years later was one of the original settlers of Dedham, Mass. His parents were Baptists, and family worship was among the objects of his earliest recollection. He was very early the subject of deep and persistent religious convictions, and along with this there was a most distressing fear that he was not one of the elect. He can never quite forgive Calvanism for what he suffered in childhood and his narrow escape from infidelity, when he broke away from it as he was merging into manhood.

In childhood he was very fond of books and escaped some of the grosser vices that are not uncommon, through his studious habits.

When but six years of age his parents moved to Ohio and settled near Granville, in Licking County. His father died when he was fifteen; two years later the family was broken up and thenceforward he was without a settled home. A Christian life began on the 7th of August, 1831, when, after weeks of agony, he "found peace with God through our Lord Jesus Christ," and along with peace came the clear conviction that his life work must be the Gospel ministry. Two weeks after this happy change, he embraced the first opportunity of uniting with the church.

In the summer of 1832 he was licensed to exhort and the year later to preach and was recommended to the Ohio Conference for admission on trial. He was received August 23, 1833, and in due time graduated to the full ministry. He has traveled circuits four years, occupied stations thirty years and been a Presiding Elder fifteen years—twenty-four in Ohio and twenty-five in Minnesota.

He was transferred from the Cincinnati Conference to Minnesota in 1857. His work was somewhat interrupted by sickness during his early ministry and the last twelve years of his life have been years of enforced idleness, but as he worked cheerfully when on the field, he has retired with the same cheerful spirit. He has been a member of six General Conferences: 1852, '56, '60, '68, '72, '76. He was a member of the Book Committee from 1868 to 1872 and chairmain of the committee the last two of those years and prepared the majority report to the General Conference of 1872.

He has been married twice and has five children, two of whom are in the Methodist ministry, three, including these, are rejoicing in the Christian life and two have "gone before."

MILTON G. SHUMAN

Milton G. Shuman was born at Thompsontown, Pa., October, 1866, of German and Scotch-Irish parentage. He was educated in the common schools and afterwards pursued a course in the State, Normal Institution. At the early age of seventeen he was able to pass a rigid examination and received a teacher's certificate, when he at once began to teach, and continued until he was twenty During this period, he worked on the farm in the summers, for he could not be induced to spend any time in idleness. He believed that work with the hand was as necessary and honorable as with the head. Failing health compelled him to leave the schoolroom.

At the age of twenty-one, he moved to Canton, O., where he accepted a situation with the Canton Gas & Coke Company, remaining three years and passing through different grades until he reached the position of assistant superintendent. In 1891 he received an offer from the Gas Street & Coke Company of Helena, Mont., and accepted it.

Mr. Shuman was reared in a Christian home, his parents being strong Lutherans. His brilliancy when but a boy led them to anticipate for him the ministerial profession and they shaped as best they could his education toward that end; but soon their hopes were to be disappointed, for, like many other young men, when he began to think and read and investigate for himself, he was caught in the meshes of skepticism and led onward until much of his religious feeling and faith in the Bible and its God were obliterated. In this frame of mind, he reached Helena, where shortly afterward he became a member and ardent worker in the Unitarian Society He subsequently explained that he accepted Unitarianism, because it seemed like the fine art of Atheism.

But his mother's prayers had gone ahead to the Throne of Grace, and this young man set aside for the work of the ministry when but a child, could not frustrate destiny. In the spring of 1893 he dropped into a revival service that was being held in St. Paul's Methodist Episcopal Church. Rev. J. Wesley Hill was the pastor. During the sermon he became greatly moved and felt a longing for something he had never experienced. At the close of the service he accepted an invitation to step into the pastor's study, where an animated discussion of religous questions followed. At the close of the conversation he promised to read the New Testament through; to read it prayerfully; to accept light, and to attend church during the progress of the special meetings. These promises were all kept, and shortly afterwards he was suddenly and soundly con-

MILTON G. SHUMAN

verted and brought to an experimental knowledge of the Christian religion.

He at once became active in church work and attracted great attention by the fervor of his prayers and the warmth of his exhortations. It became apparent among the members of the church that he was especially fitted for the ministry, and after having served his probation was given exhorter's license, and subsequently licensed as a local preacher. On the first of May, 1894, a vacancy having occurred in Grace Church, St. Paul, he was sought as a supply for that pulpit by the Presiding Elder and was finally prevailed upon to accept it.

Upon reaching this first field of his ministry, he found much of a discouraging nature: a small congregation, a heavy indebtedness and a discouraged membership. But with matchless faith in God and the courage of a true leader he undertook the arduous and difficult work at hand. At once fresh life and zeal were inspired among the people. They rallied around the young preacher, feeling that somehow success would come under his generalship. They were not disappointed. His sermons, so simple and direct, heart-searching and thoughtful, glowing with the fire of the true orator, soon attracted attention among the people outside of the church. The congregations began to increase and encouraging indications broke in from all sides. By unanimous request from the official board he was reappointed pastor at the last Conference and has started into the year with the determination, by God's help and the hearty cooperation of the people, to solve some of the problems that have embarrassed this church and people in other days.

REV. DAVID TICE

Rev. David Tice was born November 12, 1829, in Caistor, Lincoln County, Canada, being the youngest of fifteen children born to John and Elizabeth Tice. He attended school until past thirteen years of age. One day he proposed to his father that instead of giving him a farm, as he proposed for all his sons, he give him his time until twenty-one and he would not ask other help. His father was shocked at the proposal, saying he could not take care of himself, but would get into trouble and dishonor the family. But the lad insisted, until his father reluctantly consented, with this admonition. "If you think you can do better for yourself than your parents, go; but, remember if you do any wrong thing, you must not darken my door."

That night the boy lodged some miles from home; the next day he received 36 cents, for work. Soon after that he was offered 50 cts., and then a neighbor gave him 75 cents. At the end of the first year he had saved $100, and then bought a team, and soon earned $2 per day. The next year he saved several hundred dollars and went to school during the winter. Then he began

REV. DAVID TICE

to buy books. One of the most important to him. aside from the Bible, was "Watson's Theological Dictionary." Then began night study, singing, and reading and acquiring useful knowledge.

Soon he bought 120 acres of land, cleared a part, and platted the Village of Caistorville in which he became Postmaster, Justice of the Peace, Notary Public, and a member of the town council.

During the winter of 1850 he was converted. This he has often mentioned, as it was a marked event in his history, and made a wonderful impression upon his life. "About midday" he tells us he met a friend who, speaking with him in the street, said: "Do not be discouraged, light will come." His reply was: "Discouraged? never! If I go to hell I will go there praying!" And instantly light filled his soul, joy unspeakable took possession of his being. Happy day and night, he could sing:

"O happy hour   O hallowed spot!
Where Love first found me;
Where'ere falls my distant lot,
My heart shall linger round thee:
And when from earth I rise and soar
Up to my Home in Heaven,
Down will I cast my eyes once more,
Where I was first forgiven!"

He set apart the best property in the village for a Methodist Church and gave liberally for its erection; also labored as class-leader, exhorter, local preacher, leading an excessively busy life, studying nights, and all other times that could be secured.

Then commenced a mental conflict, which extended through several years. Deeply impressed with the conviction that his duty was to preach, he hesitated, hoping he could satisfy God by dividing his time between religion and secular things and giving freely to His cause. He was sincerely anxious to know what the will of the Lord was before he turned aside from business pursuits. Had he only pressed the question fully before the Lord as he did in after time, it would no doubt have been settled sooner. Having a home, he at this time was married. And then he thought the question was settled. But it only grew in complication. Soul trouble was upon him. In the woods one day he made the matter a final issue; covenanting with the Lord, if it was his duty to devote his life to the ministry, he would willingly do so, if the way would open to lay off his public duties, and dispose of his property. Soon there came along a Scotchman who purchased his property. On September 3, 1857, the question was all settled.

Having a good wife he believed it a great advantage over having none. He was a loyal Methodist. But his Wesleyan Church said "Married men need not apply." Next year was spent in exploring the western states, and assisting pastors in Canada. The next year he moved within the Rock River Conference, and was assistant pastor of Rev. John Nate.

Impaired health next spring sent him to Minnesota, and in May, 1859, he agreed to supply Stockton circuit. In October following he was ordained Deacon, and re-appointed to the same charge. Then to Marion, Austin, St. Cloud, Mankato, then agent of Hamline University, and Lake City. His health failed the second year. Then Rushford, Faribault, Taylors Falls, Clinton Avenue, St. Paul, Stillwater and then Minneapolis.

Overwork necessitated a little rest and he received a supernumerary relation which continued for two years. Purchasing property he made it possible to support himself in doing much City Mission work. Brother Tice has been called by some a church builder. Besides repairing and improving churches, he has built churches in Rushford, Marion, Austin, St. Cloud, Mankato, Lake City, Western Ave., and St. Louis Park, and helped to inaugurate the Fowler Church. At present he has charge of City Missions. As a pastor he has been usually successful in winning many souls on the charges he has served. He has contributed liberally of his means to the church.

REV. JAMES FRANKLIN CHAFFEE, D. D.

Rev. James Franklin Chaffee, Presiding Elder Minneapolis District, was born in the town of Middlebury, Wyoming County, N. Y., November 5, 1827. His parents, Chaffees on both sides, belonged to the sturdy New England stock, having been among the colonists emigrating from old England prior to 1650. They removed to Northern Illinois when the son was seventeen years old, so that the whole period of his minority was passed upon the frontiers of civilization, where in labor and study he built up a hardy frame, upon a constitution inherited from temperate and laborious ancestors. His educational opportunities were such only as the common schools afforded, supplemented by hard study and a wide range of reading. How well he improved his slender opportunities for obtaining learning is attested by the graceful act of the Illinois Wesleyan University, which conferred upon him some ten years ago the degree of Doctor of Divinity.

Dr. Chaffee was received into the ministry of the Methodist Episcopal church by the Rock River Annual Conference in the fall of 1848, at the age of twenty-one years. For the next nine years he shared the life of the itinerant ministry. His first charge was as junior preacher of the Carthage circuit, which included the city of Nauvoo. Successive appointments were at Oquawka, two years; Monmouth and Knoxville one year each, and Lewiston and Jefferson streets, Chicago, each two years. The latter was the leading Methodist church in the city with one exception.

In the meantime, during the first year of his ministry, he married Miss Calista Hopkins, who during all the subsequent years has endured with him the toils and responsibilities, and shared with him the felicities of a Methodist preacher's itinerant life.

Dr. Chaffee took up his residence in what is now the city of Minneapolis in the fall of 1857, and was stationed at St. Anthony about September 1, of that year.

During his first appointment in St. Anthony, which continued a little less than two years, though in feeble health, he conducted a series of meetings, for eight weeks, without ministerial help, which yielded one hundred accessions to the church. Throughout his pastorates the spiritual results of his labors have been fruitful in revivals of religion, and accessions to the church. In the spring of 1849 Dr. Chaffee was appointed to the charge of Jackson Street Church, St. Paul, but returned to Minneapolis in the fall of 1860, to the then only Methodist church in Minneapolis. It was a frame building at the corner of Fifth and Oregon (now Third avenue) streets, opposite the new court house.

He was appointed chaplain of the Fifth regiment of Minnesota Infantry. Severe sickness compelled Chaplain Chaffee to resign his post from before Corinth, after a service of only six weeks.

In the fall of 1862 Dr. Chaffee was appointed Presiding Elder of the Minneapolis District, which then included the whole northwestern frontier of the state, which had been devastated by the Indian outbreak of that year. For two years he traveled throughout this extensive field, strengthening the feeble churches

REV. JAMES FRANKLIN CHAFFEE

and organizing others, furnishing his own horse, paying his own expenses, upon the annual salary of $550. Two years later the Minneapolis and St. Paul districts were consolidated, and Dr. Chaffee was made Presiding Elder of the new district, continuing for the next three years; meanwhile the Methodist church in Minneapolis had been reorganized and the Centenary Church formed.

Dr. Chaffee was appointed to the pastorate of this church in 1867, continuing its pastor for the next three years. At this time the Centenary was the largest church and had the largest congregation of any of the city churches. In each of the three winters the church enjoyed revivals of religion, and its membership largely increased. In 1870 he was appointed to the Minneapolis City Mission which he accepted with a view to gaining a year of partial rest. The rest was, however, obtained by a change in the kind rather than amount of labor, for he devoted himself to the organizing of the Seventh Street Church, procuring with the aid of liberal members of the old church, the building of a convenient church edifice for the congregation, which has since become the flourishing Thirteenth Avenue Church.

For the next few years Dr. Chaffee filled a pastorate at Duluth, another at Faribault, another at St. Paul, and was Presiding Elder of the Winona District.

To the pastorate of the Hennepin Avenue M. E. Church he was by special request appointed in 1879, and continued for three years.

The next four years were occupied with fulfilling the duties of Presiding Elder of the Minneapolis District. Through these years he was largely instrumental in the organization of a number of churches, and in raising funds for houses of worship. Among these were Twenty-fourth Street M. E. Church, Simpson Church, Bloomington Avenue, Forest Heights, Western Avenue, Taylor Street, Lake Street, and more recently Fowler.

Since 1887 Dr. Chaffee has been Presiding Elder of the Winona and Minneapolis Districts.

In 1867, 1879, 1883 and 1891, he was elected delegate to the General Conference, and each time on the first ballot as leader of the delegation. The General Conference of 1892 elected him a member of the General Missionary Committee, the term of which will not expire until the meeting of the General Conference in 1896. His most important general service has been in connection with the educational work of the church. At the conference held at Mankato in 1871 he was, quite unexpectedly to himself, elected

Agent of Hamline University. For the last five years Dr. Chaffee has been president of its Board of Trustees.

A most philanthropic work which has in recent years engaged Dr. Chaffee's attention, is the organization of Asbury Hospital, which, largely through the liberality of Mrs. Sarah H. Knight, the daughter of his old friend, T. A. Harrison, has been equipped and opened as a public hospital, but under the management of the Methodist churches. Dr. Chaffee is president and financial agent of the institution.

Dr. Chaffee has been a prolific writer for the press. Besides conducting the editorial work of the Methodist Herald, he has been a frequent contributor to the local and periodical press. Not alone does the discussion of theological and church subjects engage his pen, but speculative and scientific ones as well. Especially is he strong in meeting the cavilers at religion on scientific grounds. In theology he is liberal within the limits permitted to a loyal believer in the doctrines of his church.

Of a family of nine children born to Dr. and Mrs. Chaffee, but two survive. Their daughter Carrie, is the wife of H. M. Farnham, Esq., and his son, Hugh G., is connected with the Security Bank.

HUGH GALBRAITH HARRISON

Hugh Galbraith Harrison. In 1803 Thomas Harrison emigrated from North Carolina and settled in the wilderness four miles southwest of the village of Belleville, Illinois. He was a sturdy man of Scotch-Irish descent, and a local preacher in the Methodist Episcopal Church. Here he opened a farm, and raised a family of nine children. He was not only a pioneer in the wilderness but he was a pioneer in the milling business of the Mississippi Valley. As early as 1826 he purchased for $300 an ox mill at Belleville, and his two elder sons left the farm and assumed the management of the old mill. Five years later the father removed to Belleville with his family and introduced into the mill the first steam engine that was set up in the State of Illinois. A new and larger mill was built in 1836, which was burned in 1843 with 5,000 bushels of wheat and 500 barrels of flour, and no insurance. It was rebuilt the next year, and the business so enlarged that as a local chronicle testifies, "For many years the product of the Harrison mills at Belleville was the standard of excellence throughout the commercial world. Their sales of flour and purchases of wheat reached millions of dollars." Until the introduction of the new process in

HUGH GALBRAITH HARRISON

milling, by which the superior qualities of spring wheat were developed, Belleville flour was the best in the country.

Hugh G. Harrison was a younger son of this pioneer family, born April 23, 1822. He was educated at McKendree College at Lebanon, Ill., and in his early manhood was associated with his father and brothers in the milling business at Belleville. In 1860 Thomas A., William and Hugh G. Harrison removed to Minneapolis. Each built a fine residence; that of Hugh being on a double block at the corner of Nicollet and Eleventh, then far out of the built-up part of the town, and covered with a hazel brush thicket. This remained the family homestead, and is to-day one of the most admired homes of the city. For many years the brothers made their investments and carried on business in common. In course of time the abundant opportunities for business, and perhaps diverse tastes led them to separate and pursue different lines. They were original stockholders in the First National Bank of St. Paul, and largely interested in the St. Paul and Sioux City railroad.

In 1862 they built on the corner of Washington and Nicollet avenues the stone block, still standing, at that time the most imposing building in the town, and having a hall which furnished for years the audience room for public meetings and concerts.

In 1863 they associated themselves with Joseph Dean in the lumber business. The firm of Joseph Dean & Co., for the next fifteen years became the leader in the lumber trade of the city. They bought fine timbered lands, purchased and rebuilt a large saw mill at the mouth of Bassett's Creek, and opened lumber yards. Subsequently they built the Pacific mill on the river bank just above the suspension bridge, which was for years the largest and best equipped saw mill in the city. On retiring from the lumber business in 1877, the Security Bank was organized, with the largest capital of any bank in the city. T. A. Harrison being president; Hugh G. Harrison, vice-president, and Joseph Dean, cashier. The bank from the first was prosperous, and took the lead in that line of business. The capital was enlarged as the needs of business required, until it reached $1,000,000, with deposits of nearly $6,000,000. At the death of the elder brother, Hugh G. Harrison was elected its president, and gave personal attention to its management, the bank attaining uninterrupted prosperity, and engaging in a high degree the public confidence, to the close of his life.

The business career and character of Mr. Harrison were sketched in an obituary written at the time of his death by one who had known him intimately, and been associated with him in church fellowship, from which we condense the concluding part of this notice.

H. G. Harrison was always foremost in every enterprise relating to the growth and well being of the city. He was a careful student of political questions, though not in the ordinary sense a politician. For many years during the formative and constructive period of the school system of the city he was a member of the School Board, and one of its most faithful and effective workers. Largely to his excellent judgment is due the fact that the City of Minneapolis is possessed of so much valuable school property. He was administrator of the Spencer estate, which became the foundation for the public library. He was mayor of Minneapolis in 1868, and made a splendid administration for the young and growing city. He founded the grocery house of B. S. Bull & Co., in the seventies, and later on that of Geo. R. Newell & Co. He was one of the largest subscribers and first director and treasurer of the Minneapolis Exposition. At the time of his death he was vice-president of the Minneapolis Trust Company. He always took a deep interest in Hamline University, to which he contributed large sums of money. Indeed Mr. H. G. Harrison's benefactions in this city among the churches and benevolent enterprises are a multitude. He seemed always to be giving, and he always gave with discrimination, with a liberal hand and cheerfully. Particularly was this the case in the realm of Methodism, of which denomination he had been a life long member and active promoter.

Mr. Harrison was a cultivated Christian gentleman. He was a member and trustee of Hennepin Avenue M. E. Church of this city. Always a student, an extensive traveler both in this country and abroad, an omniverous reader of the best literature, his mind was broad and his views well settled. There was nothing narrow in his disposition or attainments. He was helpful, always helpful, to young men, to worthy public enterprises, and to the necessities of men and women about him, his purse was ever open. He was an intense lover of good music.

Mr. Harrison was twice married. His first wife, Irene, died August 13, 1876. By this marriage he had five sons, all now living and grown to manhood, and successfully engaged in various lines of business. They are Edwin, George, Lewis, Hugh and Perry. October 25, 1877, he married Mrs. Elizabeth Wood Hunt, of Allentown, Pa., who, with her daughter, Helen Louise, and the sons above named, survive him. He also has three sisters, Mrs. Dovy McBride, of Bellville, Ill., Mrs. Olive Green and Mrs. Anna H. Goheen, residing in the vicinity.

Mr. Harrison had made in the latter part of July, 1891, a business trip to the East, and returning seemed in perfect health. A slight indisposition kept him at home for a few days. He was at his desk at the bank on Monday, August 10, but returning home took to his bed, and on Wednesday night went to his final rest, heart failure following a severe cold, being assigned as the fatal cause.

"His life was ripe; his end was peaceful and lovely; his rest is earned; his works do follow him."

GEN. GEORGE P. WILSON

George P. Wilson was born on the family homestead, a farm, near Lewisburgh, Union Co., Pennsylvania, on January 19, 1840. His father and mother were Methodists of the genuine type and reared their children in that faith. In those primitive days it was considered no reflection on parents to rear large families even though it involved ceaseless toil and sacrifice. Mr. Wilson was the last of twelve children, eight of whom are still living. He left the farm in 1857 to attend the Lewis, now Bucknell, University where he remained until the fall of 1858, when he became a student of the Ohio Wesleyan University at Delaware, Ohio. While here he made decided advancement: not sparing the midnight oil for the oil of an enlightened understanding.

He remained in this institution until December 1860, when he removed to Winona, Minnesota, and began the study of law. He was admitted to the bar in October, 1862, at Rochester, Minn. In 1864 he was elected assistant secretary of the State Senate and served in this capacity the following session and as secretary the two following sessions. In 1866 he was elected county attorney of Winona County and twice re-elected. In 1871 he was appointed government commissioner on the Southern Pacific R. R., and in that capacity viewed the first eighty miles of railroad from San

GEN. GEO. P. WILSON

Francisco south. In 1872-3 he was a member of the house of representatives from Winona County. In 1873 he was elected attorney general of Minnesota and was twice re-elected, serving in that capacity until January, 1880. Soon after this he removed to Fargo, in the then territory of Dakota, where he remained engaged in the practice of his profession until 1887.

Tiring of frontier life and still retaining a warm love for Minnesota, the state of his adoption in boyhood, in 1887 he removed with his family to Minneapolis where he is now prospering in his profession. He is a prominent member of the Hennepin Avenue Church, being connected with its official board. He believes in the gospel and has no patience with any attempt from the pulpit to cover its reproaches, explain away its power, or make it popular with new fangled notions. He enjoys deep spiritual truth for his own soul and insists that such preaching is the only source of power for the pulpit, and hope for the world.

GEORGE HERBERT TAYLOR

George Herbert Taylor was born in Berkshire, Vermont, on a farm situated on the eastern slope of hills running parallel with the Green Mountains and about midway between them and Lake Champlain, on the morning of May 10, 1853, of poor but refined and intelligent parents. His father was John Taylor, a Yorkshire Englishman, and his mother, Sarah Dowler, a Scotch woman. Like his father before him, Thomas Taylor, a Welshmen, his father was a farmer. With many others of his countrymen he came to this country in 1840 to better his condition and settled on the farm where the subject of this sketch was born. At the time of his settlement there it was nothing but a Vermont wilderness. For eighteen years he laid sturdy blows on the stalwart forest trees, so that when he died in 1858, more than seventy acres had been cleared and made ready for the plow.

In a little log school house surrounded by towering maples, his son George received such instructions as the teachers of that day and location were competent to impart. For six years he labored on his father's farm but was so intent on securing an education that he would study under the flickering light of the pine knot until the small morning hours. His only books were the Bible and the Seven Wonders of the World, his only tutor, nature.

At eighteen he was fully determined to acquire an education and set out alone without any assistance. For eight months he attended the academy at Richford, Vermont. In the summer following he found employment as freight brakeman on the Central Vermont Railway.

In his ambition for a bright intellect, he was not afraid to soil his hands. After working twenty-two days on the railroad he was caught between the cars and so injured that he has carried a crip-

GEORGE HERBERT TAYLOR

pled and partially useless arm, ever since. For fourteen months subsequent to this he was out of employment; all his dreams of an education disappeared, and a dark cloud of $600 indebtedness rolled up before him which was the result of his inability to work during the idleness which necessarily followed his injury.

Upon recovery, the railroad again gave him employment and for twelve years he continued in that capacity, but during this period he was not recreant to his intellectual training or indifferent to the myriad opportunities that presented themselves for his development. He was a natural student and saw a lesson on every rock, flower and shrub. He had a natural taste for history and biography and was fond of writing sketches of all he saw or heard. After laboring hard all day he would write out at night the lessons he had received. His ability as a writer soon received recognition and for ten years he was the local correspondent of leading newspapers published in different parts of the state.

In rummaging through an old attic one day, he found a copy of Blackstone which he read and re-read many times until he found himself drifting toward the legal profession. This time he removed from the East to the West and took up the study of law and was admitted to the bar in 1886 in the city of Minneapolis where he has since been a successful practitioner in all the courts of the state.

His early ability as a writer continued to develop. In 1884 he wrote "How She Hated Him", a novel founded upon fact which is widely published and won him great praise. Since then, he has written a large number of interesting stories. These stories have largely been written between the hours of eight o'clock and midnight. Many of them have been published, among them being "Fifteen Years a Mystery"; "John Ottonberg's Mistake"; "Erastus Corning, a Story for Boys"; "My Revenge"; "An Agreement and What Came of it"; "William Livingston, or, The man-with-the-white-face." Besides these, numerous other sketches, about fishing and hunting, have been published. Those attracting most attention were, "A Day in the Adirondacs"; "Hunting in Minnesota"; "A Bear Hunt in Vermont"; "Trout Fishing in Wisconsin"; and "Hunting the Ruffled Grouse in Wisconsin".

He was married in 1876 to the daughter of Hon. Daniel Tilden of West Lebanon, N. H., a wholesale flour and feed dealer and famous as a Jacksonian Democrat of the pronounced type. In 1886 Mr. Taylor united with the church and is now an official member of Wesley Church, Minneapolis. He has a commanding personal appearance, being five feet ten inches in height and weighing two hundred fifty-six pounds, yet he can tire out the ordinary man in a tramp through the woods or field with gun or rod in hand. He is always bright, versatile and interesting, and as a conversationalist has but few equals. He stands at the head of his profession and is one of the leading representatives of his church.

REV. C. C. LASBY, D. D.

Rev. C. C. Lasby, D. D., is the pastor of the St. Paul's Church, Lincoln, Nebraska, one of the leading charges of Methodism. His rare ability as pulpit orator and his success as pastor display the outcome of pluck, patience and perseverance.

Dr. Lasby was born in Canada. When but a child his mother died and he was left alone to fight the battle of life, for his father soon married again, and, discontented with a home without a mother, he started out in the world to do for himself.

Garfield says; "A boy should be dropped overboard at sixteen and if he is worth saving, he will swim to shore." Whether this is correct philosophy or not, the boy Lasby, when but eleven years of age, leaped into the angry flood of real life, breasted it, and has reached the shore of success. The best he could do at first was to accept a position as chore boy in a lumber camp in the pine forests of Michigan. There, back in the woods, sixty miles from a railroad, he spent five years among as rough a class of men as can be found. It was a wild, romantic, dangerous life. At first there were no churches or schools, but after a time, as the settlers flocked in and the country began to develop, stores and a schoolhouse were established. From chore boy young Lasby graduated to the main clerkship in a camp supply station.

At the age of eighteen he went to Long Island and learned the printer's trade. Finally he moved to New York where he continued in his trade. He boarded in Brooklyn and while there was converted, and in January, 1873, united with the South Third Street Church.

He felt called to the ministry and began a preparatory course of study. He worked hard and taught school on Long Island.

After pursuing a course in Victoria University of Canada, he entered Drew Theological Seminary and graduated in 1879: he was immediately appointed to a church at Hartford, Conn., which was about to be sold under the "auctioneer's hammer." The edifice was unfinished, poorly furnished and uninviting; some of

REV. C. C. LASBY, D. D.

the audience room windows had boards instead of glass, but the young pastor was equal to the emergency, and in two years he had raised enough money to liquidate the entire indebtedness, spent $1500 in fitting up the building, and left a large membership and congregation.

He was then transferred to John Street Church in New York, mother church of Methodism. At this church he greatly increased the membership and paid the debt within a few months. The church then sent him to Europe for rest, where he traveled extensively on the continent. In Switzerland he met a lady, Miss Cara T. Newman, who, two years later became his wife. He returned and enlarged the work at John Street, raising more money for repairing the old edifice. Then he was appointed to Flushing, Long Island. His pastorate there revived the church and liquidated a large part of an old indebtedness. At the expiration of three years, he was appointed to Ridgefield, Connecticut. The next appointment was to Green Avenue Church, Brooklyn, and after a most successful pastorate there he was appointed to the Summer Avenue Church, Brooklyn.

This church was new and weak and imperfectly organized, but through the ability and superb tact of Dr. Lasby, it developed into one of the strongest churches in Brooklyn, and increased its congregation and membership at least onefold. While pastor of this church his health became so impaired that he was compelled to seek a change of climate more suitable to his physical condition. Consequently he accepted an invitation to the pastorate of the St. Paul's Church, at Lincoln, Nebraska. Upon severing his relations with the Summer Avenue Church he was accorded a reception by Brooklyn Methodists which, perhaps, in its extent, enthusiastic greeting and profound grief at his going, exceeded any similar occasion that has ever occurred in the history of Methodism in that city. All the churches and pastors were represented. Speeches were made by many prominent men, and when Dr. Lasby replied, the hearts of all were melted to sorrow.

His pastorate at Lincoln has been one of phenomenal success. The membership has been greatly increased, and congregations have been called together that have exceeded the capacity of the large auditorium.

The elements of Dr. Lasby's strength are found in his general disposition. In manner he is refined, cultivated, warm and hearty. He charms people to him and holds them by his genial and affable spirit. He is a pastor who devotes due time to his pastoral work, especially in cases of sickness and affliction, when a pastor is most needed. He is prompt, untiring and sympathetic; he is an excellent preacher. A broad mind lifts him above all cant or sensationalism: he does not need to resort to any cheap subterfuges in order to get a hearing: he is an earnest student of books and men. For fifty two Sundays in the year he brings to his people thoughtful, logical, well illustrated and profound gospel sermons. He is sound in doctrine, and not afflicted with the fad of "progressive theology," while at the same time his scholarship keeps him fully abreast of the thought of the age.

JOHN D. BLAKE

John D. Blake was born in Marlboro, Windham Co., Vt., May 16, 1838, on a farm on which his father, B. W. Blake, was born and lived until near the close of his life. His grandfather, James Blake, was a tinner by trade and made canteens and cartridge boxes for the federal army during the war of the revolution and as a boy was with his father, Increase Blake, a revolutionary soldier and one of the Boston tea party when the taxed tea was thrown overboard from British ships into Boston Harbor, securing for his mother, who was fond of tea, by wearing his father's large shoes and filling them with the tea wasted from the broken chests on the deck of the ship, supplies to last her through the tea famine of the revolutionary war.

This mother, the great grandmother of the subject of this sketch, during the occupancy of the city of Boston by the British soldiers, sat one day in the front part of her house not far from the Old South Church, reading her English Bible, when she was visited by soldiers who asked her what she was reading. She replied: "The story of the Cross"; when one of them took his sword and cut a cross through several pages of her Bible, telling her he would leave her a cross she would not soon forget.

Mr. Blake had only the advantages of a Vermont country school education, excepting part of two terms at select or private schools where he pursued special studies outside of the common school curriculum. At the age of fourteen he left his father's farm

and commenced clerking in the country store of Houghton &
Walker, at Williamsville, Vt., still continuing his school studies as
best he could out of business hours during the year of his clerkship.
His first year's salary was $50 and board, out of which he supported
himself and divided the amount with his father to assist him in the

JOHN D. BLAKE

payment of a debt incurred in buying an addition to the old homestead farm.

When but seventeen years of age, purchasing his minority
from his father with capital provided by a wealthy bachelor who
became interested in young Blake, he purchased the interests of
the senior member of the firm and was admitted into the business

under the firm of Walker & Blake, in which he continued until the business was closed out in the spring of 1857, just in time to escape the financial panic of that memorable year. He then removed to Brattleboro and found employment with Cune & Brackett as manager of their dry goods store.

In the spring of 1858 he formed a partnership with his former employer, H. F. Houghton, under the firm of Houghton & Blake, purchasing the dry goods and carpet business of Cune & Brackett. This business was fairly successful, being vigorously prosecuted and closely attended to by Mr. Blake. Too close application to business and ambition for success, resulted in breaking down his health and in August, 1860, he came West for a trip of recreation and to look up chances for an extension of his business.

He was so impressed with the West that he settled in business at once and began the purchase and shipment of wheat and farm produce at Lansing, Iowa, at Winona, Minnesota, and during the winter at points on the Milwaukee & Du Chien Railroad. While at Winona he became impressed with the fertility and resources of Minnesota and visited Rochester, renting a new brick store then being built. He went East and arranged with his partner for a branch business under the name of J. D. Blake & Co. He then moved his family to the new western home, establishing the new business on the basis of cash payment, one price and low price. He expected to do a small business, but after six months its volume had increased to the rate of more than $150,000 a year, one year reaching the sum of $340,000.

He formed a plan of profit-sharing business by admitting those who proved faithful and meritorious to a working interest in the profit, until finally those admitted to the business had secured sufficient interest in it to take it with their own capital.

From 1874 to 1882 he was interested in the Chattanooga Iron Company, and also owned and operated a flouring mill near Mantorville, in Dodge Co., Minn. He also owned, operated and improved a large number of farms in the different parts of the state which he traded for Minneapolis property. Upon disposing of his interests at Rochester he removed to Minneapolis where he became identified with many commercial interests.

In 1878 failing health made it necessary for him to take a trip to Cuba, the Bahamas and Florida. He returned home in March, but shortly after received a spinal injury which resulted in temporary paralysis. As soon as he was able to travel he was taken to Europe where he slowly regained his health.

Since coming to Minneapolis his principal business has been real estate. He has erected a large number of houses in the new portion of the city known as New Boston and sold them on such easy payments that a large number of people have been provided with homes at a little more than they would have paid for rent. Meanwhile Mr. Blake built for himself the beautiful home at 1124 Mt. Curve avenue, on Lowry Hill.

Mr. Blake is a prominent Methodist and is a member of the Official Board of the Fowler Church. His parents and friends were all Baptists, but thrown under Methodist influence, he fell in love with its evangelical truths and finally became identified with it. He soon became interested in Sabbath School work and has always sought to promote, approve and advance methods in that line. He was for several years superintendent of the Sunday School at Rochester, and was a member of the first Lay Conference of Minnesota and also a lay delegate to the General Conference held at Baltimore in 1876. He has been a large contributor to the benevolences of the church and is a life member of the Missionary Sunday School Tract and Bible Society; he has made contributions which have built three churches on the frontier, has aided very many local churches in building or in difficulty, and has lately contributed property to the amount of $20,000 for relief and payment of the debt of the Clinton Avenue Church, of West St. Paul, saving this important church to its great mission in that city.

He was instrumental in the organization of the Sunday School and church known as Taylor Street, now Trinity, in Minneapolis, assisted in the organization of the Mission Sunday School on Western avenue and was superintendent of it until it outgrew its quarters and developed into the Western Avenue Church. He was also instrumental in organizing the Mission Sunday School of Centenary Church in old Market Hall. Special attention has been given to systematic Sunday School quarterly reviews and for some years he has written the quarterly review for the Illustrator, published at Chicago, Toronto and New York, which, with the review charts published by them, have been of great help to Sunday School teachers in aiding them in the difficult task of properly reviewing the quarterly lessons.

Mr. Blake was early connected with the Chautauqua movement and attended the first assembly in 1874. He was a delegate from Minnesota to the first International Sunday School Convention, at Indianapolis, in 1872. He has been active in the organization and maintenance of the Y. M. C. A., largely sustaining it while at Rochester, being for some time its president. He made the first contribution toward the building of the present Y. M. C. A. structure in Minneapolis.

On April 15, 1858, he was married to Julia R. Ingram, at Boston, Mass., to whom five children have been born, two sons and three daughters; of whom two daughters, only, have lived to womanhood.

BERNARD B. BRETT

BERNARD B. BRETT

Bernard B. Brett was born at Albany, New York, August 29, 1869. He was educated there, obtaining a Regent's certificate. Like many other ambitious young men he had a desire to see the West and in 1886 came to Minnesota and for two years engaged in farming.

From 1888 to 1891 he taught school, spending his vacations on the farm. In the early part of 1891 he studied stenography and, in March, 1891, he entered the law firm of H. F. Woodard, at Fergus Falls, Minn., where he began the study of law. While in Fergus Falls he united with the Methodist Episcopal Church and became quite active in church and Mission work, starting a Mission Sunday School and superintending it until December, 1891, at which time he came to Minneapolis, entering the law office of Taylor & Woodard.

He was admitted to the bar before the supreme court in 1893 and is now a member of the law firm of Taylor. Woodard & Brett. He has not permitted his professional duties to interfere with religious life and privileges. He has kept up his activity in church and mission work and is one of the leading young men of Wesley Church. He was president of the Young People's Society of Christian Endeavor when Centenary Church moved into the the new Wesley Church and is now chairman of the Christian Endeavor Mission Committee, secretary and treasurer of the Wesley Christian Endeavor Mission Sunday School, and a member of the Sunday School Board, appointed by the Quarterly Conference.

Mr. Brett is a man of unusual energy and intelligence and gives promise of future power in his chosen profession.

DR. ELIZABETH S. DALBEY-NORRED

Dr. Elizabeth S. Dalbey-Norred was born in Wells Co., Indiana, October 14, 1843. Joseph Asbury Dalbey, her father, was a native of Frederick County, Virginia, whence, at the age of four years, he moved with his father to Pickaway Co., Ohio. Here he grew to manhood and was married to Sarah H. Jennings, of Montgomery Co., November 2, 1842.

In 1843 Joseph Asbury Dalbey moved from Ohio to Indiana, where he resided until 1852, when he removed to Illinois, and opened a large stock farm, upon which the interesting childhood days of Dr. Norred were spent.

She was educated at the public schools and the North Sangamon Academy of Illinois, and on November 16, 1865, was married to Dr. Charles H. Norred, a surgeon in the 7th Illinois Cavalry. She became the mother of two children. Charles Elmer, born April 6, 1867, and William Asbury, born Dec. 21, 1869. The father, mother and two sons are all at home and constitute a most happy family.

Sometime afte rher marriage to Dr. Charles H. Norred she took up the study of her profession. In 1878 and 1879 she attended the winter and spring courses of lectures at the Woman's Medical College of Philadelphia. In 1879, 1880 and 1881 she attended winter and spring courses at the Woman's Medical College of Chi-

DR. ELIZABETH S. DALBEY-NORRED

cago, from which institution she was graduated. Her standing in the profession is represented by membership in the Illinois State Medical Society, Illinois, Indiana and Kentucky Trio Medical Society, the American Medical Association, the Society of Physicians and Surgeons of Minneapolis, Hennepin County Medical Society and the Minnesota State Medical Society, in all of which she has an honorable standing and is highly respected. She is deservedly popular as a physician. She has been one of the directors and a member of the medical staff of the Northwestern Hospital for several years, and is consulting physician to the Asbury Hospital, both of Minneapolis.

Dr. Norred is a broad minded woman in all her views and practices. Her charity and benevolence knows no restrictive lines. In her movements she only wants to be assured that her labor will be for the good of mankind and have the approval of God. While a member of the M. E. Church, attentive and laborious in temperance movements, she is not unmindful of the common brotherhood of man and the common Fatherhood of God.

REV. LYMAN EDWIN PRENTISS, D. D.

Lyman Edwin Prentiss was born in Putman County, Ohio, in 1849. He was converted in 1864 and was admitted into the Central Ohio Conference in 1873. His ministry has been marked from the first with wonderful success; he commenced at the lower round of the ladder, doing missionary work in Cincinnati, and has gradually ascended until at present he occupies one of the first charges of Methodism. Like the philosopher's stone, he has turned everything he touched into gold. Every field from circuit to station has felt the transforming power of his magic hand. Fame as a pastor soon brought him into great preeminence, he having filled some of the first stations in the Central Ohio Conference; he was sought for by the First Church, in Knoxville, Tenn., then by First Church, Chattanooga, and then transferred to Cincinnati Conference and stationed at Raper Church, Dayton, O., where he is still located.

He is an all-round man and succeeds on all lines and, being possessed of great personal magnetism, he readily wins his way to the hearts of the masses. He moves among his people like a sunbeam scattering light and gladness wherever he goes and solving the vexed question "How to reach the masses" by extending to the masses the hand of sympathy, love and help. As an organizer he builds up every department of Christian work. "Everything paid up and money in the treasury," is the report on every charge to which he has been appointed. He is a live man and does everything with dispatch. As a preacher he is sententious, vigorous. eloquent, pointed and brief. He inspires and instructs without weary-

LYMAN EDWIN PRENTISS

ing. He is an energetic pastor and needs no imported evangelist to fan the revival flames, hence, his ministry is always attended with signal revivals. He preaches a whole gospel, emphasizing all its cardinal points, yet keeping clear of anything that savors of fanaticism.

He received the degree of D. D. from Grant University in 1890. He was elected a member of the Board of Control of the Epworth League from the Sixth General Conference District, and in 1892 appointed by the Board of Bishops a member of the Executive Committee.

EZRA NORTHFIELD

EZRA NORTHFIELD

Ezra Northfield was born in Cambridgeshire, England, July 10, 1844. His parents were Methodists of the primitive type and filled the life of their son Ezra with thoughts of duty and destiny. In 1849 they moved from England and settled in Milwaukee. In 1864 he moved to Lake City and came to Minneapolis in the fall of 1887. He was converted when a young man and at the age of eighteen united with the church and is now an official member of Trinity Church, Minneapolis, and one of the influential Christian business men in that part of the city.

Foremost in every good work, he is in full sympathy with the church of his choice and always ready to contribute of his substance or time to its great achievements.

He is engaged in the meat business and illustrates the possibility of mixing business and religion, being known as a man of inflexible honesty and sterling Christian qualities.

EVERETT F. ADAMS

Everett F. Adams, physician and poet, was born April 25, 1857, Washington County, Maine. He is of English and Scotch descent. His early education was acquired in the public schools. He studied medicine with one of the leading physicians of Boston. Mass., and at a preparatory medical college, New York, and graduated at Vermont Medical College.

He practiced his profession in Lynn, Mass., three years, meeting with unusual success. He was elected vice-president of the American Health Society, Boston, November 1, 1889. He removed to New York City in 1890. Still ambitious to excel in his profession, he took a post graduate course in the Bellvue Medical College. During the same year, in 1891, he became assistant to

EVERETT F. ADAMS

the distinguished Dr. Ballou, of the Outdoor Department of Bellvue Hospital. He came to Minneapolis in 1892 where he has been identified with many of the public institutions of the city. He is a member of the Board of Trade, a prominent Mason and Knight Templar. He is also president of the American Progressive Investment Company which is mentioned elsewhere in this volume.

Dr. Adams has acquired more than local fame with his pen as a poet, and for many years he has been correspondent of the leading journals and magazines of this country. He is a man of strict integrity and unswerving allegiance to the church. He is a member of Fowler Church, also the Y. M. C. A., toward which he is a liberal contributor.

REV. JOHN STAFFORD, D. D.

Rev. Dr. Stafford was born in Nottingham, England, December 6, 1843. He came to this country with his parents in the spring of 1857 and settled in eastern New York. He was converted during the great revival of 1857-8 and joined the M. E. Church at Union Village, Washington Co., N. Y.

In 1860 his parents were attracted by the great opportunities presented in the West and moved to Minnesota traveling hundreds of miles with an ox team. They settled between Hastings and Red Wing. The settlement was called County Line and was included in the Red Wing Charge. Rev. Thomas Day was pastor. Dr. Stafford had always felt the call to preach and now surrendered fully to the great work that appealed to him. He was licensed to preach in the fall of 1862; he attended Hamline University, then located at Red Wing. In 1865 he was married to Miss Hattie R. Matthews, a young lady of culture, piety and devotion. During the years of his subsequent ministry, she has been a helpmate in the full sense of the word. For the first two years of his ministry he served as a supply under the Presiding Elder. He joined the Methodist Conference in 1867 and was ordained deacon by Bishop Simpson. Four years later he was ordained Elder and stationed at Waseosa, Anoka, Stillwater, Washington Avenue, now Foss Church, Minneapolis, Grace Church and Jackson Street Church, St. Paul.

In 1878 he was appointed financial agent of Hamline University. Upon assuming this responsibility, he was confronted by the greatest discouragement; he found an unfinished building standing alone on the prairie between the Twin Cities, its friends discouraged, and the Conference divided in its attitude toward it. Yet he was not bewildered. With that far-sightedness so characteristic of him, he set to work with a determination to win and in two years the building was finished and dedicated by Bishop Foss amid great enthusiasm.

REV. JOHN STAFFORD, D. D.

In 1882 he was stationed at Rochester. August 23, 1883, a cyclone destroyed the church and damaged the parsonage. In six months the church was rebuilt, more beautiful and commodious than before. At the close of this pastorate he was stationed at Grace Church, St. Paul, one year, and at First Church, Minneapolis, three years. While here, his pastorate was very successful. His church was always filled and the membership was greatly increased.

In the fall of 1880 he was appointed Presiding Elder of the Minneapolis District and remained in it for five years. In spite of the hard times he was aggressive. No opportunity for the usefulness or glory of Methodism was neglected. His administration was characterized by the "forward movement" spirit. Among the many good things accomplished during his administration was the founding of Park Avenue Church and Fowler Church in Minneapolis. Time will demonstrate his wisdom and commend his pluck.

At the Conference in Minneapolis, 1893, Bishop Ninde appointed him Presiding Elder of Mankato District where his efforts are being crowned by characteristic success. As a preacher Dr. Stafford is simple and plain. He preaches the Word, has no use for "claptrap" methods and hews to the gospel line. He is never tedious and always interesting and edifying.

FINLEY DeVILLE NEWHOUSE, D. D.

Finley DeVille Newhouse was born in Rochester, Fulton Co., Ind., July 27, 1857. His ancestors on both sides were of purely English stock. His father, Rev. John E. Newhouse, is a minister of the Methodist Episcopal Church, in the N. W. Indiana Conference, of which he has been a member for nearly half a century. Dr. Newhouse was educated in De Pauw University, Greencastle, Ind., and was graduated as a classical student in 1880, taking the history honors of his class. During his college course he achieved unusual success as an orator as well as student of the Greek language and literature, to which he gave special attention, reading much more than the regular course required. He received the degree of B. A. at graduation, and has since received the degree of A. M., and in 1892, the degree of D. D.

Soon after graduation he was sent by Bishop William Taylor to the American College, at Conception, Chile, S. A., where he filled the Greek chair. In addition to his college duties he did

considerable preaching both in English and Spanish, and while yet
in Chile was admitted as a minister to the N. W. Indiana Conference.

His health became seriously impaired and in the fall of 1884
he returned to the United States and was almost immediately

FINLEY DeVILLE NEWHOUSE, D. D.

appointed pastor of the church at Williamsport, Ind.   Here he was
united in marriage to Miss Ida Kate Fox.

The following fall, at the request of the missionary secretaries of the church, he consented to a transfer to British India, and
was made pastor of a large English church in Allahabad, capital of
the N. W. Provinces. The health of Mrs. Newhouse becoming

feeble, they again returned to the United States in 1889, and Dr. Newhouse was stationed at the Fifth Avenue Church, in Goshen, Ind. Still in search of health, they went, in 1890, to Huron, S. D., where the Methodist Church was served for three years.

During this pastorate a heavy church debt was lifted, a valuable parsonage property was acquired and 357 were added to the membership. In the fall of 1893, Dr. Newhouse received a call from Franklin Avenue Church, Minneapolis, which he accepted.

He is the author of a college romance entitled, "The Three C's", and has published a book of lectures under the title, "Why I Am a Protestant". He has also written much for his church papers, and several articles from his pen have been published in the magazines of the country. At the last session of the Conference, he was appointed to the pastorate of the First Church, at Red Wing, Minn.

P. A. H. FRANKLIN

P. A. H. Franklin was born in Norway, August 8, 1847. Although born of humble parentage and in lowly surroundings, he has forged ahead in the church and commercial affairs until he occupies a position of honor, usefulness and phenomenal success. When but a boy he was conscious of an ambition that could only be satisfied by the development of the rare gifts with which he was endowed. He was a student by nature and gave himself up to every book it was possible to obtain. He would work on his father's farm all day and study for hours at night so that he soon became proficient in all the common branches, although he did not have the advantages of a common school training.

He was soon able to enter the University and Medical School of Norway. There he evinced rare ability and went to the head of his classes. Having completed a course in this institution, he turned his face toward America, and, on August 15, 1873, he reached Minneapolis. Hearing of the great mineral resources of Utah, he immediately went to that territory and began work as a mining engineer.

While engaged in this work he first had a sense of his sinfulness and need of salvation. After some resistence, he yielded to the gospel call and gave himself to Christ and was genuinely converted. It changed the whole course of his life. There at once came to him a burden for the salvation of those about him. The mining camps rang with his exhortations. He stood in the mines, on the

P. A. H. FRANKLIN

street, and wherever he had opportunity, pleading with men to be "reconciled to God."

He attended one of our Mission Conferences in Salt Lake City and attracted great attention by his fervor, enthusiasm, burning testimony and complete consecration to the work of Christ.

He was given work as a missionary among his people, many of whom had fallen into the meshes of Mormonism. Success was with him from the very start, although his first field was barren and desolate, having no church, no membership, and no congregation. He grasped the situation with a master hand. The people rallied to his inspiring call, gave of their means and were converted by scores.

A church was built and all the elements of success sprung into existence as if by magic. Mr. Franklin soon became known throughout Utah. Courage and generalship never failed him and he became a leading figure in the Norwegian work. Wherever he went, churches were built, the powers of darkness suffered loss and the kingdom of Christ triumphed. Sent East to raise funds, the same success that was with him in Utah followed him among the staid and conservative churches of the eastern states. His story was so simple, unaffected and pathetic that great congregations were melted to tears and his appeals for help were responded to by contributions that aggregated thousands of dollars.

He built one of the largest and most beautiful churches in Salt Lake City. There are but few points in Utah that have not felt his spiritual touch and been benefited by his rare financial skill. But Mr. Franklin, like many other leaders did not discriminate between his own financial interests and those of the church. He not only gave away the small salary he received at different points, but in his eagerness to carry on the work and multiply churches, he assumed responsibilities that were too great for any one man and which soon began to embarrass him in his ministry. Yet he never faltered for he felt that somehow the hand of Providence would lead him through to victory.

In 1889 an opportunity came to him for acquiring some of the best mining property in Utah. Mr. Franklin regarded this as an answer to his prayers, and the way to an opening for him to meet all the obligations assumed for the church and to do even larger things for the cause of the Master. He at once went East and after laying the great project before some leading capitalists of Philadelphia, the Niagara Mining and Smelting Company was organized, incorporated and placed in full operation. Over half a million dollars was expended in purchasing and developing the properties of this new company. On April, 1892, Mr. Franklin incorporated

The New Tintic Mining & Smelting Company.

These properties are in the Tintic Mining District, about six miles from Eureka, Utah, and are said to be among the best gold and silver producers in the inter-mountain region. The company had also acquired the title to the Honorine Group, at Stocton, Utah.

Of these two properties there has been nearly $300,000.00 and this money has been raised through the efforts of Mr. Franklin together with his business associates. The mines comprising the Tintic group have already paid over a million dollars in dividends. It is a noteworthy fact that this great success has not turned the heart or head of Mr. Franklin. He is the same kind hearted, generous, self-sacrificing man and has, with increasing fortune, not only liquidated the obligations assumed while in the ministry, but has since given thousands of dollars to charitable causes.

He is not only in touch with the leading financiers of the country, but also with the leading men of Methodism. His donations are not confined to any one point; he has responded to calls from different sections of the country and always delights in helping those in need, regardless of creed, color or condition. It is not often that one can turn from the ministry to business without loss of spiritual life, usefulness and power, but Mr. Franklin feels that this new field has been providentially opened and that now with hand as well as voice he can minister to those in want and thus contribute his part toward the spread of the kingdom and the glory of the Redeemer.

PAUL DEAN BOUTELL

Paul Dean Boutell was born January 3, 1837, at Bakersfield, Vt., son of William Boutell, a farmer. Mr. Boutell worked on his father's farm until the age of fourteen when he entered the Spaldwin Academy, graduating with high honors at the age of seventeen.   Immediately after leaving college, he started for Worcester, Mass., with but ten dollars.   After paying his fare he had $2 left. Going to a leather factory he secured employment as an apprentice, receiving $5 per month.   At the expiration of three years of apprenticeship his employers showed their appreciation of his good

PAUL DEAN BOUTELL

service and appointed him foreman at a salary of $1000 per year, which they increased from time to time until it reached $3500 per year.

After serving as foreman for seven years he bought an interest in the factory.   This being just at the close of the war, when prices began to depreciate, he lost $8000 during the first year of his partnership. When the war broke out, Mr. Boutell desired to enlist as a volunteer but his employer said that they could not spare his services. Soon after, he was drafted and his employers again refused to let him go. They hired a substitute to take his place.

In 1872 he was stricken with typhoid fever which finally settled on his lungs making it necessary for him to seek the benefits of a western climate. Upon the advice of his physician he sold out his interest in the East and started for Minneapolis, where he located in the spring of 1872. He entered into partnership with George A. Hanson carrying on a furniture trade. After one year, Mr. Hanson retired from the firm, selling his interests to A. N. Trussell with whom Mr. Boutell carried on the business for three years when he sold out and started in business alone. This business has gradually increased until the large building which he occupies on Washington avenue is insufficient for its full and complete operation. Consequently Mr. Boutell has recently leased the large building being erected at the corner of First avenue south and Fifth street, where he will remove his business as soon as the structure is completed.

Mr. Boutell identified himself with the Hennepin Avenue Chuch soon after reaching Minneapolis where he is still a consistent and influential member.

WALLACE THOMAS GOODHUE.

Wallace Thomas Goodhue was born in Jerico, Vt., August 31, 1853. His father was John C. Goodhue, the youngest son of the Rev. T. Goodhue, who was a Methodist minister and a preacher of great power among the pioneers of his state.

At about the age of twelve years the subject of this sketch became interested in religious questions and soon after was happily converted and united with the Methodist Church at St. Albans, Vt. He attended St. Albans Academy where he excelled as a student; he was active in Sunday School and young people's work and was appointed leader of a large society of young people for a number of years.

In 1876 he married Miss Ellen Elizabeth Haight. This union has been blessed by one daughter who is about sixteen years of age, a young lady of rare and beautiful Christian character.

In 1880 Mr. Goodhue moved to Minneapolis, joining the Hennepin Avenue Church by letter, but afterwards changing his

WALLACE T. GOODHUE

membership to Franklin Avenue Church. While a member of this church he spent one year in evangelistic work throughout the state, meeting with good results. In 1889 he had charge of Fairview Mission and the same year united with the Forest Heights Church. He founded the Gospel Union and was one of the leading spirits in starting the Free Breakfast Mission which has done so much to reclaim the lost. He was superintendent of the spiritual work during the B. Fay Mills meetings in Minneapolis. The same year he published several tracts which have been the means of doing much good. Among them are the following: "A Peculiar People"; "Established Facts Concerning Dancing"; "Assurance by the Word of God"; "Suggestions to Young Converts"; "The Light of the World"; "Submission and Why."

Mr. Goodhue is engaged as a traveling salesman with the Century Piano Co., and is well known throughout the Twin Cities, having a large circle of friends.

At present he is superintendent of Forest Heights Mission.

M. LARA

M. Lara, the subject of this sketch, was born in Androscoggan Co., Maine. He spent the first twenty years of his life on one of those rocky farms in the town of Turner. Then, concluding that was not the most desirable place for a young man to start in life, he migrated to Massachusetts where he taught school for a couple of years, then went to New Orleans. There he was engaged in mercantile business and sugar planting with Mr. E. Heath for fifteen years, building up a large and lucrative business. Mr. Lara stood high in the estimation of the business community there, as evinced by the several positions of official trust and honor held by him.

M. LARA

During the war, particularly in 1863, the goverment distributed to the poor and destitute families in New Orleans about two hundred barrels of provisions a day in the shape of rations. He was superintendent of this distribution, and also held a position of trust in the Treasury Department in Louisiana during the war; he was also a member of the senate of the first free state legislature of Louisiana.

The yellow fever epidemic of 1878 not only broke up his business but caused the death of his youngest son, a remarkably bright boy of five years. This was so discouraging to Mr. Lara that he removed with his family to Kansas City in 1879, and in 1882 came to Minneapolis. He bought a half interest in the carpet business with Mr. A. H. Kenyon, then at 420 Nicollet Ave. When their partnership expired by limitation in 1885, he bought Mr. Kenyon's interest, and has since been doing business as M. Lara & Co. He rented the store where he is now located in the Sidle block, Nicollet avenue and Fifth street, before the block was built and while Mr. Sidle's residence was still on the ground.

He has built up a large business in his legitimate line, being the only exclusive carpet and drapery house in Minneapolis. His trade not only takes in the Twin Cities but extends throughout Minnesota, the Dakotas, Montana and portions of Iowa and Wisconsin. He does business on the principle that there are other things in the world as well as money, and that character and reputation are quite as valuable as the former. On this basis he has built a reputation that it takes the best part of a lifetime to do. In the business of carpets, draperies and interior decorations the house of M. Lara &. Co., is acknowledged to stand at the head of the list.

NATHANIEL McCARTHY

Nathaniel McCarthy came to Minneapolis from Buffalo, N. Y., where he had been for nine years in the employ of Mr. H. H. Otis, in the Methodist Book Depository in that city. Mr. McCarthy began at the foot of the ladder, his first position being that of errand boy. During the years in the employ of Mr. Otis, he was advanced from one position to another, until we find him occupying the highest position in the gift of his employer.

In the fall of 1883, a proposition to go into business in Minneapolis was made him by Mr. Orton S. Clark, and after visiting Minneapolis at that time, these gentlemen decided to establish themselves in the book business in Minneapolis the following spring. From that time until the present, the firm of Clark & Mc-Carthy has achieved success. Entering the city with an acquaintance limited to two families, former Buffalo friends, these gentlemen, by strict attention to business, have won for themselves a place in the commercial interests of the community. A large and increasing mail order department testifies to the ability of the firm to satisfy their patrons residing at a distance.

Mr. Clark retired from the business in February, 1892, Mr. McCarthy purchasing his interests.

INTERIOR VIEW OF BOOK STORE

The store is the rendezvous for clergymen of all denominations. An examination of the books is a convincing reason why a great many people find pleasure and profit in browsing in this best of book stores in Minneapolis.

Mr. McCarthy has been identified with the Methodist Episcopal Church for about twenty years. On coming to this city he placed his letter in the Hennepin Avenue Church, in June of 1884. In the following August he was elected one of the stewards of the church, and from that time to the present, has been related to the church in an official capacity, having served as Sunday School superintendent, president of the Young People's Society, and has held the office of treasurer of the church since 1890.

HOWARD AUGUSTUS BUTTERFIELD

H. A. BUTTERFIELD

Howard Augustus Butterfield, son of Cornelius A. Butterfield, was born in Ft. Wayne, Ind., July 22, 1860. He moved with his parents to Sandusky, O., when but a small child and lived there until eight years of age. At this time his father, on account of failing health, caused by too close application to business, removed to Viola, Minn., where he purchased a farm. Here Howard received a common school education and subsequently took an academic course of three years at Rochester, Minn. While here he was converted under the preaching of Rev. John Stafford and united with the church. After completing his education he returned to his home in Viola where he remained until 1886 when he took a position as county auditor's clerk in Rochester. This position he held for three years when it was terminated by a change in administration.

In 1889 he came to Minneapolis and was employed as bookkeeper for the Phelps Well & Wind Mill Co., being made manager of the same in 1891. In 1894 he purchased the stock of the business and became a member of the firm of Dean & Co. He is an active member of Hennepin Avenue Church. In 1893 he was elected president of the Christian Endeavor Society and served in that capacity for two years.

JOSEPH HENRY JOHNSON

Joseph Henry Johnson was born at Calais, Maine, January 17, 1852, where his father, the Rev. C. H. Johnson, of the East Maine Conference, was stationed. Soon after he was stationed at Bangor, where his health failed and, upon the advice of his physicians, he removed to Minneapolis in 1855. The journey across the countr

was long and tedious and he failed to rally from its effects. He
died within six months after arriving in the frontier town. After
the death of her husband Mrs. Johnson returned to Maine, where
she remained until 1857 when she married Justin S. Dow and came
back to Minneapolis to live, bringing her daughter, Kate, and her

JOSEPH H. JOHNSON

son, Joseph, with her.   Thus it will be seen that the subject of this
sketch is essentially a Minneapolitan.

At the age of fifteen he was thrown upon his own resources
by the death of his mother, thereafter making his home with the
late Judge T. R. E. Connell, during which time he attended the
public schools and business college.   He has been a member of the

Methodist Church since 1868 having united with Centenary Church that year.

He was married February 15, 1857, to Miss Louise A. Lyon, daughter of Walter Lyon, of Uniondale, Pa. They have two sons, Walter Henry and Arthur Eugene, aged respectively sixteen and nine years.

Mr. Johnson is an active and successful business man; he was early associated with George T. Vail, one of the pioneer undertakers of this city, and continued in the business thus established on Washington avenue until 1890 when it was removed to 614 Nicollet avenue. In 1891 Wm. H. Landis became a member of the firm, incorporating as The Johnson-Landis Undertaking Co. Mr. Johnson is not only an influential Methodist, but a prominent Mason, commanding the esteem of all who know him.

REV. THOMAS BILLING

REV. THOMAS BILLING

Rev. Thomas Billing was born at Swinford, Rugby, England, September 9, 1853. He was educated at Elma House school, Rugby, and united with the Wesleyan Methodist Church in 1871 and licensed as a local preacher in 1873. He served four years as District Evangelist in East Anglia and, feeling called to the work of the pastorate, came to America in 1886. He was received as a member and local preacher in old Jackson Street Church, St. Paul, and by its Quarterly Conference was recommended to the Annual Conference for admission on trial. He was subsequently received on probation in the Minnesota Conference and ordained Elder by Bishop Merrill in 1881. His appointments have been; Medford, Blooming Prairie, London, Wadena and Fisher. Mr. Billing is an able minister of the New Testament, he is a thorough Bible scholar and a very methodical and painstaking student, and his preaching is sound doctrinally, true to the Wesleyan standards, and full of instruction for the people.

Though an Englishman by birth he is a thorough American in feeling and in perfect sympathy with the progressive spirit of the great country.

His pastoral work is always faithfully performed. His own spirit is devout and prayerful, and hence his ministry is successful in the larger and better meaning of that much abused word.

W. P. PICKARD

W. P. Pickard was born in Ontario, Canada, in 1865, and was educated at Pickery College, Ontario, and Victoria University, Canada. Conscious of a call to the great work of the ministry, he entered the Toronto Conference of the Methodist Church and received special ordination for mission work. Opportunities for greater usefulness presented themselves in Minnesota, and in 1889 he entered the Minnesota Conference. Soon after this he was married to Miss Eva Trotter of Canada who has been a true helpmate to him.

W. P. PICKARD

He was first appointed to the Park Rapid Mission where his work was eminently successful, assuming such proportions that it was necessary for an assistant to be appointed and finally for the work to be divided into two circuits. Two churches remain as monuments to his two years' pastorate.

Osakis was his next field, where he reorganized Villard circuit. He held successful revivals and developed work which also necessitated division. His present charge is at Herman where he is laboring with characteristic success. He possesses in a marked degree, the qualifications of a successful pastor.

W. F. ROBERTSON

W. F. Robertson, journalist, was born April 9, 1865, near the village of Lachute, Province of Quebec, Canada. His father emigrated from Athol, Scotland, in 1820. He was one of the Robertsons of Athol, once a celebrated and powerful clan. His mother,

W. F. ROBERTSON

Mary Sinclair, was a lineal descendant of Sir William Sinclair, Earl of Caithness and head of the House of Sinclair. At the age of fifteen William was appointed Deputy Dominion Land Surveyor and was given charge of a party to subdivide a tract of drown lands in the British Northwest territories. For two years he was private

secretary to Hon. Duncan Sinclair, Winnipeg. He then moved to
the territory of Dakota and had a varied experience as merchant
and journalist, starting the Free Lance newspaper in 1886. From
1888 to 1890 he traveled extensively in Canada and the United
States. In 1891 he was a regular correspondent of the Winnepeg
Daily Tribune and was one of the commissioners appointed to set-
tle the Okase Indian trouble. In 1892 he removed to northern
Minnesota and became state attorney for the International Insurance
Co., deputy register of deeds and deputy clerk of court for Hubbard County and was also one of the editors of the Advocate, at
Park Rapids, Minn., until the spring of 1894. At this time he was
appointed secretary of the American Investment Co. and moved to
Minneapolis where he was subsequently made first vice-president
of the company. He is a member of the Board of Trade, editor of
Investor's Guide and president, secretary and treasurer of a number of religious and charitable institutions.

He is an active temperance worker, believing that the saloon
is the greatest evil of our civilization and that its destruction is the
only hope of the country. He has recently united with Fowler
Church and is one of its strong and effective workers.

WILLIAM H. LANDIS

William H. Landis was born in Tioga County, Penn.,
May 28, 1844. At the age of eighteen he entered the Union Army
and served in Company A, One Hundred and Seventy-first Regiment,
Pennsylvania Volunteer Infantry. At the close of his army service, imbued with the spirit of "Westward ho," he emigrated to
Minnesota, taking up his first residence in Le Sueur, Le Sueur Co.,
Minn., remaining there for a year and a half, then removing to
Farmington, where he took up the study of telegraphy and railroad station accounts. He was in the employ of the St. Paul, Minneapolis & Manitoba Railway for ten years as traveling auditor in
charge of station agents' accounts, leaving this branch of the service to accept a position with the North Western Elevator Co., as
superintendent of their Sioux Falls line of elevators. With the
purpose of establishing business for himself, he purchased the in-

terest of George T. Vail, of Vail & Johnson, forming the present corporation of the Johnson-Landis Undertaking Co., of which he is secretary and treasurer.

He is a firm believer in fraternal organizations from the fact that he is a member of the following: Upchurch Lodge, No. 13,

WILLIAM H. LANDIS

A. O. U. W.; Cecilian Council, No. 1367, Royal Arcanum; Fraternity Lodge, No. 62, I. O. O. F.; Ark Lodge, No. 176, A. F. & A. M.; and Geo. N. Morgan Post, No. 4, G. A. R. Dept. of Minnesota. He has been elected to many positions of honor and trust by the members of these orders. At present he is the Master of Upchurch Lodge, No. 13, A. O. U. W.; Chaplain of Council No.

1367, Royal Arcanum, and Quartermaster of Geo. N. Morgan Post, No. 4. These official stations have come to him unsought through the almost unanimous request of his associates.

Mr. Landis was converted in early life, uniting with the church at the age of sixteen and is at present connected with Franklin Avenue Church, of which he is a member of the Board of Trustees.

REV. S. E. RYAN

Rev. S. E. Ryan was born May 6, 1861, in Cannonsburgh, Washington Co., Penn. His parents removed soon after his birth to Louisville, Ky., remaining there during the greater part of the civil war, so that the earliest recollections of the subject of this sketch are of martial music and marching men.

His parents returning to Washington Co., he spent his boyhood days among the hills of Pennsylvania, where, at the age of four years, he met his first great sorrow in the death of a loving mother. When twelve years of age he was converted and soon after felt his call to the ministry. Realizing that preparation was necessary for that work he attended Waynesburg College in 1875 and in 1876 entered Allegheny College, located at Meadville, Pa., remaining there until the fall of 1880 when he was appointed as a supply to Salem, Clarion Dist., Pa. From this institution he has also received his degrees of Bachelor and Master of Arts.

At Meadville, the seat of the college, he was admitted on trial into the Erie Conference, in September, 1881; passed the course of study with credit; was admitted in full connection; elected and ordained to orders, serving meanwhile with great acceptability, Brockport, Clarington, Karns City, Fagundus and Rouseville charges.

When on his fourth year at Rouseville, he was transferred to the North Dakota Conference and stationed at Lisbon where he remained two years. In 1890, while pastor of the church at Bismark, he was elected Chaplain of the Senate, which position he creditably filled, making many warm personal friends among the senators and state officers.

From Bismark he was removed to Jamestown where, by his manly bearing, fervent spirit and earnest evangelical preaching. he entrenched himself in the hearts of the people and overcame. by skillful and wise management, difficulties which had for years been a great hinderance to the work.

REV. S. E. RYAN

In the spring of 1893 he was appointed by Bishop Fowler to the Grand Forks District and the following year, there being a change of district boundries, he was appointed by Bishop Mallalieu to his present position, Presiding Elder of the Jamestown District, which embraces about two-thirds of the State of North Dakota.

In all the responsible and trying positions in which he has been placed he has shown the same Christian spirit of love and forbearance, yet never shrinking responsibility or failing to do his part to maintain the right, win victories for temperance, convince the erring of sin and lead the penitent to the cross of Christ.

REV. C. M. HEARD, D. D.

The Rev. C. M. Heard, D. D., was to the itinerancy born, March 13, 1840, the son of Rev. Stephen Heard, of the Erie Conference. His educational advantages were such as were afforded by the best schools on or near his father's various fields of labor. He was licensed to preach in 1859 and admitted on trial into the Erie Conference. After thirteen years' service in this Conference, he was transferred to Minnesota and stationed at Lake City where he had a successful pastorate of three years. Thence he was sent to Anoka. After a delightful year there

REV. C. M. HEARD D. D.,

he was unexpectedly removed to the Hennepin Avenue Church in Minneapolis, and became its first regular pastor. This church had been organized the year preceding, but the social and business standing, culture, wealth, and Christian devotion of its members, enabled it very soon to take rank with the best churches in the city. Its spiritual growth was specially noteworthy. The membership in three years increased nearly fifty per cent. The lot where the present edifice now stands was bought and the tabernacle was moved thereon.

Mr. Heard's next field of labor was Winnebago City with a church not inferior in culture to the one he left, but burdened with an old debt of $1400 which was paid in the first year of his administration. A year later he sought a transfer to the Wisconsin Conference where he spent four years, and then, at the request of the

Anoka Church, consented to transfer back again to Minnesota. After three years at Anoka he was again brought in touch with Twin City Methodism by his appointment to Trinity Church, St. Paul.

While here he made a literary venture and won the prize offered by Bishop Vincent for the best synopsis of the Disciplinary Course of Study for Preachers. In 1889 he became the pastor of Taylor Street, now Trinity, Church, Minneapolis. Under his administration this church became self-supporting, its membership steadily increased, its Sunday School became noted for its efficiency and the congregations outgrew the house of worship.

The Minnesota Conference in 1890 organized its committees of examination and its student ministry into a Conference School of Theology, and Mr. Heard was placed at its head as chairman of the board of examiners. This new departure attracted the attention of the church throughout the country, and is being substantially adopted by many other Conferences. Dr. Heard was a delegate to the General Conference of 1892, and the same year was honored by the Lawrence University of Wisconsin with the degree of Doctor of Divinity. As a member of the editorial staff of the Methodist Herald he is a frequent contributor to its columns. He is now at Monticello serving one of the substantial and historic churches of Minnesota Methodism.

REV. EUGENE MAY, D. D.

Dr. Eugene May's birth place is Mahaska Co., Ia., date, April 10, 1852. His mother was of the Wright family of Indiana, his father, Col. Geo. May, a well known lawyer, orator, legislator and soldier. The Mays were of Virginia, proud to trace their ancestry to Patrick Henry.

The person of this sketch was educated in the public schools of Iowa and Illinois, State University and McKendrie College in Illinois, completed the classical course, a graduate of the first class in the C. L. S. C., liberally taught by noted teachers in elocution, and has pursued a post-graduate Phd. His reputation as a scholar ranks high.

At the early age of 19 he was junior preacher on an old time circuit in Illinois: twenty preaching places, a distance of one hundred and fifteen miles around. Sermons for the year. 180: travel, 4,000 miles on horseback. In turn he has been a member of the South Illinois, Upper Iowa and North Dakota Conferences, filling

REV. EUGENE MAY, D. D.

leading appointments in each, and now pastor of First Church, Fargo, directing the building of a new church, the finest northwest of the Twin Cities. In '88 he was called to Seattle: in '89 received a flattering invitation to the pastorate of the 34th Street Reformed Church, New York: in '90 asked to accept a charge in Portland,

and in '92 elected president of the Red River Valley University. Each of these were declined.

Dr. May's ability as a preacher is of a high order and he has never failed to draw large audiences. As a lecturer he is excelled by very few indeed. Bureaus have made him liberal offers, but he has never turned aside from his chosen field, the pastorate. As opportunity has afforded he has lectured widely and acceptably; his lecture on "The Ascent of the Matterhorn Mountain in Switzerland" is one of the greatest on the platform to day.

REV. GEO. W. WILLIS

REV. GEO. W. WILLIS

Rev. Geo. W. Willis was born in Ashland Co., Ohio., April 6, 1864, and it would seem as if he was hewn out of his very cradle into the preacher and evangelist. A tiny boy seeking to carry sheaves in the golden harvest field was typical of his early life.

For the past ten years he has been an acceptable and well beloved minister in the Orthodox Friends' Church. For his entire ministry he has been in the evangelistic field with marvelous success. Pastors and newspapers have spoken in most cordial and complimentary terms of his work.

Cleveland, O., is his present home and has been for a number of years. He is very highly regarded there. The Cleveland Leader says of him, "Were he to be heard and not seen he would seem like one of the old Methodist revivalists of half a century ago."

He preaches without manuscript entirely: talks to the people and not at them, but in every case it is his aim to reach at once for the heart and lead immediately to the Lord Jesus Christ.

May his life be prolonged many years to do gracious work for the Master.

REV. C. A. VAN ANDA, D. D.

C. A. Van Anda was born in Northumberland Co. Pa., October 18, 1831. In 1833 his parents moved to Knox Co., O., where he was reared on a farm in the vicinity of Mount Vernon. After a preliminary education in the public schools, he attended the Ohio Wesleyan University four years, graduating in the Biblical Department in 1854. He was received on trial in the Ohio Conference during the same year. He at once exhibited remarkable ability as a preacher. His remarkable power over men, both as a pastor and preacher, soon brought him into prominence and he has served some of the leading pastorates of the church. He has been an important element in the growth and development of Minneapolis Methodism, having served the Franklin, Centenary and First Church with great acceptability and success.

During his recent pastorate at Emanuel Church, Evanston, Ill., he was called to Minneapolis to preach the funeral sermon of H. F. Lillibridge, of the Wesley Church. He is well advanced in years, but is still in the effective rank and preaches with all his old time fervor and power.

JOHN W. THOMAS

John W. Thomas was born in Steuben, Oneida County, New York, January 14, 1844, of Welch parentage. His early days were spent on the farm in Steuben and Bridgewater, New York, until 1857 when his parents moved to Bangor, Wisconsin. He obtained his education in the district schools until about sixteen years of age when he entered Sparta Academy. After finishing his course in this institution he entered the dry goods business, clerking in Sparta, Portage and Milwaukee. In 1869 he went to Winona, managing a branch store for N. H. Word & Co., whose principal place of business was located at Portage, Wisconsin. This same year he was married to Miss Jennett Jones, of Utica, New York, by whom he has three children: two daughters and one son. In 1870 he formed a co-partnership with Geo. F. Hubbard, of Winona carrying on a dry goods business continuing two years,

at the end of which time he started business for himself on Third
street, Winona, where he remained for fifteen years and by his
untiring energy and business ability, becoming one of the leading
merchants of that growing young city as well as a respected and
popular citizen.

JOHN W. THOMAS

In February, 1883, Mr. Thomas moved to Minneapolis. The
popular dry goods house of which he is now sole proprietor, was
established by Geo. W. Hale in 1867 and is the oldest house in
this line in Minneapolis. Mr. Hale managed the business until the
winter of 1882-3, when on account of failing health he was compelled to give up. Looking around for a young man to take an in-

terest in and assume the management of the business, then making rapid strides with the boom which prevailed in Minneapolis, he fixed on Mr. Thomas as the man of his choice, depending probably very much on Mr. Thomas' established reputation, his acquaintance with him being very limited. His judgment was good, as after developments show. Mr. Thomas formed a co-partnership with Geo. W. Hale and his brother Jefferson M. Hale, in February, 1883. Geo. W. Hale died in 1889 and Jefferson M. Hale in October, 1893. In February, 1894, Mr. Thomas purchased the interests of the heirs of Jefferson M. Hale and is now sole proprietor of the oldest and probably best known dry goods house in the Northwest, having by years of generous and honest treatment of its customers, won an enviable reputation.

Mr. Thomas' parents were staunch Calvinists, earnest and consistent members of the Methodist Church. He has inherited much of their religious zeal endeavoring to live his religion in private, social and business life. He is an active member of the Westminster Presbyterian Church of Minneapolis, an Elder of the "Session" and closely connected with all branches of the work of this large and influential society.

In his home, he is a man of quiet tastes, devotedly attached to his family and enjoying nothing better than a quiet evening with his wife and children about him.

REV. CHAS. B. WILCOX, D. D.

Charles B. Wilcox was born in Fox Lake, Wis., Nov. 24, 1851. His parents, David Thomas and Charlotte Bowser Wilcox emigrated from England to the United States in 1849, settling on a farm in Wisconsin. They were devout Christians, industrious and thrifty, but at that time in meagre circumstances. They occupied what was then a sparsely settled portion of the state where few advantages offered for an education. During his childhood and youth Mr. Wilcox attended a district school in the country, but reached his majority with only the barest rudiments of learning. Converted at the age of 19, he united with the Methodist

Episcopal Church of which his parents were members. Soon after friends in the church urged him to prepare for the ministry, and convictions of duty to preach deepened. A few months after conversion he was granted an exhorter's license, and a little later urged to become a local preacher. These appeals of the church were resisted chiefly from a sense of incompetency. In the meantime he married and settled on a farm, but the conviction of duty to preach increased and a troubled conscience led him, at the age of 23, to begin preparation for the ministry. Having a wife, one child and very little means, he began a classical course in the first year of the preparatory department of the Northwestern University at Evanston, Ill. He pursued the course into the Freshman year, and then entered the Garrett Biblical Institute, completing the three years' course in two, and graduating in the spring of 1880.

Dr. Wilcox immediately joined the Wisconsin Conference, where the first ten years of his ministry were spent. He began at Pleasant Prairie, a small circuit, receiving a salary of $600. His two most important appointments were Court Street Church, Jonesville, and First Church, Oshkosh. His pastorate in the latter church extended over five years, during which a heavy indebtedness of long standing was provided for, extensive improvements made on the property and the membership largely increased. At the close of this pastorate he received a call and was appointed to the First Church, St. Paul, Minn.

This church, prominent by reason of historical associations and the character of its pastors had suffered from secession and the organization of an independent church by the popular pastor in the immediate vicinity. As a result First Church was greatly reduced both in wealth and numbers. When Dr. Wilcox came, current expenses were far in arrears and the membership scattered and discouraged. He is now serving his fifth year as pastor. Confidence has been restored, all back current indebtedness paid, and the membership nearly doubled.

Dr. Wilcox was ordained a Deacon in 1878 by Bishop Andrews, in Chicago; an Elder in 1884 by Bishop Mallalieu, in Oshkosh, Wis. The degree of Doctor of Divinity was conferred upon him by Hamline University.

J. D. MORRISON

J. D. Morrison was born April 22, 1851, in the Province of Ontario. His father, John Morrison, and mother, Eliza Ann Empey, were among the pioneers of the province. His brother Duncan R. Morrison, of the third generation is still living on the homestead. J. D. was converted in December, 1876, in the town of Madrid, N. Y. His early life was devoted to the Sunday School work. He was elected for three years in one of the rural district schools near his home. He was married to Chastin Hartwell, daughter of Joseph and Seraphina Hartwell, of

J. D. MORRISON

New York, on July 24, 1881, and moved to Dundas, Minn., where they lived two years. He then moved to Minneapolis, 2930 Fifteenth avenue south, where he now resides.

He was one of the first to organize a Sunday School near his home. Being a carpenter and builder, he drew the plans and made out the bill of material for the Bloomington Avenue Church. He has filled some of the important offices and still holds an official relation to said church.

REV. SAMUEL G. SMITH, D. D.

Rev. Samuel G. Smith was born in Birmingham, England, March 7, 1852. His parents removed to America in 1858. Rev. William Smith, M. A., a prominent minister in the Methodist church in Iowa, was his father. He graduated from Cornell College, Iowa, in the classical course in 1872, and subsequently received the degree of Doctor of Philosophy from Syracuse University, on examination, in 1882.

He entered the Upper Iowa Conference in the fall of 1872. Soon after he was elected principal of Albion Seminary. After three years he resigned to enter the pastorate. His charges have been: Osage, Ia., two years: Decorah, Ia., two years. In 1879 he removed to St. Paul to become pastor of the First Methodist Church. In 1882 he was appointed Presiding Elder of the St. Paul District. In 1883 he was elected a delegate to the General

REV. SAMUEL G. SMITH, D. D.

Conference. In 1885 he received the degree of Doctor of Divinity from the Upper Iowa University.

Failing health compelled him to retire from the St. Paul district in the fall of 1884. He spent most of the following year in Europe.

In 1885 he was reappointed to First Church, St. Paul, by unanimous request of that church. January 1, 1888, he resigned that pulpit and withdrew from the M. E. Church at the request of friends in St. Paul, and became pastor of the Peoples' Church of St. Paul, holding services in the Opera House until one of the largest and most complete edifices for working purposes in the United States was erected.

Dr. Smith has been closely identified with the social and political life of Minnesota for fifteen years. He has served for three years on the school board, resigning, when president, on account of the pressure of other duties. For the past six years he has been a member of the State Board of Corrections and Charities, having been appointed by three successive Governors. During the past three years he has been lecturer on Sociology in the University of Minnesota. He has also for many years lectured at Chautauqua assemblies and on other lyceum platforms.

During several tours in Europe he has studied the life and art of the leading nations, including a tour devoted to penal and charitable institutions in which he visited sixty of the leading prisons and asylums, by appointment of Gov. Nelson, as official visitor from Minnesota.

He is a man of genial disposition, sympathetic heart and practical turn of mind. He has no use for a theology which cannot be applied to the problem of every day life. As a preacher, he has but few equals. Having the advantage of a thorough education, coupled with unusual natural ability, he is exhaustless in his pulpit resources. His church, which is among the largest in America, is always a center of educational influence, Christian culture and spiritual power.—*From National Encyclopedia of American Biography.*

REV. J. C. HULL, B. D.

Rev. J. C. Hull was born in Fayette Co., W. Va., February 24, 1856; his parents were Joseph and Rebecca Hull and his ancestors were from New England, having come there from Leeds, England, before the period of the Revolutionary war. A

branch of the family went from New England to Maryland and
Virginia at an early date in Colonial history, and were leaders in
the educational interests of the South, the Rev. Hope Hull, of the
Southern branch of the family, having been one of the most eloquent
Methodist ministers of the Asbury period, doing effective work in
the Carolinas and Georgia, and was one of the founders of the
university at Athens, Ga. The immediate ancestors of Rev. J. C.
Hull were natives of the rugged mountains of Pendleton Co., Va.,
and were noted for their longevity, and an education quite in
advance of their unfavorable environment.

The subject of this sketch was ten years old at the time the
free school system was introduced in West Virginia, and at once
came to the front in the common schools. Without a dollar of help
he made his own way in getting an education, working as a day
laborer to purchase a library until he was able to teach school.
He attended Marshall College, Huntington, W. Va., a part of two
years, and after teaching in Fayette and Roane counties, went, in
the fall of 1879, to Kansas, and, after teaching with success near
Eureka and at Toronto, entered the South Kansas Conference of
the Methodist Episcopal Church in March, 1881, and was appointed to Madison, where he remained for two years, raising the
money and securing the erection of a new church, and in general
promoting the interests of the work. On the 21st of December,
1881, in Emporia, Kan., he was married to Miss Alice Anderson,
who had been a pupil in his school at Toronto. He was next
stationed at Yates Center, and after remaining there for two years,
with excellent results to the church, was transferred to the West
Virginia Conference, and stationed at Chapline Street, Wheeling,
and after two years to St. Paul's Church, Fall River, Mass.

During this time he had carried through courses of Hebrew
under Dr. Harper, and of Greek under Dean Wright, of Boston,
and in his second year at Fall River was graduated from the
Chautauqua School of Theology. The hard study, together with
very taxing pulpit and pastoral duties had at this time seriously impaired the health of Mr. Hull, and on the advice of physicians, to
avoid permanent injury, he took a supernumerary relation, at the
Conference held in Taunton, Mass., April, 1889, and removed to

Minneapolis, Minn., where he spent several years in comparative rest.

During this time he traveled among the mountain regions of the United States and did extensive newspaper writing. He had numerous flattering offers to reenter the pastorate, and rendered

REV. J. C. HULL, B. D.

at various times valuable service as a supply, going from Minneapolis one winter to Des Moines. Iowa, where he supplied the pulpit of the First Church for sixteen Sundays in succession.

In the fall of 1893 he accepted the pastorate of the Clinton Avenue Church, St. Paul, and during his first year succeeded in turning from the church $24,000 of debt. The church had been crushed and discouraged by the great burden; but under the pastorate of Rev. Mr. Hull it promises to become one of the strongest protestant churches of the Northwest. Mr. Hull is a fluent and ready speaker without notes, and has been a leader in the temperance ranks since his participation in the campaign for constitutional prohibition in Kansas in 1880. He has since taken an active part in the campaigns in West Virginia, Massachusetts, and Iowa; but he has studiously avoided political entanglements which might impair his usefulness in the ministry, having declined the offer of the prohibitionists to nominate him for Congress for the First District of West Virginia in the fall of 1886.

Having been deprived of many advantages in his boyhood by the seclusion of the West Virginia hills, he has sought to make up for such lack of advantages by visiting and studying the methods and work of many of the leading colleges and universities of the country, and has also visited many of the most prosperous churches both of his own and of others denominations to hear great preachers and study the methods of successful church work. For this purpose he has visited the cities of Boston, New York, Brooklyn, Baltimore, Washington, Pittsburgh, Cleveland, Detroit, Indianapolis, Chicago, Kansas City and other places, selecting one or more of the largest and most successful churches in each place and making a study of the work, and in most cases remaining over a Sunday and hearing the sermons.

The Rev. Mr. Hull is a close student, always a frequenter of the libraries and has about ready for the press a work entitled: "Our Nation's Destiny, or The Story of Ben Adam." He has also under preparation "The Life of Rev. Ernest Blackwood," which is based on his own struggles to get an education. Among his popular lectures are "Orators, Scholars and Eccentrics of Methodism," and "Knocking Against the World."— *From National Encyclopedia of American Biography.*

MART N. HILT

Mart N. Hilt was born at Indianapolis, Ind., October 24, 1868. He was brought up in the pure atmosphere of a Christian home.

His education was acquired in the public schools of Indianapolis. He completed the high school course. In 1888 he came to Minneapolis. He was engaged with his brother during the first year in the rental business. In 1889 he entered the fire insurance business for himself. He has since succeeded to his brother's rental

MART N. HILT

business. Under his careful direction the business has grown until it is one of the most representative in the rental and insurance line. He united with the Wesley Church in 1893. He has been secretary of the Sunday School for four years and is president of the Vincent Bible class.

REV. WILLIAM EVANS KING

Rev. William Evans King was born in Vermilion Co., Ill., September 28. 1847. He came with his parents to Minnesota, May 14, 1855, and spent his boyhood days on a farm near the village of Byron. He was converted at a revival conducted by Rev. Ezra Lathrop on the 14th day of February, 1859, and at once joined the Methodist Church. He entered Hamline University at Red Wing during the winter term of 1868. At the close of this term the school was suspended for lack of means to continue. He then attended other educational institutes in the state. He also taught school in the summer of 1869, and in the spring of 1870 and the winter of 1871.

WILLIAM EVANS KING

In 1872 he entered the Northwestern University at Evanston, Ill., and graduated from the Theological Department May 6, 1880. When he arrived at Evanston he had just $17 and needed $21 to enter, but being strong and healthy he was not discouraged and for eight years maintained himself at school by hard work and indomitable will. During his work in Evanston he and a fellow student organized the Mission Sunday School at the corner of Wood and Twenty-first streets, Chicago, which was continued for three years and a half. This school developed into the present Lincoln Street Church of Chicago.

In 1887 he became a member of the United States Life Saving Crew at Evanston, Ill., and was given the position of stroke oar in the crew. April 1, 1879 he was promoted to the position of captain.

He has a record of personally saving eight lives from drowning. One, a little girl who fell into a mill pond. He also swam and rescued from drowning in Lake Michigan, Robert Seaman, now a member of the Illinois Conference; then C. B. Ward, now missionary in India; next John Gillman whose boat was capsized in a terrible storm.

July 10, 1878, he was married to Miss Jennie Alsip of Chicago, who had been the organist in his Mission Sunday School. In 1880 he was appointed pastor of the M. E. Church at Windom, Minnesota, where he remained until September 1, 1882, when Bishop J. F. Hurst appointed him a missionary to Virginia City, Montana, where he remained three years. While in Montana he was stationed at Butte City, and also at Salmon City, Idaho. In 1891 he was transferred to the Minnesota Conference and stationed at his old home in Byron, where he has served a three years' pastorate.

CHARLES JACOB GOTSHALL

Charles Jacob Gotshall was born June 12, 1856, at Canton, O. His parents, Daniel and Rebecca, were both members of the First Methodist Church of Canton. His father was an honored soldier in the civil war and died in 1862 from sickness contracted at the battle of Shiloh. His mother, a woman of great faith and spirituality, died in 1891.

Charles was educated in the public schools. He was diligent as a student and made good headway during the period devoted to his mental training.

During a revival which occurred in the First Church, 1865, at Canton, O., he was convicted of sin, surrendered to Christ and was graciously converted. Hiram Miller was the pastor. He was married April 15, 1879, to Kate Steele, of Salem, O. Her parents were eminent Methodists also and she has always been active in church work.

Mr. Gotshall came to Minneapolis in 1880. For two years he had charge of the collection department of a large mercantile institution, after which he entered the employment of C. Altman & Co., of Canton, O, as manager of their Northwestern business. He had been connected with this company before coming West. In the fall of 1888, he moved to St. Paul and engaged with the St. Paul Plow Company as secretary.

While in St. Paul, he united with the Central Park Church, and by his steady, manly, Christian-going course, gathered about him a host of friends. In the spring of 1892 he returned to Minneapolis to engage in the insurance business. Owing to long experience in handling agricultural implements, he was prevailed upon to accept the management of the Northwestern Threshing Association, which position he now occupies.

Mr. Gotshall is a member of the Wesley Church. He is an exhaustless worker, whether at his desk, his home, or upon the street. He is always absorbed in his business interests and continually pushing them to the front. He does not wait until the iron is hot before he strikes, but strikes in order that the iron may become hot. He has three promising boys: Nelson Steele, Robert Warren, and Albert. His home is full of sunshine and he is happiest at its fireside. Those who know him hold him in high esteem for his faithfulness to any trust, his liberality, his candor and honesty, under all circumstances.

JOHN WESLEY TOUSLEY

JOHN WESLEY TOUSLEY

John Wesley Tousley was born in the town of Old Salisbury, Litchfield Co., Conn., on the 17th day of September, 1824. His parents were natives of the same state and zealous members of the Methodist Church. They were possessed of great piety and raised their children under strictly moral and religious influence.

J. W. Tousley was converted and united with the Methodist Church in the town of Sharon. Conn., in the year 1841, being at that time 17 years of age. It was under the preaching of the Rev. Hart. F. Pease, of the New York Conference, that he was brought to make a public confession of his faith in Christ, and has never lost his zeal or loving confidence which then brought him to the foot of the cross. He has been twice married. His first wife was Miss Samantha E. Wells of Troy N. Y., by whom he had five sons and one daughter. His marriage to Miss Wells was solemnized in the city of Troy on December 15, 1847, by Rev. George C. Bancroft, known as the sailor preacher. In August, 1890, after a long and useful life, this mother and wife, passed over to the home beyond, leaving a devoted husband and five married sons to mourn her loss.

In October, 1893, he married the second time to Mrs. Penelope Ferrell of Louisville, Ken., widow of the late Col. Lewis H. Ferrell of that state.

He received his education at Amenia Seminary at the time Rev. D. W. Clark was principal and who afterward was known as Bishop D. W. Clark. In the year 1843 he moved to West Stockbridge where the Rev. George Bancroft was pastor. He there united with the Methodist Church and was chosen in 1845 as Sunday School superintendent which position he filled for two years, when he moved to Troy, New York, transferring his membership to the North Second Street Church which was under the pastorate labor of Rev. S. D. Brown. Was there appointed class leader serving the church in that capacity for five years. Being seized with a desire to go West he soon determined to seek a new home and in 1857 he moved to Omaha, Neb., where he entered upon a pioneer life, tilling the soil and penetrating into the wilds of a new country. The first thing however, was to find a church, which was soon done. The First Methodist Church with Rev. I. M. Chivington as pastor was made his church home and for twenty years he served as class leader; was Sunday School superintendent for eleven years, trustee and steward for fifteen years.

In March, 1875, he received license to exhort and the following year was licensed by the Nebraska Conference to preach. He was chosen leader of what was then known as "The Praying Band" and a wonderful evangelistic work was done, in the outposts of the surrounding country. This work was untiringly carried on for five years, bringing hundreds to Christ. In the spring of 1879 the spirit of emigration brought him to find a home in the city of Minneapolis, Minn., where he immediately indentified himself with what was then known as Centenary Church but which has since built a new church edifice and assumed the name of Wesley Church. Rev. Dr. C. A. VanAnda was then pastor in charge. He was appointed class leader serving nearly three years, when he became interested in the organization of the Simpson Church and transferred his membership to that body in the year 1882, becoming a charter member. Rev. I. G. Teter being pastor, appointed him class leader; he was also chairman of the Building Committee until the church was finished. Was a member here four years, and then returned to his first love the Centenary and again assumed, under Rev. H. H. French, the duties of class leader. Is now residing in Minneapolis where he is successfully engaged in real estate business and is president of the Crystal Lake Cemetery Association which position he has held for the last thirteen years. He has held the office of local preacher since the year 1875 giving largely of his time and means to the advancement of the Lord's cause and the promotion of all moral reform. The temperance cause has found in him a strong and earnest advocate, as well as a zealous worker.

A. B. FELGEMAKER—"CHURCH ORGANS."

"Music hath charms to soothe the savage breast," but it delights and fascinates the educated tastes of the most refined of every civilized nation. And of all musical instruments the pipe organ, which has been so aptly styled the "King of Instruments," ranks first in the musical world. What church is completely furnished without one of these grand instruments? In briefly reviewing the history and progress of the organ during the present century, one cannot fail to be impressed with the great and manifold improvements which have been made both in its construction and tone-producing powers.

After 35 years of practical experience in the manufacture of church organs, the organs built by A. B. Felgemaker, of Erie, Pa., have attained a standard of excellence, which cannot be surpassed, and are second to none. They combine a richness, fulness and delicacy of tone, and by the arrangement and selection of stops, which are used in Mr. Felgemaker's organs, the greatest variety of power and effects are obtained, rarely, if ever, found in organs of similar cost.

In the comparatively new and extensive plant, built expressly for the manufacture of organs, this concern is enabled to do work of the very highest grade.

This firm being determined to uphold and extend its reputation to all parts of the country, allows no instrument to leave its establishment, that cannot bear the most critical examination and stand the severest tests.

It would be well for churches or persons desiring pipe organs to address A. B. Felgemaker, Church Organ Builder, Erie, Pa.

CHURCH FURNISHING

It is an excellent thing to have a church complete in every architectural detail both in exterior and interior appearance, and too much praise cannot be given to some of our painstaking architects who have made a life study of church building, and are now giving the results of their study to the churches of our time; but there is a matter of quite as much importance as this, which is too often hastily decided upon, and mistakes are made which are difficult to eradicate.

Well-devised, carefully made church furnishings are a source of continual and lasting comfort, while ill-shaped, poorly-constructed and ill-devised furnishings are a source of daily annoyance.

There is a world of difference between something that is almost good enough and that which is really perfect in construction and beyond the reach of adverse criticism.

The best methods of seating and furnishing churches are as much the result of experience and painstaking on the part of manufacturers devoting themselves to this special line of business, as are the architectural details of a church building.

There are a few concerns in the country who have devoted a quarter of a century or more to the practical details of church furnishings. They have not only been able to acquire a large amount of useful and practical information in this line from their own wide and varied experience, but they have also been brought in contact with the ideas of the very best architects in the world; and when this experience is combined with ample facilities for prosecuting the business, such a concern may be intrusted with this class of work with the most implicit confidence in their ability to produce results which will be entirely satisfactory to church people.

It is too often true that a difference of a few dollars in the original cost is allowed to out-weigh the advantages which could be derived from placing contracts for this kind of work with concerns of large experience.

It is far from our purpose to enumerate in this work the mistakes and failures that have been made by churches in the Twin Cities in this particular, but it is gratifying to know that some of our churches have been fortunate enough to place their orders with good concerns, and to secure work which has been, and is, thoroughly satisfactory, and we may be pardoned for calling attention to the work done in the Wesley Church, in Minneapolis, by the Globe Furniture Co., of Northville, Mich., and citing our friends to it as one of the most satisfactory pieces of work in this line which has ever been done in the Twin Cities.

YERXA BROTHERS

Prior to the incorporation of this firm, F. R. Yerxa, the younger brother, conducted a grocery business on Seventh street and Nicollet avenue. Under his management the business became so profitable that the present company was formed with the view of building it into one of the great commercial houses of the city. That this purpose has been fully consummated is seen in the magnificent proportions it has already attained. No longer able to confine it within one building, it has been divided into three busi-

ness places in Minneapolis, namely: one at the corner of Nicollet
avenue and Tenth street; one at the corner of Nicollet and Fifth
street, and one at 115-117 Central avenue. These stores are always
centers of the greatest activity and prosperity. The principal store
at Nicollet and Fifth street is constantly crowded with people. Five
years ago, the company extended its business to St. Paul where
they have located their cracker and candy factories and spice mills.
Fifty hands are employed in this factory alone while 235 are re-

INTERIOR VIEW OF YERXA BROS. & CO.'S STORE

quired to operate their business in both cities. They have demonstrated the wisdom and success of the cash basis in trade, upon
which principle their business stands secure. Their groceries and
vegetables are always fresh and the very best the market either at
home or abroad can afford. The houses are all manned by clerks
who are polite and attentive to the wants of the public.

The success of this business is a monument to the unflagging
energy, indomitable purpose, financial skill and phenomenal executive ability of its promoters. It should also illustrate to young

men, the truth of the adage that "patience and perseverance conquer all things." This business did not leap to its present mammoth proportions in a single day. It is the product of years of steady growth and of unremitting application to its highest interests. It is not the result of a rich legacy, but of hard struggle and unwearying patience and that determination which surmounts all difficulties.

This article is not meant to be in biographical form, else it might be shown that the Yerxa brothers have made their way through life by their own unaided efforts; that they began at the bottom and have gone forward until they at present control the largest grocery business in the Twin Cities.

Their father is an honored member of the First Baptist Church of Minneapolis, and their business is conducted upon the principles inculcated in them in early life.

J. F. RIVERS

J. F. RIVERS

J. F. Rivers was born in Marquette. Mich., in 1855. Both his parents were French Canadians and Roman Catholics. He lived in Michigan until he was of age. He came to Minneapolis in 1878. While in Minneapolis he was married, in 1880, to Miss Estella Champlin, a Christian of the genuine type, always loyal to Methodism, the church of her choice. In 1881 Mr. Rivers went to Green Bay, Wis., and engaged with the Ft. Howard Iron Works. In 1884 he went to Kaukanna to take charge of the Ledyard Iron Works. He occupied this position until he accepted a place of trust in the City Fire Department. He at the same time was engaged in the sewing machine business, also handling pianos and organs. In the spring of 1891 with four others he formed the Kaukanna Machine Co., with a capital of ten thousand dollars. Under his management this business assumed large proportions. Disposing of his interests in this company, he returned to Minneapolis and purchased the bicycle and machine shops of H. Johnson, in which business he is still engaged at 633 First avenue south.

After entering this business he purchased his present beautiful home at 3255 Fourteenth avenue south. Since coming to Minneapolis he has been converted and with his wife belongs to the Bloomington Avenue Church. He is chairman and treasurer of the Board of Trustees and a member of the Board of Stewards.

R. S. GOODFELLOW & CO.

This business house was established in 1878 by Messrs. Goodfellow & Eastman, who conducted it until 1886, when Mr. Eastman retired. W. S. Ray then became a partner. In February, 1893, Mr. Ray died. After the settlement of Mr. Ray's estate, Mr. George Loudon became a partner in February, 1894.

Mr. Goodfellow is a native of Troy, N. Y., but has resided in Minneapolis since 1878. Mr. Loudon is a native of Scotland, where he received his commercial education in one of the largest Scottish mercantile houses. He came to this city in the fall of 1882. He came direct to Minneapolis and was engaged the day after he arrived by Messrs. Goodfellow & Eastman as their bookkeeper, and has advanced with the business until he has obtained his present position. Mr. Goodfellow attends to the store proper, while Mr. Loudon takes charge of the office and financial department.

We mention Mr. Loudon thus prominently in connection with this firm, as he is a member of the congregation of the Hennepin Avenue church, of which his wife is an active member. He is in thorough sympathy with the church, and one of its generous supporters.

The firm started business in the store now occupied by Nicol, the tailor, across the way from the present location, at 247-249-251 Nicollet avenue. Under the careful, prudent and conservative management of Mr. Goodfellow, the business has gradually increased to its splendid aggregate and to-day is one of the strongest and most favorably known of the many splendid business houses throughout the Northwest.

Their business of exports and retails of drygoods, cloaks, furs and draperies has been built up on the basis of always placing before their customers the very best goods for the money, that the markets of the world have to afford. Trashy, showy goods have always been avoided as unsatisfactory to both buyer and seller.

INTERIOR VIEW OF STORE

Time and attention have been devoted entirely and strictly to their business as drygoods merchants, despite the modern tendency to turn everything into department stores. About one hundred and twenty are employed, some of whom have been with the firm since they first started, and many of them over ten years. Duly qualified managers are in charge of the various departments. They are always among the first in the West to display newest goods and latest novelties. Whatever is advertised is always to be found as described, consequently, firm reliance has come to be placed on every movement of theirs by a discerning public.

ERNEST F. SMITH

Ernest F. Smith was born August 4, 1868, Pekin, Ill. Finished his education at U. S. Naval Academy, Annapolis, Md., and Iowa Wesleyan University, Mt. Pleasant, Iowa. He joined the church at Pekin, Ill., in 1883. Both parents were Methodists of long standing. He came to St. Paul in the spring of 1887, took a position with St. Paul Storage Forwarding and Implement Co. He came to Minneapolis January 1, 1889, as secretary and treasurer of Smith Wagon and Implement Co. He united with Hennepin Avenue Church by letter in 1889. September 1, 1890, the partnership of Smith & Zimmer was formed.

ERNEST F. SMITH

L. W. ZIMMER

L. W. Zimmer was born October 16, 1868. Until December, 1889, he lived at Pekin, Ill., where he was connected with the Pekin Plow Co., manufacturers of plows and other agricultural implements. Upon coming to Minneapolis, he became a member of the firm of Smith & Zimmer. He united with the Hennepin Avenue Church in 1890.

SMITH & ZIMMER

Smith & Zimmer succeeded to the wholesale business of The Smith Wagon and Implement Co., September 1, 1890. The partnership is composed of Ernest F. Smith and Luppo W. Zimmer, who were both connected with the corporation they succeeded; the former, in the capacity of secretary and treasurer, and the latter being in charge of the books of the concern. Both are peculiarly fitted for the business that they have chosen, as they are sons

L. W. ZIMMER

of manufacturers of farm implements and wagons, and had been connected with the manufacture and distribution of this class of goods for several years before the present partnership was formed. They were, without doubt, the youngest men ever forming a partnership for the conducting of a wholesale business, both being just past their twenty-first year.

By constant application and personal attention, the business has grown from one of the smallest to one of the largest of its kind in the Northwest. The "Smith" Wagon and Pekin Plows manufactured at Pekin, Ill., a corporation in which both Mr. Smith and Mr. Zimmer are stockholders, form the foundation on which the large trade has been built. Avery cultivators, carriages and buggies are handled, and in 1891, foreseeing the phenomenal demand for bicycles, they were added to the line; being first in the field and giving that branch their careful attention, have easily held the position they still occupy, that of being the largest bicycle house in the Northwest. Their particular wheel is one made for them by one of the largest factories, and is called the "S. & Z. Special." They also have other wheels on which their trade is large.

Early in the spring of 1894, threshing machines were also added to their line and the first season's experience has proven very satisfactory, and demonstrated the superiority of their machines, the Avery engine and separator. Unless some unforseen disaster overtakes the business of this firm, the future holds greater success for them.

A. L. FUNK

A. L. Funk was born in Putnam Co., O., October 22, 1863. At the age of six years his parents moved to Kansas, where he was educated in the public schools. After this he attended the

State Normal School in Kansas, and
was made principal of his home school.
He then entered the banking and loan
business in Kansas. In 1889 he became general agent of the old Manitowoc Manufacturing Company with
headquarters at Omaha. In the winter of 1891 he came to Minneapolis as
Northwestern salesman, in which position he continued until the factories
of the company were destroyed by fire.

A new company was at once
formed, and on account of his former
valuable services he was given the position of general superintendent of sales

A. L. FUNK

in the Northwest, with headquarters in Minneapolis. Mr. Funk
a young man of striking business energy, but is never so occupied
with business as to forget the moral principles upon which it should
be founded. Although much of his time is spent in traveling, he
is faithful in his relations to the church, and avails himself of every
opportunity to enjoy its services. When but a small boy he was
impressed with his duty to preach the gospel, and the hope still
lingers with him that circumstances will yet enable him to follow
this high calling.

P. G. HANSON

P. G. Hanson was born in New York City, March 20, 1856.
When but three years of age, his parents moved into the country
on a small farm near the village of South Port, Conn. During
his earlier years, young Hanson assisted his father in work on
the farm. In 1877 he located in Minneapolis. Soon after reaching
this city, he engaged as a clerk in one of the largest retail grocery
stores.

After six months' clerkship, his employers, who were then
conducting five retail groceries, made a proposition to sell to him
and his brother the stock in the store located at 1304 Fifth street

south.   The offer was accepted and a note was given drawing interest at twelve per cent. for the entire amount of stock.   This
partnership continued until the fall of 1882, when a dissolution was
effected by the junior Hanson who sold his interest to his partner.
In the spring of 1886, having felt the need of more commodious

P. G. HANSON

quarters in order to meet the growing demands of his trade, he
procured the rental of the store at 416 Second avenue south where
he is still engaged in business.   On September 25, 1887, he purchased the stock and fixtures of the retail market at 404 Second
avenue south and since that time has conducted and managed

the largest and most prosperous combined retail grocery and meat market in the city.

Mr. Hanson is a man of untarnished Christian character. In youth he was taught to revere and respect God and religion and from his earliest days has been a constant church attendant.

His parents, while in New York City, were members of the Moravian Church, but upon moving to the country they affiliated with the Congregational Church of South Port and became very active members. When but twelve years of age, Mr. Hanson united with the same church and lived a consistent Christian life and remained in its membership until he came West. On arriving at Minneapolis he allied himself with church people and regularly attended services at the Plymouth Congregational Church, and so continued until some time after the establishment of the business in the south part of the city, when, for reasons of convenience and other influences, he attended either the Second Congregational or the Seventh Street Church. Finally, on January 1, 1879, he joined by letter the Seventh Street Church, now Thirteenth Avenue Church, and at once became closely identified with its work and success. He has ably filled various official positions in the church for the past fifteen years and has been Sunday School superintendent for the past seven years, which position he still occupies.

JOHN A. LANE

John A. Lane was born near Cablentz, Germany, on November 4, 1870, son of John and Kate Lane, who were members of the Roman Catholic Church. In 1872 his parents emigrated to America and settled in Minnesota. His early education was acquired in the district schools. His parents died during his boyhood, and at the age of eleven he was alone in the world. Although he was a stranger in Minneapolis he went to work with determination to find employment. He was not disappointed for he soon obtained a situation in Duncan's Nursery in which he continued for three years.

While thus engaged he attended the city schools during the winter, and the last winter took a course in the Curtiss Business

JOHN A. LANE

College from which he graduated. He then kept books for a fuel company, after which he was employed in the drug store of W. A. Collin. He still holds this position.

While Mr. Lane was engaged in work on the nursery he attended some revival services that were being held in the Camden Place Church, under the pastorate of Brother Atkinson. It was during these meetings that his faith in Romanism was shattered and he was able to receive Christ as a personal Saviour. He united with that church and has since been a very important factor in its development; he has been an enthusiastic worker in the Christian Endeavor Society, and has served as its secretary and president, which latter position he still holds. He has also been a leading spirit in the Sunday School, having served as secretary, treasurer and teacher. Two years after he united with the church he was given an Exhorter's license, which he still holds with credit to himself and blessing to the church.

L. A. BROWN

L. A. Brown was born near Ypsilanti, Mich., August 2, 1848. His parents were thorough-going Methodists, his grandfather having died at the age of ninety-four, praising God with his latest breath. Mr. Brown attended the public schools, the Friends' Academy, near Adrian, and the State Normal at Ypsilanti, from which he graduated in 1887.

Early in life he was thrown entirely upon his own resources; but his energy and ambition were greater than all the difficulties and we find him quietly but steadily advancing. He was so intent upon acquiring an education that he would work on the farm during vacations, sell books or do anything that was honorable. Finally he was able to pass a teacher's examination, and he then taught school. In 1879 he came to Glyndon, Minn., and took charge of the graded schools there, continuing in this position for four years, and was then elected county superintendent of schools in Clay county. This was also a four years term. At the expiration of this official position he became a travel_ ing salesman for school and church furniture. In 1891 he settled in Minneapolis, as manager for the Northwest of the Manitowoc Manufacturing Co. At the close of the year, he organized the

L. A. BROWN

Twin City School Supply Co., which has the only stock of Kindergarten materials and teachers' aids west of Chicago. In connection with this the company handles all school supplies, maps, charts, globes and books needed by school boards or teachers. Its large and well assorted stock may be found at the store rooms, on the seventh floor of the Boston Block.

In 1891, Mr. Brown was married to Mrs. Lydia A. Hewens, of Ypsilanti, Mich. She is associated with her husband in business, and is no small factor in its success. They are members of the Fowler Church.

HENRY M. FARNAM

Henry M. Farnam, lawyer, resides at 84 Twelfth street south. His professional office is at 635 Temple Court. For ten years, 1868 to 1878, he was engaged in newspaper work, serving on the Albany Argus, New York Tribune, Cincinnati Inquirer and the Chicago Inter Ocean.

He studied law with the attorneys of the Central Vermont Railroad Co., and came to Minneapolis in 1882, where he has been in the active law practice ever since.

In 1884 he was married to Miss Carrie Chaffee, daughter of the Rev. J. F. Chaffee, D. D. This union has been blessed with four children: Lynn C., Earl, Julian and Laura.

HENRY M. FARNAM

Mr. Farnam is a member of the Hennepin Avenue Church, also secretary of the Board of Trustees of the Fowler Church and secretary of the Asbury Hospital.

He is a lawyer of unusual ability, a Methodist of the helpful type and a citizen known for his patriotism and progressive spirit.

J. D. OGDEN

J. D. Ogden, son of B. V. Ogden, was born in Dubuque, Ia., March 7, 1862. His father was born in New Jersey in 1817 and died in Ackley, Ia., in 1867. His mother, Nancy Furman, was born in Pennsylvania, November 25, 1820. She is at present living with her son at his residence, 3419 Eighteenth avenue south. After his father died his mother had a hard struggle caring for the family, yet her seven children rallied around her and did all within their power to provide for the necessities of life. When but twelve years of age the subject of this sketch came to Minneapolis where he has since lived most of the time. He returned to Iowa in 1876 and from that time was the principal support of the family. He attended school when he could, but his opportunities were limited. He is, however, a wide-awake business man and an inveterate lover of books.

J. D. OGDEN

He commenced in the harness trade in the spring of 1880. Soon after this he was stricken with the sense of guilt, and found peace in Christ. He returned to Minneapolis in 1883, and started in business on Cedar avenue with less than $135; he has been in the same building ever since, with three additions, necessitated by increase in trade.

Engrossed in worldly pursuits he became careless about church matters, but was reclaimed through the work of the Y. M. C. A., and united with Centenary Church. Afterwards he changed his membership to the Twenty-Fourth Street Church where he was steward and Sunday School teacher for several years. In 1888 he moved to Bloomington Avenue Church, in which he has served in various official relations, being Sunday School superintendent at the present time.

April 8, 1891. he was married to Lulu B. Cook, a noble Christian woman, strongly attached to the church and foremost in every good work.

JOHN DOUGLASS

In the beautiful village of Ashkirk, Scotland, seven miles from Abbotsford, home of Sir Walter Scott, near the romantic Tweedside and not far from where the Aylewater mingles its silvery stream with the rippling waters of the Teviot, was born, in 1823, John Douglass. His ancestors were sturdy Presbyterians; his father, John Douglass, having descended from one of the border Douglasses, who played their part in the heroic deeds of Flodden Field and Dunbar, and whose martial spirits were kindled by the ballads of Chevy Chase and the border wars. His mother, Mary Hood, belonged to that family of Hazeldean, enshrined by Burns in his immortal song.

Business misfortune overtaking the once prosperous father, he determined to retrieve his fortunes in the New World, whither he went in 1831, settling in Montreal, his wife and three sons, James, John and George, following him, sailing from Greenock in the summer of 1832. After a voyage of six weeks, they joined the husband and father at Quebec, whence they took the steamboat for Montreal.

The family now in their new home united themselves with the old Presbyterian St. Gabriel Church, one of the pioneer Protestant churches of the city. Soon after their coming to Montreal, Mr. Adam Miller, an earnest worker and visitor in connection with the Methodist church, called at their home and invited the three Scotch boys to attend the Sabbath School. This marked their first introduction to Methodism. They continued their attendance at the Presbyterian church, but as the youths grew, parents and children little by little drifted into the Methodist fold, lured by the warmth of its services and the Christian devotion of its members.

Soon after their arrival at Montreal, the three brothers entered the British and Canadian school, where they pursued their studies for a number of years. That school was favored with the services of Mr. Minshall, a teacher of great scholarship and professional ability. Subsequently John pursued the course of the Edinburgh University under a private tutor. He was converted in his four-teenth year, and forthwith united with the Methodist church, being the last one of his family to leave the Church of Scotland. In

JOHN DOUGLASS

1842 he was licensed as a local preacher. He pursued his studies and acted as book-keeper in a book store and also in a large im-porting dry goods establishment. He was a natural student. While others were resting or recreating, he was all ablaze with the sublimities of higher education. He would often pore over his books until two or three o'clock in the morning. Upon entering the ministry he began a special course in theology, under Rev. Matthew Rickey, D. D., one of the most eminent scholars of Canadian Methodism.

In 1845 he took regular work under the Chairman of the District, and in 1846 united with the British Conference in which he remained until his Conference merged into the Canadian Conference. He maintained this relation until 1869, when he came to Minnesota. For a number of years prior to this he had been disabled from preaching by lung trouble. Upon coming to Minnesota he settled in Winona, remaining there six years. During this period he was most diligent in everything that pertained to the growth and prosperity of the church. Upon arriving there he found one little struggling Methodist Church, but when he left there were three. It seems that his coming to Minneapolis in 1875 was providential in many respects, but in none more than in the courage and able counsel he imparted to the enterprise, then in its inception, of organizing and establishing the Hennepin Avenue Church. He recognized the opportunity as the voice of God, and gave it hearty and unfaltering support. Among those familiar with these early days, and the important part Brother Douglass played in the formation of the new church, he is familiarly referred to as its father. In 1878 he was appointed special agent of the Treasury Department of the United States, which position he occupied with great honor for seven years. Since then he has been engaged in the building and loan business.

It would be interesting to follow out the history of the Douglass family and give in detail, not only the life of the subject of this sketch, but also of his two brothers. We cannot however resist the desire to make special reference to his brother George, who during his life, became the pulpit bard of Canada, and was known throughout ecumenical Methodism, as one of the great leaders of the church, powerful in his preaching ability, clear in his discernment of spiritual things, simple and pathetic in his presentation of the claims of the gospel, and always ready to testify from a heart full of the pure love of Christ to His saving power.

In 1850 Mr. Douglass was married to Miss Elizabeth B. Hatch. She is a lady of unusual grace and culture, always gener-

ous and full of sympathy, never wearying in her devotion to the
church, and in love with the great truths of the gospel. Her
father was a prominent clergyman in the Congregational Church.
Her sister was the wife of Hon. William Windom, at one time
secretary of the Treasury Department of the United States.

REV. D. C. PLANNETTE

Rev. D. C. Plannette was born December 25, 1850, in Allegheny City, Pa. In his 17th year he united with the Union Methodist Episcopal Church. In early life he had the advantages of the
public schools of the city of his birth. Having thus laid the foundations for a liberal education, soon after his conversion he began
a preparation for his life's work by entering upon a course of study
in Westminster College, New Wilmington, Pa. He was licensed
to preach in 1872, and in the following September was received
on trial into the Erie Conference. He retained his connection with
that Conference for eleven years, and his name became a synonym
for untiring energy and ultimate success. His success in building
churches and paying old debts was truly phenomenal; and some of
the best churches in that Conference were lifted out of the "slough
of despond" by his efforts. In 1883 he supplied Bismarck, then
within the bounds of the Minnesota Conference, and successfully
completed an unfinished church enterprise.

At the first session of the North Dakota Mission, Bishop
Fowler appointed him Presiding Elder of the newly formed Grand
Forks District, which at that time embraced one half of the present state of North Dakota. He entered upon the work with his
usual enthusiasm, and so well did he succeed that at the end of his
fourth year the district was divided. As an indication of the
thoroughness with which he did his work it is in evidence that no
other denomination has succeeded in getting much of a foothold
in that part of the state. In 1888 he was appointed Presiding
Elder of the Fargo District, spending two years on that field, when
he was assigned to the pastorate of Second Church, Fargo, then
a struggling mission worshiping in an old saloon. During his
pastorate of two and one half years the mission developed into

the Roberts Street Church, and erected a two story brick building. In connection with his pastorate there, he also did heroic work as financial agent of the Red River Valley University, of which institution he was one of the founders.

In the spring of 1893 he was reappointed Presiding Elder of the Fargo District, which position he still holds. In connection with his district work he also edited the North Dakota Methodist Pioneer, which has the distinction of being the first Methodist paper to nail to the mast head the motto "A Million for Missions." He was also a delegate to the General Conference of 1888, having received all but three of the votes cast.

Mr. Plannette is no less favorably known as a strong and successful preacher and faithful devoted pastor, than he is as an unusually successful church builder. He has been blessed with gracious revivals in all his pastorates. In every respect he is "a workman that needeth not to be ashamed."

MATTHEW N. PRICE

Matthew N. Price is a native of Illinois. His father, George B. Price moved from New York State to St. Louis, Mo., in 1833 and started there the first religious paper published in that section of the country. In 1835 he moved to Illinois and located at Carrollton where he became prominently identified with the early history of Methodism in that section. He established the Carrollton Gazette in 1846, which is still published under the supervision of the oldest son.

Matthew N. Price received his education in the public schools of his native town. He became converted and united with the M. E. Church when about 16 years of age. He learned the printing business in his father's office at Carrollton and when 22 years of age he married Miss Georgianna Sutton.

In the spring of 1876 he moved to Jacksonville, Ill., and in connection with a brother-in-law, Mr. H. S. Clay, established the Daily Illinois Courier.

It was at this place that Mr. Price found a much larger and more profitable field for his enterprise and business qualifications.

During his residence in that city he became identified with the educational interests and enterprising business men of that section, and was a man in whom the strictest confidence might be imposed.

In 1882 they sold out their interest in the Daily Illinois Courier and came to Minneapolis and started the Price Brothers Printing

MATTHEW N. PRICE

Company. A younger brother, who has since died, was associated with him, but the business has been continued in the same name and Mr. Price has given it his untiring attention, and through his push and energy has increased the business to its present size. There is no plant in the Northwest that enjoys a better reputation for prompt service and excellent workmanship.

Soon after arriving in Minneapolis he united by letter with the Franklin Avenue Church, of which he is still a member and has served on the official board for about eleven years.

DAVID WILLIAM EDWARDS

The magnitude of the life insurance business is only appreciated when one is confronted with statistics showing the capital invested or accumulated, the members who avail themselves of its benefits, the amount of premiums paid, and the enormous sums disbursed in fulfilling its obligations. It has become to a large number of our people a trustee of their surplus income, a reliance for support in misfortune or age, and a relief from the dread of leaving loved ones dependent when the strong arm of their support may be taken away. It has the business character of an investment and the soft and soothing touch of a beneficence.

Natural Premium Life Insurance is the latest phase of the system of life insurance, evolved after a long experience, eliminating many inequalities in the operation of a rigid system, and reducing the cost of the life insurance to the actual requirements of the obligations assumed.

This brief history is thus epitomized in the words of Doctor Edwards, president of the Northwestern Life Association of Minneapolis addressed to the Sixteenth Annual Convention of Mutual Life and Accident Underwriters held at Minneapolis in June, 1891:

"When these conventions were organized, this system of life insurance was, in this country, in its infancy. Few there were who dreamed of its possibilities. Mountains of prejudice rose up to meet it on every hand. It was held up to ridicule and contempt by the representatives of the old system, which practically held the field, entrenched behind breastworks of gold. To meet such a competitor successfully upon the business arena, called for men— men of brave and honest hearts, men of the finest intellectual and moral fibre, careful, calculating men of undaunted courage and iron will; and when such men were needed they came and took the infant and nourished it through childhood and youth, until now it stands before us clothed in all the dignity of a noble and perfect manhood, enjoying the confidence of the world.

"Facts show that this system paid, during 1890, to the widows and orphans of the country, the enormous sum of $46,500,000, and that it now has its strong arm of protection round nearly 3,000,000 of our people, protecting the beneficiaries in the fabulous sum of $600,000,000."

The Northwestern Life Association, which Dr. Edwards so successfully administers, is the leading Natural Premium company in the West, if not the entire country, and is the best exemplification of his minute knowledge of the subject, and of his care and fidelity in the application of the principles of scientific insurance.

Dr. Edwards was born February 1, 1849, near Beaver Dam, Wis. His father, David Edwards, belongs to the line of descent which includes the famous New England divine, and has been represented by a David and Jonathan in every generation. He was born at Hadley, Mass. His mother's maiden name was Mary H. Allen. She was born, raised and educated at New Haven, Conn. David W. is the oldest son of a family of seven children, and was ushered into life in a log farm house. His early life was mostly spent on a farm, where he acquired habits of industry and frugality. He was early taught that his mission was to assist his parents, which he faithfully did until 22 years of age, receiving only such education as he could get by attending school winters. He then started for himself by taking a course in a commercial college. Among other acquisitions he learned telegraphy, obtaining the position of station agent at Heron Lake, Minn., where he continued for four years, putting in his spare hours in reading books on dentistry, which profession he had decided to enter.

He located at LeSueur, Minn., in the spring of 1878, in the practice of dentistry, where he remained for nearly ten years. The estimation in which he was held by the profession is shown by his election at first as secretary, and afterwards as president of the Southern Minnesota Dental Society, and later as secretary of the Minnesota State Dental Society, of both of which he is an honorary member to this day.

While satisfied with his professional success, and without at all contemplating engaging in life insurance as a pursuit, he was attracted to the study of the science and eagerly read all the literature of the subject which came in his way. He listened with attentive ear to the tales of agents setting forth with voluble tongue the merits of their systems, or the marvelous success of their companies. His attainments as an insurance expert came to the

DAVID WILLIAM EDWARDS

knowledge of several life insurance companies, which tendered him positions in their service of more or less importance. These were declined. Not until 1887 did he yield to the solicitations to enter the business, when he was elected a director of the Northwestern Life Association of Minneapolis, and at the first annual meeting was chosen vice-president. This was soon followed by his election as president of the company and by becoming identified in the management of its policy and affairs.

Dr. Edwards has more than a local fame in life insurance circles. He is a member of the National Convention of Mutual Life and Accident Underwriters of America, has served on their important committees and participated in their discussions. In 1892, at Buffalo, N. Y., he was elected vice-president of that organization, and at the annual convention held in Boston, September, 1894, he was elected president. At the annual convention held in New York in 1890, upon his invitation, the next annual convention was appointed at Minneapolis, where it assembled in June, 1891, and was practically the guest of Dr. Edwards and his associate officers of the Northwestern Life. On this occasion he showed himself no less able as a public speaker than he was known to be skillful as an administrator. His welcoming address was greatly admired for its graceful periods, its forcible dealing, and its wise counsels. In addition to his official labors, he has for seven years edited the Anchor, a quarterly publication devoted to the interests of his company, and the general science of life insurance.

Dr. Edwards married, October 21, 1875, Miss Mattie James, who was an accomplished teacher in the public schools of Columbia Co., Wis., where she was brought up. In 1882 they were greatly afflicted by the loss of two daughters, then their only children, in an epidemic of scarlet fever. At present they have a son of ten years, and two daughters of six and eight years of age. The family occupy their own pleasant residence at No. 2502 Garfield avenue.

Dr. Edwards took up life insurance at a period when the new system was emerging from the embryonic stage into a natural scientific system, and to its perfection he has contributed in no small degree by the accuracy of his knowledge, the soundness of his judgment, and the comprehensive scale of his thought.

Because this sketch has dwelt upon the professional character of its subject it should not be considered that he possesses only such characteristics as are employed in material interests. It is a commendable fact that he has employed his gifts as a teacher of revealed truth in the Sunday Schools where he has lived. He was superintendent of the first M. E. Sunday School organized at Heron Lake, and he was honored with that position for ten years in LeSueur. He has always been active in church and temperance work and is now trustee in two different churches in Minneapolis, superintendent of the Hennepin Avenue Sunday School, and a member of several temperance organizations. It is such unselfish devotion to a noble work that develops the true character of a man, showing that above the sordid pursuits of the world he cultivates the sweet grace of the inner spirit.

BISHOP W. X. NINDE, D. D., LL. D.

Bishop William Xavier Ninde, D. D., LL. D., was born June 21, 1832, in Cortlandville, N. Y.; consequently he is now in his sixty-second year. He graduated from Wesleyan University in 1855, where his scholarship was of high rank. After graduation he taught a year and then joined the Black River Conference, and served several churches with increasing acceptability. In 1861 he was transferred to the Cincinnati Conference, and for some eight years was successfully pastor of some of the principal churches in that city. He spent a year or two traveling in Europe and the East. On his return, in 1870, he was transferred to the Detroit Conference and stationed at the Central Church in Detroit. At the close of this pastorate he was elected to the chair of practical theology in Garrett Biblical Institute at Evanston, Ill., of which institution he became president in 1879. He was elected Bishop in 1884.

Bishop Ninde might more naturally than most have sat for the episcopal portrait in the Epistle to Titus: "Blameless, * * not self-willed. * * a lover of hospitality, a lover of good men, sober, just, holy, temperate; holding fast the faithful word. as he hath been taught, that he may be able by sound doctrine both to exhort and to convince the gainsayers." He is a scholarly man, with a well-balanced, well-trained mind, a thorough thinker of wide reading, and a conscientious student. There are few better or more symmetrical minds in the church. He is also a man of unusual modesty, apparently almost shrinking from publicity, but never from duty. He is exactly the man who would never have been elected to high office but for his sterling merit, which makes

itself felt in spite of himself, becoming known to others long before
the subject begins to suspect it.　There is a charm about his character which makes him very attractive to all who come in contact
with him, and which renders his presence a delight in any circle in
which he is found.　But this is not mere amiability.　There is a

BISHOP WILLIAM XAVIER NINDE, D. D. LL. D.

positive element in his constitution, a force of character and a vigor
of intellect, that are altogether admirable.　He has in excellent
proportions the "sweetness and light" of Matthew Arnold's ideal
man.　Of course it is implied in all this that he is a man of careful
culture, refined, gentle, with a spontaneous kindness that is always

felt wherever he is. A more genuine gentleman in the highest sense of that term is seldom seen.

Bishop Ninde is a superior preacher. His matter is always full of interest and full of spiritual suggestion, convincing, persuasive, instructive; his manner is winning and free from all that is unpleasing; graceful, simple, natural: his style is neat, chaste, and yet vigorous, with a simple rhetoric drawing attention not to itself nor to the speaker so much as to the thought which it clothes. There is a seriousness and earnestness and sincerity eliciting attention and producing conviction. It is Biblical and orthodox, and at the same time in deep sympathy with all that is human. As a pastor he has, we may truthfully say, always been enthusiastically loved by his people, entering into their interests and their lives, and in all their afflictions showing himself most tender and helpful.

It has been the privilege of the present writer to see Bishop Ninde as the presiding officer of a Conference: and we run no risk in making the assertion that he is a man in that position of great dignity, self-poised, commanding respect without effort, and conducting the business with an orderliness and dispatch that invariably give the heartiest satisfaction.

TRAFFORD N. JAYNE

Trafford N. Jayne was born November 3, 1868, near St. Charles, Minnesota. His father was Havens Brewster Jayne. The name Brewster indicates that he is a lineal descendant of William Brewster, of the Mayflower. When but a small boy, Mr. Jayne's father died leaving him to the care of his mother, who, with no resources but her head and hands, supported himself and sister. For five years after his father's death he lived on a farm, attending the country school. He then attended the High School in Winona. At twelve years of age, he was a freshman in the high school proper and at the end of that year left school and learned telegraphy. Upon acquiring this knowledge he went to work at once taking at first a night office, but, by promotion, was, at the age of fourteen years, cashier of the C., M. & St. P. Railroad, at Winona, at $65 a month. At sixteen years of age, he was cashier of the C. & N. W. Railroad at Mankato, and there made $75 per month. While here he began preparation for the University of Michigan. He resigned his position as cashier and studied from that time until September 28th of the same year, when he entered college at Ann Arbor, Michigan. He took three years of the

TRAFFORD N. JAYNE

course in the regular Literary Department and one year in the Law Department, taking the four years' course in three years. He was also fairly prominent in athletics, being a member of the University Base Ball Team and, in 1889, beating both the champions of Michigan and Ohio at tennis. He received many college honors, all being granted at the hands of the students, there being no scholarship honors in the institution. At the age of twenty he was President of the Republican Club, numbering 600 members.

In 1889 he left college, having exhausted all his funds, and returned to Minnesota. Upon returning home, he was offered a position in St. Paul as chief clerk in a law office, which he accepted. In January, 1890, he was admitted to the bar having just passed his twenty-first year. He practiced alone in St. Paul until November, 1890, when C. B. Palmer, one of St. Paul's prominent attorneys, entered into partnership with him, and he was thus able to have much practice in court from the start. In December, 1891, Mr. Palmer concluded to go to New York and Mr. Jayne was offered the attorneyship of the Wilber Mercantile Agency in Minneapolis, on January 1, 1892. He at once moved to Minneapolis where he is still engaged in his profession. His new work was too much for one man so he formed a partnership with Robert G. Morrison, under the name of Jayne & Morrison. Since then his business has increased immensely and he now has a force of eight assistants in his six offices in Temple Court. He has had charge of several large cases, the amounts involved running up to hundreds of thousands of dollars. He has already had over 550 cases, though he has been in Minneapolis but two years and a half.

Mr. Jayne is one of the most active and influential members of Wesley Church. At the age of twenty-three, he was elected President of the Minnesota Christian Endeavor Union, numbering in membership about 30,000 at that time. This work brought to him new opportunities. He traveled throughout the state and made many public speeches. As a speaker, he is forcible and eloquent. When once upon his feet his hearers forget whether he is young or old and are swayed by his impassioned eloquence and carried by the light of his varied and appropriate illustrations into the realm of truth which he so clearly portrays.

BISHOP DANIEL AYRES GOODSELL, D. D. LL. D.

Bishop Daniel Ayres Goodsell, D. D., is one of the most conspicuous, honored and influential members of the Episcopal Board. The son of Rev. Buel Goodsell, long a useful and beloved member of the New York Conference, performing important services both as pastor and Presiding Elder. He was born at Newburg, Orange Co., N. Y., Nov. 5, 1840. From a child his life was devoted to study, and ere he had passed his nineteenth birthday he completed the courses in the New York University. In 1859, the year of his leaving college, he united with the New York East Conference, of which he remained a foremost member, filling important charges, with ever-growing popularity, down to 1888, the year of his elevation to the episcopacy. In Brooklyn and other chief cities where he served, his ministry was more and more sought by the most cultivated audiences. In Middletown, the seat of Wesleyan University, he had a fruitful pastorate, and at the date of his election he had just closed an important building enterprise in the university city of New Haven.

In the Conference to which he belonged he became a distinguished member, even though the body contained many notable men. Evidence of the esteem in which he was held by his brethren is found in the fact that they elected him four times in succession to represent them in the General Conference—in 1876, 1880, 1884 and 1888—and in that great council of the denomination he became known as a judicious counselor and a careful and wise legislator. His qualities were those of a statesman rather than of a politician. His views were comprehensive: the interests of to-morrow, even more than those of to-day, were taken into account. Local and personal advantages received less consideration than what concerned the general cause in every part of the field. As a law-maker he was as broad as the great church to which he belonged.

Meantime he became known to the church not only for his abilities as a preacher, but also for his scholarly attainments. Well and largely read in theology, he had given also much attention to science, philosophy and literature, and had become master of a clear and vigorous style. He knew how to put solid thought, in his various lines of investigation, into incisive and forceful English. Many of his articles in the Christian Advocate are models of robust statement and masterly disquisition. The knowledge of these facts led the Wesleyan Association, in the spring of 1887, to select him as editor of Zion's Herald. The position was accepted, and its duties were to be entered upon the ensuing January. During this interval there was a strong demand for his services as secretary of the Board of Education. The urgency of this demand induced the Wesleyan Association to relinquish its claims, and he entered upon the duties of his secretaryship in July, 1887.

In the General Conference of 1888 he was chosen to the Episcopal office; and in this high position he has honored the church in the exercise of his rare administrative abilities. In his Episcopal make-up the elements are admirably distributed and proportioned. He has no hobbies. He is a specialist in no single line. He is adapted to the entire work of a Methodist superintendent. He can preach and write with the best, as well as administer.

As a preacher he is both intellectual and earnest. With a wide and strong grasp of his subject, he warms and glows as he advances in his discourse, taking hold on the sympathies and hearts, as well as the understandings, of men. In his sermons are found the leading truths and principles of the Gospel in their modern settings and adaptations. He deals with a practical, experimental gospel for the current world and hour. In his physical and mental endowments he is eminently Episcopal. Standing over six feet in his shoes, with a strong and compact build, he presents a portly and commanding presence. His qualities of mind are judicial and masterful. He knows men as individuals and as constituent parts of the great social web, and comprehends truth in its manifold parts and relations. With depth of conviction and clearness of purpose to conserve the interests of the church, he is generously sympathetic with the men and women who are engaged in the itinerant work, taking into counsel his heart as well as his head in arranging the schedule of services for the ecclesiastical year.

WILLIAM HENRY EUSTIS

William Henry Eustis is a native of the state of New York, born July 17, 1845, at the little village of Oxbow, near the boundary line separating Jefferson from St. Lawrence county. His father, Tobias Eustis, was born at Truro in Cornwall, England, and emigrated to America while a young man, and learned and followed the trade of wheelwright. His ancesters were sturdy miners of Cornwall. His mother was Mary Markwick, also of English descent. William Henry was the second born of a family of eleven children. The boy was a robust scion of laborious and healthy parents, who had the ambition to make him a blacksmith. At an early age he assisted his father and picked up such jobs of work as the neighbors offered, chief of which was grinding bark in a village tannery. At the age of fifteen, while pursuing some daring diversion, an accident produced an affection of the hip, which laid him aside from outdoor life, and nearly cost him his life. For seven years he was a great sufferer, going about only with the aid of crutches. His recovery, deemed almost miraculous, was due to a naturally strong constitution, a resolute will, and careful treatment, which his own study and thought taught him to apply to himself. Having attended, during a few of the winter months, a district school, he found his way to Governeur, St. Lawrence Co., where he entered a seminary. His parents thought at this time that he might be able to follow shoemaking, or possibly become a harnessmaker, but he had other inspirations. He applied himself to learn book-keeping and telegraphy, while beginning studies preparatory to a more complete literary education. Besides his physical infirmity, he was without means, and could only hope to pursue a higher education through his own earnings. He left the seminary, and for several winters taught a common school. Among other studies, he took up physiology, and carefully applied the science to his own treatment.

He now obtained a situation in the seminary to teach book-keeping and telegraphy, and with some practice in soliciting for life insurance, earned enough money to pay his way at the seminary and through a preparation for college. In 1871 he entered the Sophomore class of Wesleyan University at Middletown, Conn., and keeping up with his class which he entered, while absenting himself winters to teach school, and recruit his finances, graduated with the class in which he entered college in 1873. He went immediately to New York and entered the Columbian Law School, at which he graduated in the spring of 1874, having done the work of two years in one. He was now master of a profession, but without practice, and in debt $1,000. He, therefore, as the best expedient that offered took a position as teacher in one of the grammar schools of New York City. Having been brought up in the school of privation, he had learned the lesson of economy, so that he was able at the close of the year to pay off the debt incurred in obtaining his education, and had money enough to buy a railroad ticket to Saratoga Springs, a new suit of clothes, and a surplus of fifteen dollars, with which to commence the professional work of his life.

Now occurred one of those circumstances which devout men are wont to call providence, but others accidents, upon which the course of life sometimes turns. While at Saratoga Springs in attendance upon a college regatta, at which a younger brother held the captaincy of the Wesleyan University crew, he made the acquaintance of John R. Putman, a practicing lawyer of that place, who was deeply interested in the boat races. Mindful of his new acquaintance, Mr. Putman wrote him at New York, offering him a partnership in his law practice, which was accepted, and he soon was installed in the office at Saratoga, with plenty of work to keep him busy. This was in 1875. He remained at Saratoga and with Judge Putman for six years. These were busy years. The practice of the office was large and lucrative.

The competition at the bar was such as to stimulate the best powers of the practitioners. The eloquent Henry Smith the acute Esek Cowen, and the erudite William A. Beach, were in active practice and often met at the Saratoga bar.

In the spring of 1881 Mr. Eustis was at Washington at the inauguration of President Garfield, and soon sailed for Europe, intending to spend two years in travel and rest. The assassination of the president made such an impression upon him that he cut short his trip, and returned to America. It may not be easy to explain the psycological connection in the events. Mr. Eustis was an ardent republican and had been enthusiastically engaged in the campaign which gave New York to the republicans, and placed Garfield in the presidential chair. We know that the assassination shocked the country, and awoke strong solicitude as to our political destiny. We may not wonder that a patriotic American, in a foreign land should become heart sick.

The keen perception of a successful lawyer had not failed to discern the signs that political supremacy in the nation was fast tending westward. He decided to follow the star of destiny, and set out for the West. After visiting Kansas City, St. Louis, Du-

WILLIAM HENRY EUSTIS

buque, and other ambitious cities, he came to Minneapolis early in October and was favorably impressed with its appearance. Returning to Chicago, he ordered his baggage checked for the place which has since been his home and the scene of his great professional and financial success. He arrived on the 23rd of October,

1881, and at once entered an office with an old acquaintance, Dr. Camp; was admitted to the bar of the state and commenced the practice of the law. With the exception of two years he has had no professional associate. His legal practice has been fair. He brought with him the savings of his earlier years, which constituted a fair capital. By judicious investments he was gradually drawn into business enterprises, which soon occupied much of his time, and yielded large financial results. He built the block on Sixth street and Hennepin avenue, which became headquarters of the Union League. The fine brick office opposite the Chamber of Commerce, the Corn Exchange, was erected in 1885, and later a more stately office building went up under his direction upon another corner in the same locality, the Flour Exchange. He was a director and member of the Building Committee of the Masonic Temple Co., which has erected upon Hennepin avenue one of the stateliest structures in the city.

Mr. Eustis was one of the original corporators of the Minneapolis, Sault Ste. Marie & Atlantic Railway, and was upon its Board of Directors. He was also largely interested in the Land and Town Site Co., organized in connection with that great enterprise. He was also one of the originators of the North American Telegraph Co., and was a director and secretary of the company. This Minneapolis enterprise, having telegraphic connections from the Atlantic to the Pacific coast is one which the great Western Union Telegraph Co. has been unable to absorb or crush, and gives to the commercial world a recourse from an otherwise overwhelming monopoly.

The physical infirmities of his earlier life have given place to a condition of robust health. He is a fine example of bodily perfection. His manners are cordial, his temper enthusiastic, and his bearing almost courtly. His conversation is most entertaining, sparkling with humor, apt illustration and solid learning. He has an artistic taste, and a manner of expression enriched with grace imbibed by familiarity with the treasures of literature.

No one of our public spirited citizens has entered with greater resolution into projects for building up the city, than he. When discredit was attempted to be cast upon the accuracy of our census enumeration in 1890 by a rival city, his spirit was aroused; although the charges urged with persistency, brought a recount in both cities, Minneapolis preserved in the final result her relative supremacy.

Mr. Eustis is an ardent republican. He believes in republicanism with all that the name implies. He was a most enthusiastic admirer of Hon. James G. Blaine, and it would have been the greatest joy of his life to see him occupy the presidential chair.

In the fall of 1892 he was elected mayor of Minneapolis. His term of office, drawing to its close, has not been free from the usual criticism of public officials, but it has marked an advance over all previous administrations in its independence of policy, practical handling of vexed questions, sympathetic spirit toward the weak and fallen, decrease in criminality and patriotic allegiance to the principles of good government.

Mayor Eustis is a Christian gentleman. His charity is boundless and his creed is "do good unto all men." While a member of the Methodist church, he is liberal in feeling toward all churches and is ready to help in any movement that has for its object the moral and intellectual enthronement of man.

REV. EDWARD S. PILLING

Edward S. Pilling was born in Philadelphia, Pa., September 4, 1858. Both parents were members of the Methodist Episcopal Church, teaching him from earliest infancy to love and serve Christ. When about thirteen years of age, he made a public profession of his faith in Christ, uniting with the Arch Street Church. From that time until the present, he has been identified with the same denomination, at once becoming greatly interested in and occasionally leading the Young People's meeting, then (1871) a well established and popular service. He is now one of our enthusiastic and interested workers in the Epworth League.

He was appointed a Sunday School teacher when about twenty years of age, and soon after, as class leader. He had charge of a Sunday morning class, both lines of work being kept up until called to the ministry in 1882.

He entered the public schools of Philadelphia before he was six years of age, and when not quite twelve years old, was qualified to enter the Central High School.   One and a half years were spent, however, in the senior grade of the Grammar School, work-

REV. EDWARD S. PILLING

ing upon advanced studies, and two years were given to High School work.

Business life was entered before he was sixteen years of age. First, with a book and publishing house, then, for a short time, working as book-keeper for his father, then as assistant secretary of the Board of Trade, until in 1879 he became head book-keeper and cashier for one of the large wholesale houses of the city, remaining at this work until July, 1882.

Having received at this time a clear call to the ministry, he entered Drew Theological Seminary, at Madison, N. J., graduating with the class of 1885, but being desirous of further special work, he took one year of post-graduate studies. He felt clearly called of God to go to Minnesota, and entered the Minnesota Conference on trial in 1886, passing subsequently all the examinations at the highest grade and at the head of his class. For several years he was treasurer of the Conference. He is now secretary and a member of the Executive Comittee of the Hamline University.

His work has been in churches in the neighborhood of, or in the Twin Cities, except for two years, when pastor of Grace Church, Duluth. In 1892 he was appointed as pastor of Richfield Church, one of the oldest appointments of the Conference, the church being on Lyndale avenue south, just beyond the Minneapolis city limits.

He has very successfully used the stereopticon in his church work to illustrate the gospel, finding it a valuable help. He also occasionally lectures for our churches on such illustrated topics as, "The Beautiful Bermudas": "The World's Fair"; "Glimpses of American Wonderland"; "Death Valley and the Mojave Desert," believing that the church should, so far as possible, give clean, wholesome and educational entertainments to help crowd out harmful attractions. The many testimonials given to him, show how much his work in this line has been appreciated and how it has proved of profit to the churches.

BISHOP ISAAC W. JOYCE, D. D., LL. D.

Bishop Isaac W. Joyce, D. D., LL. D., was born in Hamilton Co., O., October 11, 1836. In 1850 his parents removed to Tippecanoe Co., Ind., and from that time until 1880 the Hoosier State was his home and the field of his labors. He was converted and joined the Methodist Episcopal Church, July 22, 1852, when only sixteen years of age. After completing the course of study at Hartsville University, he was admitted to the Northwest Indiana

Conference, October 4, 1859. From that date until his election to the episcopacy in 1888, with the exception of four years spent in the office of Presiding Elder, he was continuously in the pastorate. During this period he filled the most important appointments in his Conference, and in 1880 was one of its delegates to the General Conference. In the fall of this same year he was transferred to the Cincinnati Conference, and stationed at its most conspicuous appointment, St. Paul Church, of the city just named. After three years of most successful labor in that charge, he was appointed to Trinity Church in the same city. At the close of the pastoral term there, he was returned to St. Paul, and was in the midst of an unusually successful second pastorate in that important church when elected to the episcopacy.

Bishop Joyce was preeminently successful in the work of the pastorate. While stationed at College Avenue Church, Green-castle, Ind., his influence for good upon the students in attendance upon the then Asbury University was unbounded. Through his earnest labor and wise counsels scores of the young men were led into a Christian life and started upon careers of great usefulness in Christian work. While pastor of St. Paul, Cincinnati, that church enjoyed the most extensive revival Cincinnati Methodism had known for many years. An almost equally great awakening attended his ministry at Trinity Church. It is safe to say that no Methodist minister ever stationed in Cincinnati made a greater impression upon the city at large than did Dr. Joyce. His influence was felt throughout the Conference, and to a large extent throughout the state. So great had been the impression made by his labors, that after eight years of service within its bounds he was elected by the Conference one of its delegates to the General Conference of 1888.

As a preacher Bishop Joyce is naturally inclined to be somewhat metaphysical, but his love for souls and earnest desire for their salvation never fails to set his metaphysics on fire. He is always thoughtful, clear and logical, but the predominating trait of his preaching, and that which oftentimes renders it glowingly eloquent, is his intense zeal for the salvation of men.

As an administrator Bishop Joyce is wise, firm, and yet exceedingly kind. He is possessed of a great heart which beats in profoundest sympathy with every itinerant Methodist preacher. He has himself passed through almost every phase of an itinerant's life, with its accompanying trials and preplexities, and therefore can enter deeply into the experiences of his brethren. He is always easily accessible to the humblest minister, and without patronizing effort makes every member of the Conference over which he presides feel that he is indeed a friend and a brother.

REV. T. W. STOUT

Rev. T. W. Stout was born at Morristown, Ill., July 28, 1868. His father died when he was but two years of age. When two years old his family removed to Elysburg, Penn. There he spent the years of his childhood, receiving the rudiments of his education in the public schools of that state, removing to Minneapolis in 1882.

His preparatory education was completed in the schools of that city. He entered the University of Minnesota, graduating from that institution in 1891. While in the University he supported himself in a large measure

REV. T. W. STOUT

by his own efforts. By natural inclination he devoted himself especially to history, languages and literary study, and excelled particularly in those lines.

During his Junior year he was editor of the "Ariel," the University paper. His work was such as to call forth words of signal approval from President Northrop. He was active in the debating societies, and is a member of the Beta Theta Pi College Fraternity.

After graduation he turned his attention to teaching. For two years he was principal of the High School at Howard Lake, in this state. In those years this school rose rapidly, more certificates were issued for studies completed than in any other years, and three-fourths of the graduates that the school has ever produced, were sent forth then.

Leaving the work of teaching, he entered the ministry in 1893. Converted in childhood, he has always felt the call to preach, but unwilling to enter on that work, it was only after a severe struggle that he did so and was set to work in his present field at once.

The society of the Park Avenue Church had been organized in the spring. In July, when he assumed charge there were about twenty members. There was no church building, but services were held on Sabbath afternoons in the edifice of a sister denomination. Since then the membership has risen to eighty; a neat building has been erected and all indebtedness on it has been provided for.

Various departments of the church are in a good state, and a young and vigorous Epworth League promises much for the future.

Situated in a splendid residence part of the city, this church is sure to grow to great strength. Already the audiences fill the building and a larger one must be provided.

CHARLES HITCHCOCK FOWLER

Charles Hitchcock Fowler, son of Bishop C. H. Fowler and Myra Hitchcock Fowler, and grandson of Rev. Luke Hitchcock, D. D., was born in Evanston, Ill., August 24, 1873, while his father was president of the Northwestern University. His tastes and habits as a student and scholar conform to his environment. He has the genius of scholarship which consists in two special gifts, first, capacity and disposition for tireless and interminable work, and second, an ambition, not to go through a book or subject, but to have the book or subject go through him.

His advantages have been exceptionally good. His youth was spent in New York City. He has been drilled in private and public schools of New York City and of San Francisco, Cal., and in the High School of the latter city; in the University of California

for his Freshman work and in the University of Minnesota for
Sophomore, Junior and Senior work, where he is now a Classical
Senior. In the regular order of events he will complete in this
university year, the studies of the classical course, and also the
studies of the scientific course. He has also a full share of favor
with the students having represented the university in a debate

CHARLES HITCHCOCK FOWLER

with the students of the University of Wisconsin. He is now president of his class.

He has traveled much with his parents; he has gone round
the world in the usual route, visiting Japan, Corea, China, India,
Africa, Russia and the countries of Europe. He has visited South

America, going south almost to the borders of Patagonia. He has gone north to Alaska, America, and to the North Cape in Europe. These years of travel have been years of earnest and painstaking study. His letters to the press concerning some of these countries have been well received, reprinted and highly commended. He is known in his literary work as Carl Fowler. Tall in person, quiet and gentle in manner, and unobtrusive, yet exceedingly full of conversation, he is welcome in society.

WILBRA W. SWETT

Wilbra W. Swett was born December 12, 1839, at Bangor, Me. His father, Thomas Jefferson Swett, was a Free Baptist preacher and preached throughout Maine for about fifty-six years. His eldest brother, C. D. Swett, is a Baptist minister in Massachusetts; another brother prepared for the ministry, but died before he realized his ambition. Besides these, there were many other Baptist ministers in the Swett family. The subject of this sketch is the only Methodist in the family and yet at an early age he would resist the Calvanistic fatality of his church, and argue against it with his father by the hour. After he had left the Baptist Church he gave as his reason for the change that "Methodism is the embodiment of the most effective form of evangelizing the world." He was converted when ten years of age, but made no open profession until 1870, when, under the pastorate of Rev. James Dimmick, in Danville, Ill., he united with the North Street Methodist Church. He left his home at twelve years of age. First he worked at the carpentering trade. In 1854 he learned watchmaking; in 1859 he entered the jewelry business for himself. When the war broke out he enlisted in the Ninth Massachusetts Three Months Regiment serving in the state. He was also engaged in the government service, going to the front with the Twelfth New Hampshire Regiment from which he was detached after reaching Washington, for special service. He was relieved from this service in the fall of 1863 in consequence of ill health. He immediately moved to Springfield, Ill., and re-engaged in the jewelry business. While at Springfield he was present at President Lincoln's funeral. In 1868 he went to Danville, Ill. In 1871 he moved to Kansas, spending the time from the spring of 1872 to the fall of 1875 in Kansas, Texas and the Indian Territory. From 1875 to 1882 he was engaged in the jewelry business and watch factories in Illinois. From 1882 to 1888 he was agent for the

WILBRA W. SWETT

Equitable Life Insurance Company with headquarters in St. Louis. October 1, 1888, he became manager for the Massachusetts Mutual Life Insurance Company for the Northwest with headquarters in Minneapolis. He united with the Franklin Avenue Methodist Church in 1890 where he has served in most of the official positions of the church. He has been very active in missionary work, establishing, and for some time, maintaining the Seven Star Mission at Seven Corners.

It need only be said in conclusion that Mr. Swett is a progressive citizen, a loyal Methodist, a consistent Christian and a manly man. He is always reliable, ready to be called upon for any service, and full of zeal for the cause of Christ.

JAMES NELSON BEARNES

JAMES NELSON BEARNES

James N. Bearnes was born in Licking Co., Ohio, in July, 1854. His father was a Methodist preacher of the genuine type. strong in his logical ability, profound in his moral convictions and stainless in his Christian integrity.

These predominating traits of his father, coupled with the gentleness, self-sacrifice and tender sympathies of the mother, entered largely into the character of the son. He was educated in his boyhood in the public schools and in 1878 graduated from the classical department of the Ohio Wesleyan University. While a student he took high rank among his classmates, always devoted to his books, true to his responsibilities as a student, and animated with a determination to have a thorough preparation for the work of life. During his senior year he was assistant professor in Mathematics. Although reared in the Methodist itinerary his mind was early turned toward the law and while yet a student at the Ohio Wesleyan University, he began its study. Upon graduation he accepted the superintendency of the schools for one year, at Mt. Gilead, O. He then occupied the same position for one year at Upper Sandusky, after which he took charge of the schools at Sidney, O., for three years. He entered the law office of Gen. Jones, at Delaware, Ohio, and prepared for the legal profession, into which he was admitted in 1881. He practiced successfully for a while in Ohio. In 1882 he came to Minneapolis and has been since that time actively engaged in the practice of law.

He has in his care, cases of all classes and is known in the profession as a man who gives the strictest attention to the interests of his clients.

He is a lawyer of marked ability, is well versed in all that pertains to the profession, and commands the unqualified respect of his associates.

He was married in Indianapolis in October, 1882, to Miss Mary E. Gray. Her parents were leading Methodists and she is an active member of the Hennepin Avenue Church.

BISHOP LEONIDAS LENT HAMLINE

If you visit Rose Hill Cemetery, near Chicago, you may find there a grave marked by a plain slab of gray syenite bearing the inscription, "Leonidas L. Hamline." Only that and nothing more, for so the sleeper willed it. Was he born and did he die? Had he titles and was his life a blessing? Why should these questions be

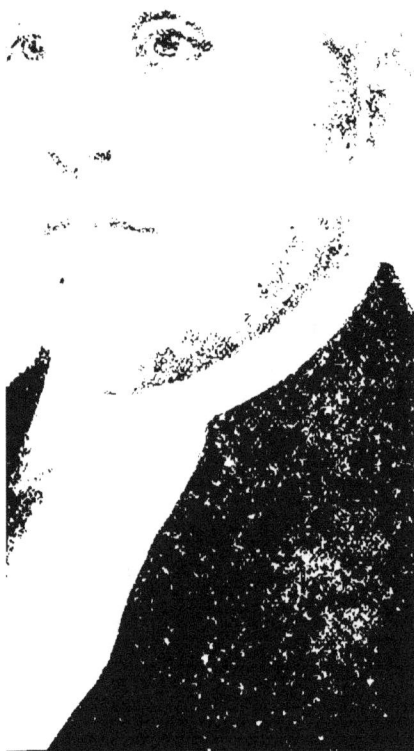

BISHOP LEONIDAS LENT HAMLINE

answered on stone? Dates and titles avail not: deeds only live in
history, and deeds at last are all gathered up into the name of him
who wrought them. It was thoroughly characteristic of the man,
and represents not self-consciousness, but humility and self-depre-
ciation, which marked his entire religious life. Let us turn from
the marble slab to the scant records of the life of this great man.

Leonidas Lent Hamline was born in Burlington, Conn., May 10,
1797. His early studies were pursued with a view to the Christian
ministry, but later he studied law, and was admitted to the bar in
Lancaster, O. The death, however, of his little daughter in 1828
changed the whole course of his life, for it led to his conversion,
membership in the Methodist Episcopal Church, and later to the
ministry, and his subsequent brilliant career in that profession. He
was received on trial in the Ohio Annual Conference in 1832, and
only two years later was stationed at Wesley Chapel, Cincinnati,
which then ranked among the most important charges in the
Methodist Church. In 1836 he was appointed assistant editor of
the Western Christian Advocate and in 1841 was made editor of
the Ladies' Repository. In both these positions he achieved
marked success. In 1844, only twelve years after he was admitted
on trial, he was elected Bishop in the Methodist Episcopal Church.
Though this was his first appearance in a General Conference, his
fame as a preacher and his power as a writer had made him well
known throughout the church; but it was not so much that as it was
his great speech on the "Powers of the General Conference," to
which must be attributed his election to the office of Bishop.

It was, indeed, a stormy session, and in the great debate on the
slavery question, which was involving both our itinerancy and our
episcopacy, the great speech of L. L. Hamline was *facile princeps*,
But he did not long remain a Bishop. Already his nervous constitution had been shattered, and even then he was entering that
period of suffering which was practically to make his sun set at noon.
He resigned his office of Bishop in 1852, and ceased to live on earth
February 22, 1865.

Such is a brief sketch of Bishop Hamline. He was a man
cast in one of nature's largest moulds. His physical presence was
noble and commanding. Henry Clay said of him, "I have never

seen such dignity in human form before." And yet his was the dignity of a polite, well-bred gentleman, whose presence in any company would immediately attract attention. But nature did not bankrupt herself in giving to Mr. Hamline his physical make-up, magnificent as it was, for his intellectual endowments were quite as remarkable. His training for the law did much to make him precise in his statements, orderly in his processes and logical in his deductions. As a debater he had few equals; prudent, fearless, searching and critical, yet perfectly fair and honorable.

He was a man of fine presence and voice; the English language has had but few writers of better style; he was a master of logic, argument and oratory; his imagination was vivid, yet well in hand. All this, combined with an earnestness and unction quite unusual, made him a preacher of great power. His was not, indeed, the unction, pathos and overmastering eloquence of Simpson, though falling but little below him in these respects; his thought and argument were far better, with the general impression and results more permanent.

Doctor Olin was, doubtless, the greatest preacher Methodism has ever produced, and yet Doctor Hibbard does not hesitate to say that Hamline was not a "whit behind Olin" as a preacher. Contrasting them, he says, "Hamline was impassioned; never boisterous; Olin was vehement; Hamline was earnest; Olin, impetuous; Hamline was like the even, though often rapid flow of a beautiful stream, bearing its buoyant burden safely and gracefully onward; Olin was like the torrent, or the whirlwind, hurrying all before it. With him the hurricane was inevitable, but he rode upon it in majesty, and, like the spirit of the storm, directed its forces. Hamline never suffered the storm to arise, but checked it midway, and if the sweep and force of his eloquence were less, the auditors were left more self-controlled, and the practical ends not less salutary."

Bishop Hamline was devout and intensely earnest in his religious life. When I saw him in 1850 he seemed to me like a man on earth trying to live wholly in heaven. As Carlyle said of Edward Irving. "He was trying to look into the face of Deity and live."

There was nothing "put on" in the make-up of his piety, for

he went through eight years of severe affliction with great resignation, and declared in the midst of it all, "I am far more contented and cheerful than in the best days of my youth." The comfort of his life, it was also his staff in the supreme moment of death, for he exclaimed, "Oh, wondrous, wondrous, wondrous love!"

The subject of our sketch was a man of benevolent intentions and deeds. He and his wife made at least two donations of twenty-five thousand dollars each for the founding of Methodist colleges. Hamline University is one of these, and was named in token of that fact. The property received from him is in Chicago, from which we get an annual rental of three thousand four hundred dollars, so that to that extent, at least, he is paying the tuition of the young men and women who are students in Hamline to-day, and doubtless will continue doing so for many generations yet to come. Being dead he yet speaketh; and though in heaven, he is still at work here on the earth. The unique inscription on the plain slab in Rose Hill Cemetery has its justification and completion in the holy temple builded of "lively stones" which he himself is helping to polish. For him, and for all such as he was, costly mausoleums are out of place. They are neither suitable homes nor monuments. The monument is elsewhere and far more enduring, and the home is in heaven.

Faculty of Hamline University

PRESIDENT GEORGE H. BRIDGMAN, D. D.

President George H. Bridgman, D. D., was born in Ontario, Canada. He graduated from Victoria University in 1864 and at once entered upon the work of the Christian ministry. He continued in the pastorate in Canada for nine years, occupying pulpits in Brantford, Hamilton and Toronto. In 1873 he accepted a call to the principalship of the Genesee Wesleyan Seminary at Lima, N. Y., and remained at the head of that institution for ten years. He was called to the presidency of Hamline University in 1883. The degree of Master of Arts was conferred upon him by his Alma Mater in 1867 and the degree of Doctor of Divinity by Syracuse University in 1878.

REV. GEORGE S. INNIS, Ph. D.

Rev. George S. Innis, Ph. D., passed his early years in his birth-place, Columbus O., graduating at the high school in 1869. He graduated at the Ohio Wesleyan, at Delaware, in 1872, and took a course in the Boston University School of Theology, graduating in 1876. In 1877 he entered the Minnesota Conference and in 1881 was elected Professor of the Latin Language and Literature in Hamline University. A. M. and Ph. D., were conferred by the Illinois Wesleyan in 1885. In 1889 Professor Innis was elected to the chair of history, upon the duties of which he entered after travels abroad. Prof. Innis has had personal supervision of our library, and under his untiring efforts it has become an honor to Minnesota Methodism.

PROF. LOREN H. BATCHELDER, A. M.

Prof. Loren H. Batchelder, A. M., was born in Montpelier, Vt., of Puritan ancestry. He prepared for college at the Vermon Methodist Seminary and was graduated from Middlebury College in the class of 1874. After graduation, he was elected Professor of Mathematics and Chemistry in the Newark Conference Collegiate Institute at Hackettstown, N. J., where he was soon admitted to the bar, having prosecuted his law studies while teaching. He was married to Miss Gulick, daughter of Rev. J. G. Gulick, of Elmira, N. Y., in 1882. In 1883 he was elected to his present position. He has been for three years professor of Analytical Chemistry and Lecturer in Electricity in the Summer School of the Chautauqua College of Liberal Arts, Chautauqua, N. Y. He is also a lecturer in the Chautauqua University Extension courses.

PROF. ERASTUS F. MEARKLE, LL. B.

Prof. Erastus F. Mearkle, LL. B., took the Normal Course at Pennsylvania State Normal School and afterward graduated in the Scientific Course. Read medicine—partial course—at University of Michigan, at Ann Arbor. In 1877 took Classical Course and then studied in the Law Department. Taught various schools in Pennsylvania. Taught four years in Peddie Institute, Hightstown, N. J. Was principal of Peoria Public Schools for two years. Has been professor of Mathematics at Hamline from the opening of the university in September, 1880, until the present time, excepting the year of 1882-83.

PROF. MILTON J. GRIFFIN, A. M.

Prof. Milton J. Griffin. A. M., was born in Michigan but spent his boyhood in Pennsylvania. He prepared for college in Genesee Wesleyan Seminary, Lima, N. Y., 1864-67 and entered Genesee College, Lima, in 1867, remaining there three years. Instructor Genesee Wesleyan Seminary, 1869-70. Principal of Grammar School, Rome, N. Y., 1870-71. Professor in Genesee Wesleyan Seminary, 1871-72. A. B. conferred by Syracuse University, 1874; A. M., 1876. Professor of Latin, Greek and German, Chamberlain Institute, Randolph, N. Y., 1873-75. Principal of various schools in New York from 1875-79. Studied and traveled in Europe, 1879-81. Professor of Classical Literature, High School, Syracuse, N. Y., 1881-86. Professor of Greek Language and Literature, Hamline University, since 1886.

PROF. HENRY L. OSBORN, Ph. D.

Prof. Henry L. Osborn, Ph. D., was born at Newark, N. J., 1857. Prepared for college at Drew Theological Seminary, Madison, N. J. B. A. conferred by Wesleyan University, Middleton, Conn., 1878. Ass't Professor of Biology 1878-80. Fellow in Biology, Johns Hopkins University, receiving degree of Ph. D. in 1884. Employed by U. S. Fish Commission in the summer of 1879, to spend three months in studying the natural history of the codfish, the results of which researches were published in the 10th census report. In 1880 was with the Fish Commission and in 1882-84 he was with the Chesapeake Zoological Labratory. 1884-87 at Purdue University, Lafayette, Ind. Editor of and contributor to several scientific journals. Hamline University, 1887.

PRESIDENT GEORGE H. BRIDGMAN, D. D.

PROF. WILLIAM E. THOMPSON, A. M.

Prof. William E. Thompson, A. M., was born at Bristol, Rhode Island. Graduated from Bristol High School [and the Rhode Island State Normal, and then taught in the public schools of his native state. Deciding to enter college, he prepared at Wilbraham and Phillips Exeter Academies and entered Brown University, Providence, R. I., where he graduated in 1873. Received his A. M. in 1876. Elected a member of the American Philological Association in 1877, having previously, in June, 1873, been elected to fill the Chair of Ancient Languages at Genesee Wesleyan Seminary, Lima, N. Y., where he remained for a period of sixteen years, up to the time of his call to the Latin Chair in Hamline University in 1889.

MISS HANNAH L. SHOEMAKER, A. M.

(Extract from first fifty years of Cazenovia Seminary, 1876.) Miss Shoemaker, A. M., was elected Perceptress, and still holds the place. Her administration of the Ladies' Department has been unsurpassed. No one of her predecessors has made a deeper impression upon the students or added more to the reputation of the Institution than she. An exact scholar, an apt teacher, a thorough disciplinarian, her recitation room is a distinctive feature of the Seminary. The high character which the school enjoys is a part of her unstinted contribution." In 1883 Hamline University secured the services of Miss Shoemaker. Her life among us has been all we should expect from the above extract. Active, earnest and sympathetic, her talents and culture have contributed much toward the formation of refined and noble character among our students.

PROF. ARTHUR Z. DREW, A. M.

Prof. Arthur Z. Drew, A. M., was born at Thornton's Ferry, New Hampshire, in 1860. Attended various schools until his removal to Le Sueur Co., Minn., in 1875. He taught in the public schools at Ottawa, Minn. Worked at various employments, including the position of operator in the telegraph companies, until he entered Hamline. After taking a preparatory course he entered the college in 1882, graduating in 1886. He was retained as instructor in Latin and English. Was married to a member of his class, Miss Stowers, in 1887. Was ordained a minister of the Gospel. Received his A. M. from Hamline University in 1889. Elected Assistant Professor of Mathematics in 1890.

THOMAS C. ALDRICH

Thomas C. Aldrich was born in Brunswick, O., in 1842, of Scotch-Irish parentage. He was reared in a good, Methodist home, being one of nine children, seven brothers and two sisters. His father, Charles M. Aldrich, is still living in Ohio, and is in his eighty-seventh year.

His early life was spent on a farm, where, in the district school, was laid the foundation of his education. He subsequently entered college, but at the breaking out of the rebellion, he abandoned his studies and took up arms in defense of his country. His record as a soldier during the war, was characterized by the same energy, courage and patriotism, that have played so prominently in his subsequent career.

At the close of the war he went West, where he has contributed in no small degree to the growth and development of the various sections in which he has labored and lived.

He has been an ardent supporter of the church. He united with the Methodist church in 1874 and has always identified himself with it wherever his lines have been cast.

He has recently accepted the position of general agent of

The Mutual Life Insurance Co., of New York.

E. W. Peet & Son are the state managers, with their central office in St. Paul.

This company began business in 1843. It is the oldest company in the United States and the largest in the world.

Its total assets are $186,707,680, being $17,651,283 more assets than any other American life company has: its assets and surplus are twice as large as the capital and surplus of the Bank of England. The total number of policies in force December 31, 1891, was 273,213, insuring $802,867,478.

THOMAS C. ALDRICH

It is purely mutual, having no capital stock. All profits of the business are paid to policy-holders, and its entire accumulations and surplus belong to them exclusively.

Up to December 31, 1893, it had paid to its policy-holders $367,351,640.26, which is double the amount ever paid by any other life company; the death claims paid amounting to $141,281,

671.09 and the amount paid living members to $226,069.969.17. Its total surplus, as shown by the official report to The Minnesota Insurance Department, is $25,314,206.92.

Including present surplus, it has earned for its policy-holders over one hundred millions ($105,466,533.34) in dividends of profits, which is .42 per cent. more than the earnings of any other company.

The receipt in 51 years of nearly $635,000,000 for the benefit of the members of only one Life Insurance Company is, in itself, a most wonderful demonstration of what this business is capable of in the future.

Taking the entire 51 years, it appears that nearly one-fourth of its income was from the interest and profits earned by its invested funds, which now amount to nearly one-third of all the moneys it has ever received. Nearly 60 per cent. of its entire income has already been used in paying claims due to its members under contracts that have matured, or in dividends paid to policy-holders, and for surrender values allowed to discontinued policies. It has paid $87,413,924.43 in dividends, and still has $25,314,206.92 accumulated for distribution when due. $544,137,700.07 of its income has been for the exclusive benefit of its insured members.

The miscellaneous profits, realized over the interest and rents received, have amounted to nearly $8,000,000, which has more than paid all the salaries of those who, for 51 years, have managed the company and produced its phenomenal results.

The interest, rents and profits have amounted to $144,904,-194.51. The death claims to $141,281,671.09,

It follows that the earnings made by the company on its invested funds, have exceeded the death claims by $3,622,523.42 and the total expenses by $55,992,365.18. A record never equalled by any other company.

The company issues every approved form of Life and Endowment policies, also special contracts by which an annuity for life can be secured to the beneficiary, or payment of an annuity after the death of the insured to the beneficiary for 20 years and the full amount of the policy at the end of 20 years, or any time previous if so desired.

Its rates and premiums are the same as all other standard companies, and the surplus returns in the past has been greater than those of any other company.

All forms of policies in this great company not only afford protection to the family of the insured in case of death, but a good investment for the policy-holder in case he lives a certain number of years. The advantages of endowment and insurance are combined in the ordinary life insurance policy of this company.

JACOB FRANCIS FORCE

Jacob Francis Force was born March 2, 1843, at Stillwater, Saratoga Co., N. Y. He received his education in the public schools and academy of his native village; in 1860 removed to Newark, N. J., and was engaged for two years in mercantile pursuits; returned to Stillwater in the spring of 1862, and on the 13th of August, 1862, enlisted in Captain Vandenburgh's Company K, of the One Hundred and Twenty-fifth Regiment New York Volunteers, then being raised at Troy, N. Y. He was mustered in with the regiment and left with it for the front, August 30, 1862. Was with the regiment continuously from that time until January 8, 1864. At Martinsburg, Va., he was made corporal and was promoted to fourth sergeant at Union Mills, Va., January 8, 1863, by Levin Crandall, Lieutenant-Colonel comanding regiment; on the 22nd of April, 1863, he was made first sergeant of the company. He was the first orderly sergeant of the regiment to call the roll of the company from memory, which being noticed by Colonel Willard, an order was issued requiring all first sergeants in the regiment to commit the roll of names to memory. December 31, 1863, he was discharged as an enlisted man by order of the War Department in order to accept an appointment as first lieutenant in the Twenty-second United States Colored Troops, then organizing at Philadelphia, Pa. Before leaving the regiment, January 8, 1864, he was presented with a sabre, belt and gloves by the members of K Company, the presentation being made by Chaplain E. D. Simons. After joining the Twenty-second U. S. Colored Troops, he was assigned to H Company; May 3, 1864, he was promoted captain of the same company, and with his regiment participated in repulsing attacks on Wilson's Wharf and Fort Powhatan on the James River, and on June 15, 1864, was with the advance on Petersburg, his regiment leading the first charge. He performed duty in the trenches and on picket continually from this time until in September, when his regiment was ordered to Dutch Gap Canal to assist in its construction. September 29, he took part in a charge on New Market Heights, and on September 30, while re-

JACOB FRANCIS FORCE

pulsing the enemy in their attempt to retake Fort Harrison, he was wounded in the left shoulder. Complete removal of several inches of bone from the upper portion of the left arm was the result, from which a fair recovery was made, and on April 10, 1865, he was discharged from the service by Special Order War Department "on account of wounds received in action."

After the war Mr. Force acquired a thorough preparation for the medical profession. In 1872 he came to Minnesota and settled at Heron Lake, where he practiced medicine most successfully for thirteen years. While at Heron Lake he was appointed postmaster.

He was, also, from 1872 to 1875, examining surgeon of the United States Pension Bureau. In 1885 he moved to Minneapolis, where his rare professional ability and his manly Christian bearing brought him additional evidence of public esteem.

He was soon made vice-president and lecturer of *Materia-Medica* in the Minneapolis College of Physicians and Surgeons. He was also elected a member of the State Medical Association. Dr. Force is an official member of Foss Church and superintendent of its Sunday School, having occupied that position with great acceptability for a number of years.

He is treasurer of the Northwestern Life Association, a director in the Metropolitan Bank, chairman of the medical section of the National Association of the Mutual Life & Accident Underwriters and an honored member of the Minnesota Commandery of the Loyal Legion. He is thoroughly identified with the many interests of Minneapolis and has contributed in no small degree to their development. As a Methodist, he is in touch with all the movements of the church.

FREDRICK C. SAMMIS

FREDRICK C. SAMMIS

Fredrick C. Sammis was born in New York City, November 21, 1867. While yet a small boy his parents moved to the country and built a home in Westchester Co. He attended the public schools and Bradford preparatory school at Rye, under the direction of Charles Jewitt Collins, a retired Presbyterian minister and a warm friend of Dr. McCosh, of Princeton College. Here his first ambition was aroused for an education and a place among the successful men of the country. His parents were Congregationalists but attended the Methodist Episcopal Church While attending school, Dr. M. B. Chapman was called to the pastorate of the church and during his ministry Mr. Sammis united with the church. During the pastorate of Dr. Chapman he took a special interest in this young student and not only gave him excellent counsel and advice but opened his home to him, where, in fellowship with the members of the family and under the influence of strong Christian care, he made decided progress, not only in his literary work, but in his soul growth and spiritual life.

At seventeen years of age, Mr. Henry Griffen, treasurer of the New York Bowery Fire Insurance Company, offered Mr. Sammis a position which he held until he came West in June, 1887. Since coming to Minneapolis he has engaged in various enterprises and held positions of importance and trust. He is a member of the Hennepin Avenue Church and an active worker in the Christian Endeavor Society.

EMERSON WESLEY WHEELOCK

Emerson Wesley Wheelock was born in Lewis Co., N. Y., in 1862, of godly parentage. His early education was in the public schools. In 1872 he left his Eastern home and friends and came to Minnesota. He entered the Congregational School at Northfield, Minn., in 1880, where he remained until 1885. While attending this institution he was converted and identified himself with the Congregational Church. In 1887 he united with the old Centenary Church, Minneapolis, and is still a faithful member of Wesley Church. He is at pres-

E. W. WHEELOCK

ent engaged in the United States Mail Service, but never becomes so absorbed in business that he has not time to perform the duties of an upright Christian and avail himself of the privileges and services of God's house.

JAMES T. WYMAN

The subject of this sketch was born October 15, 1849, in Millbridge, Washington Co., Me. He was one of a family of twelve children, ten of whom are still living. His parents were John and Clarinda Wyman, descended from old Puritan stock, the family having first settled at Woburn, Mass., in 1640. After the close of the Revolutionary war, his great grandfather removed to Maine.

Mr. Wyman lived in Millbridge until 1868, and received a good common school education. In the spring of 1868 he came to Minnesota, and located at Northfield and attended Carleton College for one year. In 1869 he engaged in business in that village with his brother, operating a sash, door and blind factory and saw mill, but was burned out March 12, 1871, a most serious loss, as they had no insurance. His character for integrity was even then so well established, and his business habits so well formed, that he was able to borrow money on his own name and paid off every debt.

In March, 1871, he came to Minneapolis and became superintendent of the sash, door and blind factory operated by Jothan G. Smith and L. D. Parker, then located on the west side sawmill platform. In that capacity he developed such marked business ability that in 1874 he became a partner, under the firm name of Smith, Parker & Co. In this business he has been an active partner ever since, the firm name since 1881 having been Smith & Wyman, his partner being H. Alden Smith.

It will thus be seen that Mr. Wyman has been a manufacturer for upwards of twenty years, and during the most of that time a proprietor in the business. The firm's business has been extensive, for many years having on its pay roll from 200 to 250 men, and on such just and equitable principles has their business been conducted, that rarely, if ever, has a complaint been heard from an employe.

On September 3, 1873, Mr. Wyman was married to Miss Rosetta Lamberson, the daughter of a Methodist clergyman of Northfield, Minn. Seven children have been born to them of this union, four boys and three girls, as follows: Roy L., Guy A., Grace Alice, James C., Maud Ethelwynne, Earle F. and Ruth Wyman, all of whom are now living.

Mr. Wyman, while a most active and successful business man has by no means confined his energies to the prosecution of his private business. He has a strong faith in and love for the city of his adoption. Whenever and wherever he has seen opportunity to aid in advancing the general interests of the city, he is always among the foremost to seize it and push it to a successful

JAMES T. WYMAN

issue. He early became an active member of the Board of Trade, and did service for several years in that organization as chairman of the Committee on Manufactures. He was vice-president of the board in 1887, and was unanimously elected president in 1888 and also in 1889, and declined another re-election. He was one of the original members of the Business Men's Union, organized in 1889, and also a member of the Board of Directors.

Mr. Wyman was one of the most prominent in the organization of the Metropolitan Bank of Minneapolis in the spring of 1889, and in a few months after its organization he became its vice-president. At the first annual meeting of the bank he was elected president and has held the office ever since.

Mr. Wyman is an official member of the Hennepin Avenue Church; and also for many years has been a trustee of Hamline University, the most important educational institution of that denomination in Minnesota, and for the last four years has been vice-president of the Board of Trustees of the college.

The Associated Charities of Minneapolis is doing a most important benevolent work for the city, in which Mr. Wyman has always taken a deep interest. He was chosen one of the first directors of the association, afterwards its president, and still holds the office of vice-president of the Board of Directors.

With all these multiplied activities, to each of which he devotes its full share of time, it may well be inferred that Mr. Wyman is an unusually busy man. But these by no means comprehend the full measure of his public services. Other public organizations might be mentioned to which he has devoted no small amount of time Hardly any important public gathering is held, looking toward the advancement of the moral or material interests of the city, at which he is not invited to be present and participate. While he makes no pretensions to oratorical display or rhetorical effect, yet he never fails to command and hold the attention of his audience, and is a most convincing speaker on any subject he undertakes to handle. As an after-dinner speaker he is especially happy and never fails to "bring down the house," by his humor and wit, whose flavor does not require the adventitious aid of champagne (which he eschews) to make it truly enjoyable and delightful.

Mr. Wyman has in politics always been recognized as a consistent republican. In 1892 was nominated by the Republican Party for the legislature from the 30th Legislative District. The nomination was greeted with enthusiasm by the people of his district and he was elected in the fall by a handsome majority.

That he was the man peculiarly adapted to represent this district in which is the State University, was demonstrated by his record in the legislature. His University Bill, the most popular that has ever passed, placed the university on a footing with the public schools. He also received an appropriation for the university of one hundred and fifty thousand dollars.

It is not strange after such valuable service, that at the last election he was elected State Senator from the 30th District by an overwhelming majority.

The character of Mr. Wyman, taken as a whole, illustrates the best traits of that New England race which has become the founder and builder of cities and states. Intelligence, enterprise, sagacity, public spirit, business integrity and honor, founded on a strong moral fibre, are characteristics of the man, standing out with remarkable prominence. He is yet comparatively a young man, hardly having reached the full maturity of his physical and mental powers, and a higher measure of success than he has yet achieved, is morally certain if his life is spared.

Mr. Wyman has a delightful though modest home as a permanent residence, on Fourth street southeast. He has also a very pleasant summer residence at Lake Minnetonka, where his family usually spend the summer season, surrounded with all the enjoyments for which that romantic lake has become famous.

REV. FRANK PEABODY HARRIS

Rev. Frank Peabody Harris, now pastor of the Methodist Episcopal Church of Marshall. Minn, was born in the town of Danvers, Mass., July 15, 1858.

When three months old his parents removed to Annapolis county, Nova Scotia. Here upon his father's farm he spent the first eight years of his life, returning to Danvers at the age of nine. At the Boston St. Lynn Church he was converted at the age of fourteen. He was educated in Danvers and Lynn common schools, Lynn High School, Fort Edward Collegiate Institute and graduated from Wesleyan Academy in 1883. The same year he entered

REV. FRANK P. HARRIS

Boston University, graduating from the Boston University School of Theology in 1888.

His ministerial services have been Bridgetown, Me., where for six months he supplied, and where his first labors were blessed with a glorious revival in which over ninety souls were converted. Returning to Boston University he established a new mission in Wyoma, Lynn, where his efforts were successful, and in two months the New Broadway Church was organized with a membership of eight in full connection and fifty probationers. In this mission Mr. Harris received the special training in evangelical work that has so eminently fitted him for a successful career in the Christain ministry; he learned to successfully reach and save the masses of the people.

He served this church three years and in 1889 was appointed to Byfield, Mass.; joined the New England in April, 1890, and at the same session transferred to the Minnesota Conference and was appointed to LeSueur charge to fill the unexpired year of the former pastor who had transferred to an Eastern Conference.

In this Conference he has been pastor at Fairmont one year, Blue Earth City two years, and in 1893 was appointed to the Marshall charge. He inaugurated a series of special services on December 26, 1893 that continued to April, 1894, in which two hundred persons were converted. Mr. Harris believes that each congregation has a distinct mission, that pastor and people should together engage in special service to save souls. For this reason he does not favor a so-called union revival service, employ any sensational methods, or a traveling evangelist, but endeavors to enlist every member of his congregation in the work. His remarkable powers are shown in the fact that he preached twice a day and more for one hundred successive days, and held prayer and song services during this period. His remarkable gift in song and earnest exhortation reaches the hearts of the people.

His revival efforts at country places were continued till July 2, and a hundred souls at these appointments have professed conversion, and two flourishing societies with a membership of one hundred and twenty have been organized.

MRS. ANNA GOHEEN

Mrs. Anna Goheen was born in Bellville, Ill., or rather near the present city of Bellville, for at that time Illinois was a wilderness. She is the sister of Hugh, Thomas Asbury and William Harrison and like her deceased brothers, has devoted her life to the cause of Christ and the upbuilding of the Methodist Episcopal Church.

Her father was Thomas Harrison, born December 13, 1779, in York Co., S. C. When he was quite young, about two years old, his father removed to Rutherford Co., N. C. About the time of the removal to Rutherford county, his mother died. When he was about ten years old his father removed to the state of Georgia. Here the family remained until he was 19 years of age when his father again removed to North Carolina. In the year 1800, he was married to Miss Margaret Gilbreath, a lady of bright intellect, broad sympathies, deep consecration, and noble Christian character.

Although her home was in the South, she could not tolerate slavery. She could not endure the thought of rearing children in the midst of such moral blight and social degredation. This explains the fact that, in 1804, young Harrison and wife removed to the then Territory of Illinois, County of St. Clair. Here in their wild, western home, they struggled together against many obstacles and natural disadvantages. But they were more than equal to the emergency. The soil was cultivated, the wilderness conquered, the savage pacified, and the foundation of a great family was laid. Children were born. So anxious were the parents that they should be educated, that out of their scanty savings, the elder son was sent away to school that he might teach the other children. Their married life was of fifty years duration, when it was terminated by the death of Mrs. Harrison. Writing of her death, the Rev. John Scripps, says, "Another mother in Israel. in the person of Mrs. Margaret, wife of Rev. T. Harrison, of Bellville, aged 70 years, whose house in the long gone by of Western Methodist pioneering, was the welcome home of the weary itinerant. We found it such forty years ago, when our now sainted sister used to minister to our comfort, refresh our weariness, talk of heaven and even when

THOMAS A. HARRISON

difficulties were before us, mount her horse and pilot us to our next appointment. Blessed saint. Long shall we cherish thy memory."

Mr. Harrison was converted in 1802. It was a real conversion, permeating his whole being with the Christ life, and impelling him to a career of self-sacrifice and heroism for the Master. For a period of fifty-five years, he acted as steward, class leader and local preacher in the church. In 1860, he came to Minneapolis and made his home with his daughter, Mrs. Goheen, at 1115

Nicollet avenue. He was a member of the Centenary Church until he died in 1867. His funeral was attended by a large concourse of friends. Drs. Chaffee and Quigly conducted the services.

The daughter of such parents, it is not strange that the subject of this sketch has played such an important part in the growth of Minneapolis Methodism. She began early in life to serve the church. When but a girl she was converted under the preaching of Dr. Wentworth and immediately united with the church. From that time she has been animated with the one ambition of building up the church of her father, and spreading the Redeemer's kingdom. In 1846 she was married to Dr. S. M. E. Goheen. He was practicing medicine in Lebanon, Ill., and was also professor in the McKendree Collage at that time. Dr. Goheen was a man of unusual ability in his profession, and devotion to the church. He had already become known throughout the church on account of the heroic spirit that led him to consent to an appeal from our Missionary Secretaries, to go to Africa and act as physician for the missionaries. In 1839 he started upon this, at that time, perilous mission.

Upon reaching Liberia, he became such an important factor, not only as a physician, but as a Christian worker that the affairs of the mission were practically placed in his hands. He stood at this post of duty for five years, and then returned to America.

After his marriage to Miss Harrison, they settled in Lebanon, where he met with gratifying success in his profession. Later they moved to Bellville on account of the failing health of her parents. In 1852 Dr. Goheen went to California; this was during the great gold craze. Upon reaching California, Dr. Goheen had such a demand for his professional service, that he consented to practice for a while. This work proved fatal. His practice absorbed all his time, calls for help crowded upon him and although in a strange climate, his own health not the strongest, he found no rest. He was suddenly prostrated with a sickness from which he did not recover. He reached California in June and was buried the following January.

Just twenty years later, Mrs. Goheen visited California and
stood by his lonely grave. She came to Minneapolis with her father
in 1860. At the first opportunity she united with the Centenary
Church, in which she soon became preeminently useful. Her
generosity never failed. She gave of her money without stint,
and of her time and talents with enthusiastic love. Providence
made her a central and efficient figure in the formation of the

DR. S. M. E. GOHEEN

Hennepin Avenue Church. Her work is of the quiet order. She
sounds no trumphet. She cannot be induced to talk about anything she has done. She walks alone with God and does his work
without ostentation.

It is doubtful whether there is a Methodist Church enterprise in Minneapolis toward which she has not contributed. This
liberality is not without sacrifice. She denies herself in many
things in order to help many worthy causes. Her home is at 1125
Nicollet avenue. She formerly lived at 1115 Nicollet, but sold it

for a mere nominal sum, in order that Minneapolis might have an Episcopal residence. She is always bright and cheerful and scatters sunshine wherever she goes. May she be spared to Minneapolis Methodism for many years.

REV. JOHN W. HILL, D. D.

Rev. John W. Hill, D. D., is an honored member of the Central Ohio Conference, having continuously served in the active pastorate for over forty years. He is at present pastor at Dunkirk, Ohio. His grandparents on both sides were natives of Virginia, of sturdy stock, resolute and courageous, known for their patriotism and sterling qualities. His grandfather, William Hill, distinguished himself during the war of 1812 for rare valor and patriotism.

He and his wife emigrated from Virginia to Ohio at an early day and settled in Ross county. They were Methodists of the heroic type. Their house was a preaching place as well as a resting place for the pioneer Methodist preachers of that period.

John Hill, the father of the subject of this sketch, was born in 1802. He was converted in childhood and became a preacher. His education was limited to the opportunities of the wilderness, but he had great natural endowments, both mental and muscular, and with all, a heart full of the love of Christ, set on fire by the Holy Spirit. He heard the call of the Master, and without hesitation or reservation, he swung his saddle bags onto his horse, leaped into the saddle, and started out through the dense forests and across the prairies as the embassador of Christ, preaching, praying and pleading with men everywhere to "be reconciled to God." His was not the artistic pulpit of modern times, set in a temple of magnificence, where the mellow notes of the stately organ mingle with the praise and prayer of comfortable communicants. It was his saddle, or a box or stump, or improvized platform, or the bare ground, from which he preached to those hardy pioneers, brave men and women who left friends, home, comfort and happiness behind, and plunged out into the picket line of the nation, there to carve order out of chaos, transform the wilderness into a garden, grapple with nature, conquer the red man with fire and powder and love, build cities, enlarge commerce, found states, and create civilization. His voice was soon heard throughout the state, and he was known for his courage, conviction and consecration.

It was during this ministry that the subject of this sketch was born, January 23, 1831, in Fayette Co., O., whither his father had moved after his marriage. Soon after this the family moved to Vanwert Co., O., and settled in the depth of a wilderness, which up to that time had been penetrated by but few white men. It was still the play ground of wild beasts and the camping ground or the battle field of painted savages. Yet it was civilization, for mother and home were there, and morning and evening a godly father would open the Book that has opened the ages, and read of deity, duty and destiny, hope, happiness and heaven, and then bow with his loved ones in prayer and commit all their interests into the hands of the sleepless Watcher.

Reared under such environment, pinched by poverty which was clean and independent, surrounded by hostile Indians and confronted with all the obstacles of an undeveloped country, there were great opportunities for physical development, but none for mental training. Nature seemed to say, "Hew down the forests, cultivate the soil, modify the climate, annihilate the beasts of prey, civilize the red man, 'prepare ye the way of the Lord,' and the church, the schoolhouse, the court of justice, the bank and the factory will follow." The admonition was heeded, and the Hill family, of which young John was no faltering spirit, went to work with a will to conquer the wilderness and make a place for their posterity. The father would lead the boys in their arduous labors during the week, and on Saturday night, start out into the darkness on his horse, following the bridle path for miles in order to reach his preaching points on Sunday. During his absence the mother would expound the Scriptures to her boys, show them the way of eternal life and plead with them to become followers of Christ. It was while the father was absent from home on his circuit, that his son John, named after him, was converted. It was a primitive conversion. He did not enter the kingdom of Christ by card, but by a change of heart. He was but a boy, but felt called to preach.

He realized his lack of education, and the more discouraging fact, that no opportunities were within his reach for acquiring an education. Besides he felt obliged to stay on the new farm with the family and contribute his part toward bringing it into a state of productiveness. But all his days were visions of one great duty, and at night it hung over him like a pillar of fire. It would not vanish. It seemed like a great hand pointing the way of usefulness, holding the promise of power and offering the key to eternal success. The untutored boy of the wilderness, who had never seen a college, nor dreamed of a theological seminary, yielded to the Divine call, and promised the Lord he would proclaim his gospel.

He immediately began to prepare for the great work. He determined that he would become skillful in the few books that he possessed, viz., the Bible, a grammar, an arithmetic and a spelling book. The very poverty of his library, became the wealth of his intellect. He wore those books thread bare. They were pulverized and ground into the tissue and blood of his being. He could spell the book through both ways. He could recite grammatical rules, declensions and conjugations, parse with ease and analyze anything. He gained the reputation of a mathematical expert, and as for the Word of God, he was triple-plated with it. It honeycombed his soul, body and spirit. It electrified his brain, clarified his vision, quickened his conscience, purified his heart, and burned along the fibres of his spiritual nature like celestial fire. His Harvard was before the old-fashioned fire place where he would work at his books under the light of the burning wood, frequently until morning would lift the curtain of night.

He began preaching before he was twenty-one, and from the very start he handled the Word with great skill. His assertions were all backed up with the "Thus saith the Lord." His was the logic of eternal verities, more axiomatic than syllogistic. His early ministry was in the polemic period of theology. Heretics were going about determined to tear down the "faith once delivered to the saints." The young preacher could not remain an idle spectator. His heart was in the fierce strife and his head must follow. He had no training in dogmatic theology, and this was a new field: but he resolved to master it, and go into strict and rigid training for the conflict at hand. He procured a large volume of Lee's Theology, a work setting forth and establishing all the great fundamentals of Christian theology, perhaps more tersely and clearly for its size than any other book then extant. Within a few weeks the young theologian had completely mastered this volume. He ate, digested and assimilated its contents from

REV. JOHN W. HILL, D. D.

beginning to end, and could, without any hesitation, at a moment's notice focalize all its logical and scriptural argument on any controverted point in theology. Thus armed for the fray he entered the arena, where he engaged in several important discussions with Campbellites, Universalists, Unitarians, Atheists and Infidels. He displayed great valor in every encounter. His logic, spontaneous wit, burning sarcasm, glowing eloquence and clear knowledge of the Scriptures never failed him; he was invincible. He seemed like one in a chariot drawn by steeds of fire over the heads of his antagonists. His fame as a debater became wide spread and he was called for from many quarters by the friends of the faith, to come and "lift up a standard against the enemies coming in like a flood." Not only was his early ministry thus marked by polemic success, but if possible, in a greater degree it was successful in arousing the public conscience on the slavery question, convincing and convicting sinners of their sins and leading them to the fountain of cleansing. Burdened for the salvation of souls and empowered from on high, he feared no danger, turned from no hardship, postponed no duty, missed no appointment, sought no comfort, took no rest, nursed no selfish ambition, and with unflagging energy, unwearying patience, unfailing love and a faith incapable of bewilderment, he gave himself to human need, sorrow, tears and sin, in order to supply the need through Christ, bring comfort for sorrow, joy for tears and pardon for sins. Before he was thirty years of age, many hundreds had been converted under his ministry.

In 1862 he was married to Miss Elizabeth Hughes, of Kalida, O.; her parents were natives of North Wales. They were strong Calvinistic Methodists, never missed morning and evening devotion, were rigid observers of the Sabbath, great lovers of the Bible, and intensely religious in all their daily walk and life. Coming from such a home, and having acquired a good education during her girlhood, she was well-fitted for the work and worry of a Methodist preacher's wife. Reared in the Calvinistic faith, she was very quiet in her religious life, having been taught that "woman should adorn herself with modesty" and not be heard in the public congregation. This training, however, was soon to be revised in the light of Methodist fire and experience. She had been in the work but a few years when she saw that it was her privilege to be free in Christ Jesus, in whom the Apostle declares "there is neither male nor female, but every man a new creature." Acting under this light, she was enabled at the Arbana campmeeting in Ohio, after a struggle lasting for several days, to cut loose from pride and early training, timidity and unbelief and make a complete and lasting consecration of herself to God. That was an epoch in her life. It was the starting point of an experience that has widened and deepened with the passing years, and from which sweet streams of influence have flowed forth to turn moral aridity into flowering garden and verdant vale.

During the twenty-five years that have interlapsed since then, naught has disbursed her soul's sweet peace, and there has been no time in which she was not ready and willing to do or suffer the will of God. Clothed with such spiritual power, she has been of inestimable help to her husband in all the departments of his work; especially in revival work is she most gifted. We have seen whole congregations visibly affected by her pathetic appeals. In prayer she sweeps the whole catalogue of practical theology; yearns, weeps, agonizes, pleads with piercing tenderness and pathetic love, grasps the promises, lifts herself up to enlarged vision of human need and possibility, and to great visions of God and the Divine resources, and with the boldness of assured faith, importunes at the door of mercy, until all her needs are supplied, "according to his riches in glory by Jesus Christ."

It is a noteworthy fact that at the same camp-meeting where his wife entered into the "valley of blessing so sweet," Dr. Hill came into an experimental knowledge of the doctrine of perfect love as taught by John Wesley and as held by the Methodist Church. That experience wrought a great change in his ministry. He was able more than before to preach Christ as a perfect Savior and to offer salvation as a gift from God. His preaching, with the advance of time, has become richer, clearer, more spiritual and consequently more effective in converting sinners and lifting the church into a higher realm of religious experience. Wherever he has gone, spiritual victories have crowned his work. His preaching never creates strife or division in the church. He has witnessed over two thousand conversions, and received as many into the church. He has resolutely steered clear of cant, censoriousness and fanaticism. He preaches holiness as moral soundness—as the habit of agreeing with God. For many years he has been one of the prominent camp-meeting preachers of Ohio. His sermons on these occasions have been baptised with pentecostal power, and not unfrequently have the vast multitudes broke into rejoicing and praised God in such a shout that the preacher was compelled to stop and wait for the spiritual storm to subside. He is a member of the Ohio State Holiness Camp-meeting Association.

He has been an extensive writer for the periodicals of the church. He is most at home in the discussion of doctrinal subjects, which he does with the style of originality, the ease of familiarity and the skill of the logician. He is now in his sixty-third year, but has never been more effective with voice or pen. He has been a close student all his life, never allowing himself to lose step with the most advanced thought, or to advance so far as to lose sight of the great columner truths of revelation. At the last commence-ment of the Taylor University of Indiana, he received the honorary degree of Doctor of Divinity.

He has traveled extensively in his own country, having crossed the continent several times and preached from ocean to ocean.

As the time approaches for him to retire from the effective ranks, he is beset with glorious visions. The past is full of rejoic-ing, a picture of fidelity, made golden by the love that transfigures drudgery into glorious privilege. The future is resplendent with the light of "many mansions," streaming through the veil of the invisible, to cheer with the hope of celestial dawning. The present is the vision of lingering opportunity to "fight the battles of the Lord" and help to usher in the millenium.

Added to the comfort of such visions, is the joy of having two sons and one son-in-law engaged with him in the fields "white for the harvest."

DR. LEVI HALL

Dr. Levi Hall was born in Delaware, O., October 26, 1833, of Episcopal parentage. He attended the public schools, and after-wards pursued a regular course in the Ohio Wesleyan University, located at Delaware, graduating and receiving the degree of Master of Arts. At ten years of age he was drawn into a Methodist re-vival, and became greatly exercised over religious questions. Although but a child he saw his need of something more than baptism, the catechism and confirmation. He had a sense of guilt and felt his need of Christ. Before the meetings closed he was converted. So great was the change that occurred in him, his parents were not able to deny him the privilege of becoming a

DR. LEVI HALL

Methodist. To the contrary, on the day that he united with the church they also handed in their names. Thus converted and brought into the church, he became very active in all the movements of the church. He had a real experience and it was a fountain of perennial enthusiasm, love, faith, hope and self-sacrifice in the cause of Christ. He was not content simply to be saved himself, but felt a longing for the salvation of his playmates. He would plead with them, pray for them, and hold on to them with the tenacity of a real spiritual leader, and many of them were thus, through his agency, brought to a saving knowledge of Christ. It was soon seen in the church that young Hall had rare gifts. It was whispered about long before he had reached his majority, that he was to be a minister. Finally, at the age of twenty, he was licensed by the church as a local preacher.

In 1854 he united with the Ohio Conference. His great ability as pastor and preacher soon brought him to the front and he occupied many of the best appointments in his Conference. Wherever he went revivals occurred, old debts were liquidated, large congregations were gathered together and the church was built up in deep piety.

Dr. David Moore, D. D., editor of the Western Christian Advocate, visited him during the Missionary Meeting that was held in Minneapolis, and in writing back to the Advocate, referred to Dr. Hall as the "popular and very successful pastor of the Ohio Conference."

In 1873 he came to Minnesota where he continued in the active pastoral work until 1881. During this period he served the following charges: Austin; Foss Church, Minneapolis; Dover and Litchfield.

During his ministerial days, he was constantly engaged in the study of medicine. He had a natural aptitude for it. He thus became well versed in medical science before he stopped preaching. So well informed was he that he frequently prescribed for his parishioners while he was in the regular pastoral work. Upon taking superannuated relations in his Conference he decided to complete his medical education as soon as possible. He attended lectures at the Hahnemann Medical College and in one year from the time he gave up the active work of the ministry, he received the degree of M. D. Since then he has practiced with great success in Minneapolis. His office is at his home, 77 Highland avenue.

He is a member of the Wesley Quarterly Conference and is one of the leaders in that church.

He is in love with the Gospel. In the pulpit, he preached it in all its fulness, and now that he is in the pew, he is satisfied with nothing less than the "Old, old story."

COLLINS HAMER

Collins Hamer was born in Lancaster Co., Pa., September 4, 1822. His parents were Solomon and Elizabeth Hamer, thoroughly set in the Methodist faith and enthusiastic in their devotion to the church. Their son Collins was given public school advantages and reared under the purest Christian influences. At the age of twenty-five he was converted and united with the Methodist Church. In 1852 he was married to Miss Mary Jane Rockey. In 1857 they came to Minneapolis. At that time Minneapolis was a village of less than 500 inhabitants. They at once united with the Methodist Church at the corner of Fourth street and Third avenue south, services being held in Woodman's Hall; J. D. Rich was the pastor. Mr. Hamer afterwards became a member of the Centenary Church. When Hennepin Avenue Church was organized he was one of the leaders in the movement; he has since then served Hennepin in various official capacities.

He is an earnest Christian and is greatly interested in the prosperity of his church. He is engaged in the real estate and rental business.

J. S. WOODARD

J. S. Woodard was born in New York in 1824. He points with pride to his staunch Methodist parentage, and doubtless this in part explains his great love and loyalty to the church. His secular education was acquired in the public schools, while in the Sunday School the seed was sown which is now bearing such fruitage in ripe, Christian character. Reared in a devoted, Christian home and brought up by pious parents under the influence of the church, it is not surprising that his life has been one of fidelity to duty, consecration to Christ and faithfulness to the church. He was converted when twenty years of age and without any delay connected himself with the church of his parents. Thus it will be seen that Brother Woodard has been a Methodist for fifty years, and we may add that this has been a period, not of shirking or complaining of the church, or of its usages, but of activity, self-sacrifice and burning ambition to build up Methodism, and through it the kingdom of the Lord Christ.

J. S. WOODARD

He has served in all official capacities in the laity of the church, but has been especially gifted and successful in Sunday School work, having been Sunday School superintendent thirty years. At the age of twenty-three, he was united in marriage with Miss Freelove Baker of Lake Co., O., whose deep piety, unusual common sense, great courage. tireless energy and beautiful Christian bearing, are like threads of gold in the fabric of their home. In 1858 they came to Minnesota and settled in Rochester. where they remained for a period of twelve years. They then removed to Coldwater, remaining five years and then to Owatonna, where they lived prosperously for five more years. In all these places they were active and influential in the Methodist Church. In 1881 they came to Minneapolis, which has since been their home.

RESIDENCE OF J. S. WOODARD

During the great activity in real estate Mr. Woodard went into that business and was able to more than hold his own with all competitors. Their home is at 2214 Bryant avenue, which was the first house built in the Sunnyside Addition.

Mr. and Mrs. Woodard have been connected with the Hennepin Avenue Church since coming to Minneapolis, but owing to the convenience of the Fowler Church to their residence, they have united with it. Mr. Woodard is one of the trustees, and has been very active in the promotion of the enterprise.

They have three children living: Dr. F. R. Woodard, their son, is one of the leading physicians in Minneapolis. Their daughter, Grace, is a pianist of rare skill and ability; she has devoted several years to the study of instrumental music and she is well and favorably known in the highest musical circles of Minneapolis. She is now engaged in teaching and has a large class of bright and promising pupils.

Upon retiring from the real estate line, Mr. Woodard returned to the drug business, to which he has devoted the best years of his life, and purchased the **Western Avenue Pharmacy.** This is, without doubt one of the best equipped, and most attractive drug stores in the city of Minneapolis. It is located at 2 and 4 Western avenue and is easily accessible from most parts of the city. Its stock of drugs and instruments is the best that can be placed upon the market; in connection with this stock, a fine assortment of school supplies is carried, also a full line of novelty goods. All prescriptions are carefully compounded by an experienced and competent druggist. This store has been but recently opened and we bespeak for Brother Woodard a goodly share of the patronage of Minneapolis Methodism.

DR. CHARLES H. NORRED

Dr. Charles H. Norred is a native of the state of Virginia, where he was born in 1841. His parents removed to Illinois while he was a small child, and his early years were spent on his father's farm in that state. After leaving college he read medicine at Springfield with Dr. R. S. Lord, and received his medical education at Pope's Medical college, St. Louis. Early in 1865 he enlisted as a private in the One Hundred and Fourteenth Illinois volunteers, and organized the first regimental hospital. He had been in the ranks but a short time when he was commissioned as assistant surgeon, from which time he served in various military hospitals, until he was ordered to the Seventh Illinois cavalry, and placed in charge of the medical department of the regiment, where he was on duty until the close of the war. The doctor afterwards graduated at Jefferson Medical College of Philadelphia, and also at the School of Anatomy and Surgery of Pennsylvania. Dr. Norred came to Minneapolis from Illinois about four years ago. He had practiced medicine in that state some twenty-five years, and

DR. CHARLES H. NORRED

his efficiency as a physician and surgeon is evidenced by the highest indorsement from many of the most eminent citizens of that state, who have known the doctor for many years, including men of high rank in the United States army.

Dr. Norred was United States Examining Surgeon, under President Harrison. During this incumbency, his broad sympathies, generous attitude toward the old soldiers and faithfulness to the duties of his office, placed him in high repute with the administration, as well as with every soldier in his district. He is at present Examining Surgeon for and Consulting Surgeon to the Minnesota State Soldiers' Home. As a physician he is fully abreast with the times. He is imbued with the unction of his profession, and places it above mercenary motives. In his practice he never stops to inquire into the financial ability of those who call him. His only question is "Can I render help?" Himself and wife are members of the Fowler Church.

CHARLES CARROL CURTISS

In the spring of 1874 Minneapolis was a different community than to-day. The entire county of Hennepin contained about forty-eight thousand inhabitants. Compared to the Minneapolis of this time the city then presented the appearance of a crude and unfinished but ambitious village. All of our great industries were in the period of infancy. The city's jobbing trade was small and insignificant. The East Division, formerly known as the city of St. Anthony, had only a year or two before laid down its corporate existence to become a part of the city proper. The old suspension bridge, constructed in 1852, was still the only means of inter-communication between the two divisions. Pence Opera House was the largest audience room and the only place of popular amusement in the city. None of the large and beautiful church buildings which now adorn our streets and avenues were then built. Nearly all of the commercial and financial transactions of the city were done within walls of inferior brick or rude and primitive wooden structures. No street in the city had been paved, and foot passengers were compelled to be content with sidewalks of pine lumber, while dim and distant gas lamps pointed the local burglar to his prey. The Street Railway System existed only within the vivid imagination of Col. W. S. King, and the reportorial tramp: from Bridge Square to the court house was a Sabbath day's journey. Altogether we were a wild and woolly western village with large ambitions and a city charter.

Several unsuccessful attempts had been made to found commercial colleges and business schools in Minneapolis prior to 1874; but the effort had usually proved abortive. In 1873 the Barnard School of Business was located in what was then known as Harrison's Hall, which occupied the third story of the large stone building still standing on the southeast corner of Washington and Nicollet avenues. The Barnard School was drifting slowly toward an early death, when, in the summer of 1873, Charles Carrol Curtiss arrived, filled with visions of the future commercial and financial prominence of the city.

The hour had arrived: Mr. Curtiss was to prove that he was a man for the hour. He first entered the Barnard School as principal. A few months later, in 1874, he bought Mr. Barnard's interest and laid the foundations of the present commercial college.

Five years later, or in 1879, he established the twin school in St. Paul, and has since filled the want felt by the Twin Cities for high and judicious commercial and financial training.

Fitted by nature and training for work of this character, Prof. Curtiss' institution has since kept pace with the industrial, financial and commercial development of the two cities. Wherever, throughout the northwest, business training is sought after, the Curtiss Commercial College is, and has been for two decades, a household word.

Prof. Curtiss took his first professional steps in the public schools of central New York, finishing as a pupil of Hamilton Academy. In 1855, at the age of eighteen years, he adopted teaching as his life profession. This resolution once formed, he entered the Normal School, supporting himself by teaching until he was graduated in 1859. His first employment as a teacher was in the country school of his neighborhood. Later he was assistant principal of the House of Refuge, in New York City, an institution similar to our State Reform School at Red Wing. In 1860 we find him principal of the public schools at Tarrytown, N. Y., which position he resigned in 1863 to become the principal of a high school at Sing Sing. Later he resigned this position and became accountant of the International Insurance Company, of New York City, and in this last position he was discovered by the celebrated

CHARLES CARROL CURTISS

commercial college firm of Bryant & Stratton, who employed him as principal of their school at Poughkeepsie. From Poughkeepsie he was transferred as superintendent of a similar institution in Brooklyn, N. Y. From Brooklyn he went to Oswego and was engaged for a time to superintend the Department of Accounts in the State Normal Schools of that city. In 1868 he came to Minnesota and first cast his fortunes with the city of Rochester, Olmstead Co., where he was appointed superintendent of the the city schools. He resigned this position to accept the Department of Accounts in the Winona State Normal School, a position which he held for four years, while for one year he was in the service of the state, having supervision of the Department of Accounts in the three State Normal Schools of Winona, Mankato and St. Cloud. This employment he left for the purpose of establishing the Curtiss Commercial College in Minneapolis and St. Paul.

There is probably no branch of human knowledge where quacks and pretenders may so easily wax and grow fat as in the establishment of so-called commercial colleges. Professions of law, divinity, and medicine, have each thrown around their guild the protection of the law, or are guarded by social habits of fixed customs. The quack in medicine, the petifogger in law, an imbecile in the pulpit, are all readily recognized; whereas, it may take years to tear the mask from the reputation and character of a scoundrel who seeks to rob the people of their money, under the pretense of instructing young men and women in the established rules of business. The pretender will always be exposed, but too often, not until his false and ignorant methods have done incalculable harm to the untrained and unsuspecting young people who have been deceived into trusting him.

The first few months of the existence of the Curtiss Commercial College demonstrated that it was to be a fixed institution of the cities. The professor had become known to the educators of the entire state as an able and conscientious trainer of youth; his work received the cordial stamp of approval of the State Superintendent of Public Instruction, from the president and professors of the University of Minnesota: of the principals and teachers of all the State Normal Schools whose fellow-worker he has been. From

one of the best known colleges in central New York he had, un-
solicited, received the degree of Master of Arts. In short, from
the day he arrived in Minneapolis, his school was recognized by
every trained educational intelligence, as a legitimate institution of
technical training. Twenty years of active usefulness has only
confirmed this reputation.

The Curtiss Commercial College does something more than
teach the established and technical rules which are supposed to
govern and direct men and women in the active pursuit of gain.
Especial importance is given, in the institution, to the ethics of
trade, commerce and business generally. Systematic, methodical
rules are popularly supposed to be essentially truthful. So well
understood is this proposition that it has grown into a universal
proverb that "figures" cannot lie. The proverb is wrong. Figures
not only can lie but they are perpetually made the medium through
which the scoundrels of the world perpetrate every variety of ras-
cality. No man knows so well as the trained statistician how simple
it is to make arithmetical signs express half truths which deceive
with more facility than absolute prevarication.

It is the conscience of honest men and women that will not lie.
When entire rectitude sits behind the figures then there is no chance
for mendacity or deception.

REV. EDWARD L. WATSON

Rev. Edward L. Watson, pastor of Hennepin Avenue Church,
Minneapolis, was born in Baltimore, Md., February 6, 1861, of
other than Methodist parentage. When about fifteen years of age
he attended Methodist revival services and was converted. His
education was received in the public schools of his native city, and
in the John Hopkins University. Afterwards he pursued post-
graduate studies in Shemitic, Philosophy, History and Sociology.
In 1881 he entered the Baltimore Annual Conference of the M.
E. Church, the Rev. Bishop Matthew Simpson presiding. He has
served charges as follows: Hancock, 1881-1882: Montgomery,
1882-1884: Patapsco, 1884-1885. In 1885 he was associated with

the Rev. John F. Goucher, D. D., in the pastorate of the First M.
E. Church, having special charge of the Royer Hill Church. After
a pastorate of six years he saw the erection of the present Twenty-
fourth Street Church in Baltimore. Lutherville, Md., was his
next appointment, where he remained for three years, 1891-1894.
During this pastorate, for a time, he taught in the Woman's Col-

REV. EDWARD L. WATSON

lege. February 6, 1894, he was united in marriage to Miss Edith
C. Hann, of Baltimore. At the session of the Baltimore Conference,
March, 1894, he was sent to Frederick, Md., from which place,
after a pastorate of seven months, he was transferred by Bishops
Foss and Fowler, to his present charge.

COOPER W. LANDIS

Cooper W. Landis was born in 1866, near Paris, Tenn. His parents were members of the Disciple Church. His father stood at the head of the medical profession in that state, having occupied the chair of demonstrative anatomy in the Memphis Medical College. He began the study of medicine when but a boy, and its practice when he was nineteen years of age, continuing in it for thirty years. The subject of this sketch was left alone in life at a very early age. His mother died when he was a child, and his father, when he was but twelve years of age.

COOPER W. LANDIS

But coming from such ancestry he could scarcely do otherwise than get on in the world. He was all ambition. It was not that type of ambition, however, blind to the necessity of thorough equipment for the work of life. After his father had died, Mr. Landis would devote hours to looking over his books and reading the papers which he had prepared for his college classes and medical societies.

While engaged in this pastime there came to him the conviction that his life must be a blank unless brightened by the educational acquirements that had given his father such poise in his profession. He began at once the struggle for mental and moral mastery. Perhaps it was the vow then taken that has kept him from the many vices that have precipitated the downfall of multitudes of young men. He attended the public schools until his resources were exhausted and he found it impossible to continue by his own unaided efforts. About this time he heard of a Shaker settlement in Kentucky where boys were taken and educated for the work they would do upon the farm. This was just such an opportunity as he craved, and his name was soon enrolled on the record of the members of the Society of Shakers. He remained here for a year, diligently pursuing his studies, and faithfully performing the work to which he was assigned. Upon leaving the settlement, he entered the Murray Institute at Murray, Ky., and without friends or money, worked his way through it.

We next find him in Kansas, engaged in journalism. His work in this department soon attracted the attention of some of the prominent men of the state, and drew about him many admirers and friends. He not only gained for himself the reputation of industry and frugality, but he became known as a young man of unswerving integrity. It was doubtless this reputation that lifted him into a prominent position in the Meade County National Bank, in which he remained for three years. He then went to Davenport and completed the regular course of the Iowa Commercial College. He was met at graduation with an urgent invitation to accept a position with the American Mortgage Trust Company, which he did. He afterwards became identified with the Citizens' Investment Company, of Kansas City.

In 1890 he removed to Ogden, Utah, where he entered the fire insurance and loan business for himself. It was while he was at Ogden that he was converted, during a series of revival services which were being held in the First Methodist Episcopal Church. He soon became very influential in the church. His faithfulness to the church and everything involved in consistent Christian character attracted the attention of more than religious people, and he became known throughout the city as a godly young man. In the meantime his business was growing beyond all expectation, and soon became the strongest in its line in Ogden. In 1893 he was sought by Governor J. E. Rickards, of Helena, Mont., to take charge of his important real estate and insurance business. This position Mr. Landis accepted and occupied with great acceptancy for nearly a year. He then returned to Utah and resumed his former business. He has recently accepted a position with the Corser-Belknap Fire Insurance Agency, of Minneapolis. Their office is at No. 211 New York Life Building. As this is perhaps the largest company of the kind in the Northwest, it gives Mr. Landis a large field for the exercise of his rare ability in the insurance line. The Corser-Belknap Agency represents the leading insurance companies of the United States and the world, and has gained a reputation that requires no special comment or commendation. Mr. Landis and wife are members of the Fowler Church. We bespeak for him the success which he deserves in his new business field.

THOMAS TAYLOR DRILL

Thomas Taylor Drill was born in Birmingham, England, and comes of a musical family. He first commenced singing as a boy in the great choirs of New York City, viz: Old Trinity Church, and St. John's Chapel, where he was leading soprano boy several years, After his voice changed and he became a basso, he commenced singing in the choir of St. John's Chapel, Trinity Parish, New York., which was in the latter part of the year 1871. After this he became a member of the St. Ann Protestant Episcopal choir, Brooklyn, where he remained until the 1st of May, 1880, resigning to accept the position of second solo bass in the choir of Grace P. E. Church, Brooklyn Heights. In addition to this, he received the position of solo bass in St. Luke's Church, Brooklyn. The organist and choir director of St. Luke's, was Prof. A. H. Mersiter, who was also organist and director of old Trinity Church, New York. Mr. Drill sang his first solo as a basso in St. Luke's, December 12, 1880, it being, "Look Down on Us," from Mendelssohn's Elijah. While there he also sang, for the first time, the bass part in Haydn's Creation.

He resigned his position in St. Luke's, March 26, 1881 to accept a position in St. John's Chapel, Trinity Parish, New York, then and now, under the directorship of George F. LeJeune, one of the most famous hymn writers in the world. On October 1, 1881, Mr. LeJeune, who also had charge of the Church of the Transfiguration, better known as the "Little Church Around the Corner," having become thoroughly satisfied with Mr. Drill's work, gave him the more important position of solo bass in this time-honored church. Mr. Drill resigned this position December 1, 1882, to become solo bass in the choir of the Church of the Redeemer, Brooklyn, where he sang nearly a year, when he was recalled to the choir of Grace P. E. Church, on Brooklyn Heights, from which he resigned in March, 1884, and after competition with several well known and good baritone and bass singers, he was engaged as solo bass in the University Place Presbyterian Church. The committee of this church, which engaged Mr. Drill, consisted

THOMAS TAYLOR DRILL

of two famous publishers, viz: Mr. Moses W. Dodd, of the firm of Dodd, Meade & Co., and George R. Lockwood, of the firm of George R. Lockwood & Co. May 1, 1885, Mr. Drill accepted an engagement in Christ's P. E. Church, Brooklyn, in which church, he was subsequently married. The tenor in this choir was the celebrated tenor and vocal teacher, Mr. William Courtney.

In the early part of 1885, Mr. Drill was elected a member of the Apollo Club of Brooklyn, which was under the leading writer of church music—Dudley Buck. May 1, 1888, Mr. Drill accepted his first engagement with the Methodist Episcopal Church, which was the St. Pauls Church, of New York City. During the season of 1887 and 1888, he sang with George F. LeJeune in his St. John's Chapel choir, at the grand choral services, which he gave every Sunday afternoon in the Church of the Holy Spirit. Among the works rendered were Rebecca, Stabat Mater, (Rossini); Holy, City, (Gaul); Ruth (Gaul); Elijah, (Mendelssohn); Abraham (Molique); Moses in Egypt, (Rossini); Creation and Seasons, (Haydn); Athalie (Mendelssohn).

Mr. Drill has had the finest possible advantages in the development of his voice. He began to study with Ivan Morawski, and continued with him for one year and a half, and then placed himself in the hands of Mr. William Courtney, who stands without a peer, as a teacher of oratorio and artistic singing with whom he studied for about three years, during which time he made a specialty of the study of Oratorio Music.

During the visit to this country of the great baritone, M. Jaques Bouhy, (the original "Toreador" in Bizets's opera "Carmen") Mr. Drill had the advantage of a thorough course of voice culture and dramatic singing, as he studied with him steadily, taking never less than three lessons every week. Mr. Drill was well and favorably known in New York City and vicinity, as a glance at his scrapbook will show, and received many fine engagements there. He was chosen by the great composer, Dudley Buck, to create the very important and trying role of "Christopher Columbus" in his dramatic cantata, of that name, and after the performance, which took place at the Academy of Music in Brooklyn on December 7, 1886, Mr Drill was highly complimented by Mr. Buck on his artistic work. He was again engaged by Dudley Buck to repeat his performance at the "Festival of American Music" given in Chickering Hall, New York City, during the week commencing November 16, 1887, under the direction of Frank Von Der Stucken. Upon Mr. Buck's learning of Mr. Drill's intention of leaving New York and removing to Minneapolis he wrote him a letter from which we quote the following: "I learn that you have finally decided to go West. You will be a musical loss to us, but a gain wherever you may locate. You will doubtless soon find your musical affinities and make the mark your voice well deserves."

The newspapers of New York, Brooklyn and vicinity speak in the highest terms of Mr. Drill's ability as an artistic vocalist. His voice is a basso cantante of large range and power; sympathetic and dramatic. He makes a specialty of enunciation and pronunciation, as those who have heard him can testify. His work as a vocalist and teacher in Minneapolis, where he has been very successful, is well known.

He has won for himself the high esteem of the public and made an enviable name. On great occasions, when the best ability is in demand, he is invariably called upon for service. He conducted the Harvest Festival Chorus a few years since at the Grand Opera House, and also had charge of the male chorus of the Republican National Convention in 1892. He is at present, and has been since his arrival in Minneapolis, the solo basso and director of the music in the Hennepin Avenue Church, and his choral services in that church have been thoroughly enjoyable. Since taking charge of this choir, he has made a specialty of choral services. He has produced at different times the Creation by Haydn; the Stabat Mater, by Rossini; the Daughter of Jairus, by Stainer; Ruth, by Gaul, and The Passion, by Haydn; the last three of which being thus produced for the first time in the Northwest. Mr. Drill also organized and put the boys' choir into the St. Paul's Episcopal Courch on Hennepin avenue. As a teacher he takes first rank. He has given to Minneapolis and the public some of the brightest talent.

Mr. Renssalaer Wheeler, who is singing with great success in Great Britain, Miss Maude C. Kelley, Mrs. W. S. Thomson and Mr. George N. Tate, of the Hennepin Avenue choir and Miss Grace FitzGerald, daughter of Bishop FitzGerald, all owe their musical popularity to the faithful tutorage of Mr. Drill. As a man he is broad in his views, liberal in his feelings, energetic in his work, faithful to every duty and intensely enthusiastic in his sphere.

He is known better than any other vocalist west of Chicago, and being but a young man, his many admirers anticipate for him a career of unusual success and renown.

BENJAMIN FRANKLIN NELSON

A generation has passed since the close of the' war of the Rebellion. The survivors of its contests in arms, have crossed the meridian of life. Their animosities have softened, their judgments matured, and their love for a common union, strengthened, or if once alienated, has been restored. Those who once wore the blue fraternize with those who donned the gray, and the acrimonies which were once bitter between them, have melted into a common respect. Minneapolis entered into the struggle with enthusiasm, and sent her choicest citizens to the front. But she has always been kind and tolerant to those who were on the other side. Her cosmopolitan population cherish neither bigotry nor proscription. Thus, she made a celebrated confederate general her city engineer, and elected one who bore arms against her in Virginia to her chief magistracy. With similar courtesy and forbearance she received Mr. Nelson, after the war was over, and has entrusted to him her dearest interests, and placed upon him her chief honors. And no one, born within her own limits, and following her tattered flags, could more loyally and honorably bear them than he.

Benjamin F. Nelson was born in Lewis Co., Ky., on the 4th of May, 1843. His parents were natives of Somerset Co., Maryland. His father was in infirm health, and the support of the family devolved upon the sons. · The necessities of earning a living turned his early efforts into industrial lines, and left but fragmentary times for attendance at school. At seventeen years of age he engaged with a partner in the lumber business, which at first promising success, was after two years broken up by the war. An attempt at farming shared the same fate. It will be remembered that the state of Kentucky was debatable ground in the early part of the war. She was a slave holding state, and most of her citizens sympathized with the confederacy; but the state was held by the strong arm of the federal power from actual secession. Hence such of her people as chose to join the rebellion, had not the excuse of loyalty to the state. Nevertheless a large part of them chose to join the south in arms. Among such was young Nelson, who at nineteen, with a firm conviction of doing right, and animated with the contagious spirit of his section, enlisted in 1862 in Company C. of the second Kentucky battalion, and went immediately into active service, under the command of General Kirby Smith.

During the next two years his campaigning was active and laborious, extending into Virginia, Alabama, Tennessee and Georgia. He served successively under Humphrey, Marshall, Wheeler, Forrest and John Morgan, and participated in the battles of Chicamaugua, McMinnville, Shelbyville, Lookout Mountain, Sterling and Greenville. The marchings were rapid and exhausting, the raids spirited and the fighting severe; but he escaped all the perils of the march, the field and the camp. In 1864 he was detached upon recruiting duty in Kentucky, and venturing within the federal lines, as far as the Ohio river, he had secured a few recruits, and returning was captured and sent to Lexington and placed in close confinement. There two of his unfortunate recruits were executed, and it was for a time uncertain but that he might be treated as a spy. He was, however, held as a prisoner of war, and sent to Camp Douglas, in Chicago, where he was detained in custody until 1865, when he was sent to Richmond; and at the close of the war, in accordance with the liberal terms accorded by General Grant, upon Lee's surrender, he was paroled.

After the war he returned to Lewis Co., Ky., where he remained through the summer working in a saw mill until the latter part of August, when he decided to try his fortune in the far west. The south, with its sleepy manners and customs was too slow for the man of ambition and enterprise that young Benjamin now was, and on the 3rd day of September, 1865, he set foot in the then little town of St. Paul, Minn. Only one day did he remain there, but came on to the Falls of St. Anthony to look for work in the mills, if possible. While walking about the village of St. Anthony that day he wandered down near where the university now stands and lay down on the grass. In this position he studied the Falls of St. Anthony, which were before him, and estimated their power, which was then going to waste. He fully made up his mind that he was lying on the site of a city that would some day be a great one, because of the power in the falls. He estimated the power at 100,000 horse power, and it has since been proved that the estimate was right.

BENJAMIN FRANKLIN NELSON

Fully resolved to make St. Anthony his home, Mr. Nelson went to work rafting lumber, to be sent down the river, as there were then no railroads into the city. When the season was over he took up a claim near Waverly, built a house, and staid a few nights, but again decided that he did not care about farming. That winter he chopped wood at Watertown, Minn., and when the spring opened up he came back to Minneapolis and went to work in the saw mills. The next winter he contracted to haul logs at Lake Winsted. This venture was not a success, and so in the spring he began to work in a shingle mill, where he remained two years. He then took the contract for making the shingles by the 1,000, and continued it for seven years. The mill was owned by Martin & Brown at first and the firm was then changed to Butler & Mills. In this venture Mr. Nelson saved some money, and in 1872 he formed a partnership with Warren C. Stetson.

This firm started a planing mill, and as the business grew, the St. Louis mill was built. The partnership was dissolved a few years later, Mr. Stetson taking the old mill, called the Pacific, and Mr. Nelson retaining the St. Louis mill. Through the planing work he entered the lumber business, taking lumber as pay for planing. The trade increased until the year 1881, when Mr. Nelson took into business with him W. M. Tenney and H. W. McNair, under the firm name of Nelson, Tenney & Co. This firm continued, H. B. Fry entering a few years later, and Mr. McNair retiring. W. F. Brooks afterwards was added to the firm, which in 1882 bought the old Fred Clarke saw mill, and began the manufacturing of lumber on a small scale. Only a few millions of feet were made at first, but the business grew with the city, until last year 50,000,000 feet of lumber were manufactured by the firm.

The plant contains two large mills and a smaller one, together capable of cutting 100,000,000 feet if necessary. Thus it is seen how a man of ambition and energy, as B. F. Nelson, was able to work upward, starting without a dollar, until now he is at the head of one of the largest lumber manufacturing enterprises in the Northwest.

Mr. Nelson is also interested in the Nelson Paper Company, being founder and president, as well as president of the Hennepin Paper Company, at Little Falls, Minn.

While giving his attention primarily to his large business affairs, Mr. Nelson has been called to perform important civic duties. In 1879 he was elected alderman of the first ward of the city of Minneapolis, and served as a member of the City Council until 1885. He was elected a member of the Park Board soon after the organization of that important branch of the municipal government in 1883, and was an active participant in adopting the park system which has added so much to the beauty of the city. He also served as a member of the Board of Education for seven consecutive years, from 1884 to 1891, a service of little eclat before the public, but one of the most useful and responsible in the city government.

Mr. Nelson has been twice married, first in 1860 to Martha Ross who died five years later, leaving two sons, William E. and Guy H. His present wife was Mary Fredingburg, who bore him one daughter, Bessie E.

His religious connection is with the Methodist Episcopal Church, of which he is an active member, administering one of its most important educational trusts, as trustee of Hamline University. He is an official member of the First Church.

His social and charitable inclinations have found abundant occupation in Masonic affiliation, in which mystic order he has received the highest degree.

In politics he is a democrat, not of the demostrative sort, but quietly and firmly holding the political doctrines of Thomas Jefferson. These led him in youth to take up arms in defence of state rights, and throughout all his years of active life he has steadfastly adhered to the idea of a simple, honest, democratic government.

Take him all in all, Mr. Nelson is a unique man. His counterpart is rarely found. Accepting the lot of common labor, his integrity, industry and sagacity have raised him to the front rank of business men and made his career a conspicuous success. Coming to an unsympathizing community without prestige or friends, he has been here entrusted with the most responsible public functions. In a city whose dominant majority do not espouse his political views, he occupies a position of influence and dignity. Simple in demeanor, unostentatious in manner of life, quiet, thoughtful, almost sombre in aspect, he has attached friends of whom the most gifted might be proud. He is spare, erect, sedate. Not yet in his climacteric, there is yet unattained success before him.

A. B. RUGG

A. B. Rugg, the popular photographer of this city, was born in South Lancaster, Mass., September 11, 1853. When he was 10 years of age his parents moved to Fitchbury, Mass., where he received a common school education. In 1870, when 17 years old he apprenticed himself to Mr. J. C. Moulten, of Fitchburg, the most prominent photographer of that place, and one of the leading photographers of Worcester Co. Three weeks had hardly elapsed after his entrance into the studio, when circumstances happened that tested his resources and ingenuity to quite an extent. Mr. Moulton was taken suddenly ill, and at that time the only other employe was a young lady clerk who did the finishing. Thus suddenly dropped upon the shoulders of young Rugg, the responsibility of a photographic studio in full blast. Plates and chemicals were not furnished ready to hand in those days, and you can imagine it was something of a task for a young man of 17 years, who had hardly learned to develop plates properly, to try and take the place of a man who had made the first daguerrotypes in that section, and who was familiar with photography from A to Z. But Rugg had come to learn the business and this was his opportunity; by taking proofs and negatives to Mr. Moulton's sick chamber every night, and getting criticisms and instructions, the business went on as usual during the three weeks that the proprietor was ill. Thus Mr. Rugg demonstrated his ability to save a business man even before he had acquired any experience or knowledge of the profession.

In 1873 he went into business for himself in a small inland town, but not proving very successful he sold out and went to Boston where he served as operator for two years, at the end of which time he was induced to go to Florida for the purpose of becoming an orange grower; but this proved an entire failure and he lost everything, and he was obliged to work his way to New Orleans where he got a situation at the old business with W. W. Washburn, in one of the leading galleries of that city. Owing to malarial troubles he was obliged to come north, and came up the Mississippi river to LaCrosse, Wis., where he was operator in the leading studio for a year and a half. In 1879 he came to Minneapolis and in the fall of that year purchased the studio of Wm. Brown, then situated in the old Merchant's Block, corner of First avenue south and Washington. When this block was torn down

A. B. RUGG

Mr. Rugg fitted up an elegant studio in the Dolly Varden Block on Nicollet avenue; later, as business moved up the avenue, he fitted up the first ground floor studio of any size at 56 Fifth street south. where he soon became one of the leading photographers of the city. This studio was lately removed to make room for the large Olson Block, and Mr. Rugg can now be found at his elegant ground floor establishment at 116 Sixth street south, where anyone wishing to avail themselves of his large and varied experience will find it to their advantage to do so.

Mr. Rugg's experience in photographing people of all nationalities, coupled with his skill as an artist, will insure satisfaction to all his patrons, and his large studio at 116 Sixth street south, fitted expressly for the art, should be seen to be appreciated.

SAN ANGELO HOTEL

This house ranks among the very best family hotels in Minneapolis. It has been under its present management for seven years and has steadily increased in popularity. It is under complete hotel equipment, is modern in all its conveniences and appliances, and in its service and appointments meets the demands of the most fastidious. It has seventy-five large, well lighted, clean, comfortable and well arranged rooms. The rooms are all exposed to the sunlight and are not only convenient within, but afford an excellent outlook. It is located near the corner of Thirteenth street and Nicollet avenue and owing to its central location is easily accessible from all parts of the city. M. C. Shomburg, the popular proprietor, has had years of experience in the hotel business and seems to have an instinctive, as well as acquired ability to meet all the requirements necessary to the most successful prosecution of the business. He is genial and wide-awake. He takes special delight in accommodating his guests and meeting their every want.

Without great advertisement of effort beyond that involved in maintaining a first-class house, the San Angelo has become favorably known among the best boarding families of the city, and has drawn to itself a large number of patrons of this class.

M. E. WALLACE

M. E. Wallace stands at the head of the leading millinery house in Minneapolis and the Northwest. His successful business operated at 515 and 517 Nicollet avenue is the creation of his rare tact, unsullied integrity, public spirit and phenomenal business genius. He began on Nicollet avenue about six years ago, at that time just struggling into commercial life. The attractive view appearing with this sketch shows at least in some degree, the result of his arduous efforts. Mr. Wallace has won the reputation of being an honest man. He has not only made it a rule to sell for the smallest possible profit, but also to handle first class goods, and correct styles. This, with the qualities above referred to, explains

INTERIOR VIEW OF STORE

why, in the face of hard times, his business has outgrown the double store at 403 and 405 Nicollet avenue. The new store in the Syndicate block has been fitted up regardless of expense, in elegant, artistic fixtures; the parlors and French pattern rooms are a perfect palace, fitted in beautiful designs of cherry cases, mirrors and imported carpets. The ladies highly appreciate these beautiful select pattern rooms where they can take their time and comfort in selecting from the choicest imported millinery in the market. It is the pride of Minneapolis that such a magnificent house has a place in her commercial circle. Perhaps no house in the country displays more exclusive designs in imported novelties and patterns. It also has a large assortment of medium priced goods. The large and elegant rooms are always filled with an appreciative and patronizing people, which, within itself is a sufficient and most substantial recognition.

THE JOURNAL

The making of a great daily newspaper involves the expenditure of a great deal of effort and a great deal of money. The Journal, as it stands to-day, is the project of years of hard and careful work, and has cost large sums of money. That the effort and the money have been wisely expended, however, is demonstrated by the success which the paper has attained. With a daily circulation of 40,000 copies, it stands far in the lead of any of its contemporaries in the Northwest, and by reason of the extent of its circulation and the quality of its reading constituency it enjoys the finest advertising patronage accorded to any paper in Minnesota.

Probably no paper published anywhere in this country covers its own field as thoroughly as does The Journal. The territory in which it circulates, including Minneapolis, comprises Minnesota, the northwestern half of Wisconsin, northern part of Iowa, a large section of Northern Nebraska, South Dakota, North Dakota, Manitoba, Northern Idaho, Montana and westward to the coast.

For the printing of a paper of this character the best mechanical devices are required. The Journal is up to the times. It is set on the Mergenthaler Linotype, or typesetting machines. Eleven of these marvels of mechanical ingenuity are required to set the type for The Journal. Each machine has a keyboard not unlike that of a typewriter. At the top of the machine, spreading out somewhat like a fan, is a large magazine, divided lengthwise into compartments which contain small, flat pieces of brass. These pieces of brass are each stamped upon the edge by a die with a letter of the alphabet, or some other character used, in printing.

The operator playing upon the keyboard, by mechanical action, releases one at a time these small pieces of brass, or matrices, and they fall by gravity into their proper position in line. Spaces to fill between the words are brought down from a separate magazine in the same way as the matrices, and when a line has been set and adjusted, that is to say, made of the exact length required by the the adjustment of spaces, it is taken automatically to a casting box, where a stream of hot metal is injected into the face of the matrices and an impression taken of whatever words they contain. The casting is in the form of a line of type all in one piece. When the line is cast the matrices are automatically lifted from the casting box, carried to a distributor, which is a revolving screw, and each one is deposited in its proper compartment, the selection being made by the machine in accordance with a system of nicks, much upon the principle of the conbination of notches on the edge of a Yale lock key. These machines are ordinarily operated at a speed of about 4,500 ems an hour. This is equivalent to the work of at least four printers setting movable type by hand.

Not only has The Journal recently equipped itself with the Mergenthaler typesetting machines, but it has substituted for three presses, of a capacity of 12,000 an hour each, two new presses, each having a capacity of 30,000 8-page Journals, or 15,000 of a large size, an hour. Each of these presses prints from three continuous rolls of paper, each roll weighing 600 pounds. It cuts, pastes, folds and delivers the papers counted in bundles. It will print 6, 7 or 8 columns to a page, and will print as many as 24 pages inserted in regular book form order, the first and 24th pages being on the same sheet. And they are the only presses that will do this. These presses are also built to print in colors, and will print, as desired, one, two or three different colors while the paper passes through the press once. Two of these presses are in operation, and a third has been ordered. The builders are the Seymour-Brewer Printing Press Company, of Chicago, Ill. These presses may be seen in operation by the public every afternoon from 4 p. m. to 6 p. m., an elevated platform being erected in the press room, where visitors may watch the working of these wonderful machines without annoyance to the pressmen.

But the rapid printing of news is no more essential then the free delivery of the papers after they are printed. The Journal has in the city of Minneapolis over 100 regular carriers.

Between 400 and 500 newsboys sell The Journal on the streets of Minneapolis every evening. The Journal is comfortably established in its own building, erected five years ago, and arranged with especial reference to its requirements and convenience. It views with satisfaction the progress that it has made thus far under its present management, and, from the vantage ground of the highest point in its success and prosperity, it looks to a more prosperous future and to greater achievements than it has ever attained.

JASPER W. EARL

Jasper W. Earl is a native of Carthage, Hancock Co., Ill., and was born in the year 1849.

His parents were Harry and Eunice Howd Earl, who were natives of Camden, Oneida Co., N. Y. The father, through many years of his life, followed the occupation of farming. For some time he followed this business in the state of Illinois, and in 1856 migrated to Minnesota, settling near Mankato. He died February 19, 1894. His father was John Earl, a native of Germany, who, on coming to America, settled in New York State, where he followed the business of farming. He reared a family of nine children. The mother of the subject of our sketch was the daughter of Joel Howd, a native of one of the eastern states, and by occupation a farmer.

His parents, who were patriotic Americans, reared a family of six children, four of whom are now living—Sarah, now Mrs. Denison; Cecelia, now Mrs. Hanson; Theresa, now Mrs. Kneutson, and Jasper W. The father was formerly a republican in politics, but in later years joined the prohibition party. He was a member of the Methodist Episcopal church. The mother died August 12, 1887.

The subject of this sketch was reared on the farm, remaining under the parental roof until he was 19 years of age. He received a good common school education, and also took a course in the Bryant & Stratton business college, of Chicago, Ill. After completing his course in this institution he was engaged as book-keeper for Lloyd & Hunter for two years. At the end of this time he went to Montana Territory, where he engaged in book-keeping for three years, and during this time was in the employ of Dahler, Armstrong & Co. He was also the first republican elected to office in Beaverhead Co., Montana Territory; that of county clerk and recorder.

In 1875 Mr. Earl was married to Miss Ophelia Stowell, of Faribault, daughter of Paschal and Minerva Joslyn Stowell.

In February, 1876, he came to Fergus Falls, Otter Tail Co., Minn., where he engaged in the insurance, loan and real estate business, in which he met with rare success. The popularity of Mr. Earl as a citizen is evinced by the fact that while at Fergus Falls he filled the office of city clerk and alderman, and was twice elected mayor, each time on the prohibition ticket.

In 1889 Mr. Earl moved to Duluth, where he built up a prosperous life insurance business. In 1891 he came to Minneapolis, where he has since lived, his home being at 2300 Aldrich avenue south.

Mr. Earl and his wife are faithful members of the Methodist Episcopal Church, he being a member of the Official Board of the Fowler Church.

Since coming to Minneapolis, he has been appointed to the responsible position of manager for the state of Minnesota, of the Bankers & Merchants Life Association of Illinois.

CHARLES D. STRONG

Charles D. Strong was born in Somersetshire, England, June 19, 1808; the son of John and Elizabeth Strong. His parents emigrated to America in the spring of 1819, and located in the city of Montreal, Canada, where the subject of this sketch was educated and grew to manhood. Mr. Strong served an apprenticeship with Mr. H. H. Cunningham, the largest bookbinder and stationer in Montreal, and being employed in its various departments he had thoroughly mastered the business in 1828 when he removed to Boston. In 1829 Mr. Strong established himself as a bookbinder, and a few months later he opened a bookstore for the sale of religious books principally for the use of the Methodist denomination. This was the first store of that kind in New England. He started in a modest manner but soon increased his

CHARLES D. STRONG

operations by publishing a large number of books of various descriptions. He led in the organization of the Wesleyan Association, which had for its object the establishment of a Methodist paper, to be published in the interests of New England Methodism, and he assisted in the re-establishment of Zion's Herald, in Boston, where that organ of Methodism is still published. Mr. Strong became engaged in the specialty of issuing books to be sold by subscription. He was one of the publishers of Mr. S. G. Goodrich's "Peter Parley"; the former well-known American author. Mr. Strong, was a brilliant writer, and has done very efficient work with his pen for Methodism. In the summer of 1859 he removed to St. Paul, where he engaged in buying country produce and pork packing, being the first regular pork-packer in that city. Shortly after, he opened a retail grocery store which he conducted for two years. In 1860 Mr. Strong purchased a retail hardware store of Mr. C. L. Grant which proved very lucrative. He was the founder of the extensive hardware store of Strong, Hackett Co.

Mr. Strong has contributed extensively towards the growth of the city. He was one of the incorporators of the Chamber of Commerce, and was its vice-president for several years. Mr. Strong married Miss Frances Wyman Gill in 1828. She died September 19, 1843, leaving him nine children. His second marriage was to Mrs. Abigail S. FitzGibbon. He united with the Methodist Episcopal Church while a boy, and was always actively engaged in her cause. He was one of the strongest members of the Central Park Church of St. Paul and was for years president of its board of trustees, and was one of the most honored members until his death. No one knows the extent of Mr. Strong's private charities. His strong and generous heart was always ready to help the poor. His kindly nature and his uniform, generous and sympathetic conduct added to the purity of his private life, and his honorable record as a citizen and a Christian, have endeared him to all who knew him, and his memory will be long and gratefully cherished by posterity. He died in 1890.

MRS. ABIGAIL SPURR STRONG

Mrs. Abigail Spurr Strong, one of the foremost women in all reformatory and charitable work, was born at Annapolis, N. S., August 23, 1811; daughter of Robert and Sarah Harris Jefferson, who were leading Methodists. Their home was always open to ministers of the Gospel and to the poor and friendless. Mrs.

Strong inherited the good qualities of her parents; she was converted and united with the Methodist Church in 1831. She was united in matrimony August 24, 1835, to John J. FitzGibbon who was educated for the Episcopal ministry of the Church of England, and was a graduate of Trinity College, Dublin. She moved to

MRS. ABIGAIL SPURR STRONG

Boston, Mass., with her husband, where he began to prepare for missionary work and she identified herself prominently with the various organizations of her denomination.

Her husband died September 28, 1839; on October 29, 1844, she was married to Mr. C. D. Strong, a prominent Methodist, and publisher of religious works. Mrs. Strong continued in religious and charitable work in Boston until 1860 and then removed to St. Paul, Minn., where she immediately identified herself with the old Jackson Street Church, of which Rev. Dr. Chaffee was pastor. The very first Sunday she attended this church she took charge of the infant class, and shortly after began to teach the Bible class and was superintendent of the female department. One morning when Mrs. Strong returned from church she found four little boys playing marbles in the street. She was so touched by their manners and appearance that she stopped and asked them why they did not attend Sunday School. The children replied, "we would like to attend Sunday School if we knew of one." Mrs. Strong invited them to come to her home the following Saturday. In the meantime she arranged with a good lady for music, and out of this small beginning grew the Mission Sunday School which was built the following year, Grace Church, two German Methodist churches and two Swedish Reformed Lutheran churches.

In all this work Mrs. Strong was the inspiring leader, and she was not satisfied with anything short of real, genuine, vital, spiritual life and victory.

One day a drunken woman was found on the street by a lady and she at once wrote to Mrs. Strong requesting the privilege of an interview. As the result of this interview the Home for the Friendless was started; Mrs. Strong was the first secretary of the institution. It was clearly seen that there must be a reformatory department to this work and the Magdalene Home, since changed to the name of the Woman's Christian Home, was organized and placed in operation, Mrs. Strong was made president. Perhaps this was the germ of the Bethany Home; for the ladies of Minneapolis, after recognizing the good effect of the movement, requested the ladies of St. Paul to assist in organizing the Bethany Home, which is now such a successful institution; Mrs. Strong materially aided in this work. In fact she has been identified with every movement of a philanthropic nature. She has been a member of the "Daughters of Rebecca" for several years. In 1829 she became a leader in temperance reform. This work brought her into active membership in the order of Good Templars, of which she is Grand Worthy Vice Templer of Minnesota. During all these years she has been an effective worker in the Central Park Methodist Church, toward which she has contributed of her time and money without stint. She has been an important factor in the Woman's Foreign Missionary Society.

Having performed her work so faithfully during the days of her strength, she now rests peacefully in her comfortable home, the object of the solicitous love and care of her former associates and co-workers.

INTERIOR VIEW OF DYER BROS.' STORE

W. J. DYER & BROTHER

It is with pleasure we call attention to the firm whose warerooms are reproduced on this page.

For a quarter of a century they have been identified with the best development and growth of music throughout the Northwest, and particularly in this city. No individuals have done more for the development of music as an art than the Messrs. Dyer, who have built up the great business of the firm of W. J. Dyer & Bro. The name of this firm is recognized throughout the Northwest as a synonym of all that is best in the music trade. They have gathered together the productions of the best manufacturers of this continent, and probably no other music house in the country is able to offer to its patrons such an assortment of strictly first class instruments and publications as is found in the storerooms of this firm.

With large stores in both St. Paul and Minneapolis, and extensive connections both at home and abroad, the firm is in a position to meet every imaginable need in the musical line. It is, moreover, a matter of congratulation to the people of Minnesota, that a house of sufficient capital and enterprise exists in our midst, to bring to our very doors, as it were, everything in the musical line, including most magnificent specimens of the piano maker's art, Steinway, Knabe, Mehlin, Ivers & Pond, Gabler, Everett, and other instruments at prices equalling those obtainable in New York and other eastern cities. From basement to roof, their warerooms are crowded with musical instruments and merchandise, including the most complete stock of music and publications.

To those who live at a distance from the two cities, and are therefore unable to make a personal investigation, and personally negotiate for the purchase of an instrument or musical goods, the editor and compilers of this work would most heartily recommend the firm of W. J. Dyer & Bro. We can add every assurance that any confidence reposed in them will not be misplaced, and we bear personal testimony to the integrity and upright dealing of this firm.

The American Progressive Investment Co.

of this state is an institution doing a national business covering a number of the most important states in the union, in the west and northwest. It has a capital stock of $100,000. Its shares are issued to the amount of $10.00, and it has $40,000 of the same for sale upon which a regular dividend of 6 per cent. is paid annually. It issues certificates of investment representing a par value of $250 upon which a payment of $5 is made, and a monthly payment thereafter of $2.00 until the same has matured, which expert authority estimates will mature in about seven years. Fifty per cent. of the moneys received goes monthly towards the Redemption Fund. The company also issues certificates of $1,000 each upon which an admission fee of $6.00 is charged, and a monthly payment thereafter until maturity. These certificates will be expected to mature in 15 years. Actuarial investigation by leading experts demonstrates that at the end of seven and fifteen years the company will be enabled to mature the same, and if they choose make guarantees to that effect. The funds are handled entirely by the Metropolitan Trust Company and are under direct control of the certificate holders themselves, and cannot be paid without their consent and that of the Metropolitan Trust Company. The same absolute safety is offered to certificate holders by this company as is guaranteed by the Metropolitan Trust Company to its discriminating investors and patrons. The high rate of interest prevailing in this state in certain securities, and the compounding of the same enables The American Progressive Investment Company to offer absolute assurance of redemption of certificates at the estimated period. In order to more fully strengthen the company, thirty per cent. of the total amount received is set apart as a Reserve Fund. This, with the fifty per cent. placed in the Redemption Fund; the entire eighty per cent. deposited with the Metropolitan Trust Company, of Minneapolis, one of the strongest financial institutions in the state, makes the payment of certificates absolutely secure. After two years, holders of certificates can obtain paid up certificates with 5 per cent. interest annually and the entire amount of said paid up certificate payable at the end of five years out of the Reserve Fund. Twenty per cent. of the gross receipts is set apart for operating expenses. The officers of the company are: Dr. E. F. Adams, president, a prominent citizen; W. F. Robertson, secretary, a veteran journalist, and well and favorably known in the state; O. C. Lindman, treasurer, a resident of Minneapolis for 17 years, and likewise favorably known.

WARREN H. HAYES, ARCHITECT

Minneapolis, for upwards of a decade, has been noted for its modern church edifices of the better class. In their evolution and design there is one prominent characteristic in plan, viz: the DIAGONAL PULPIT arrangement originated by Warren H. Hayes, church architect, eleven years since.

Nineteen of the Twin City churches are built in this manner from his plans. As arranged by Mr. Hayes, a typical church, on his DIAGONAL PLAN, has an octagonal auditorium, with the chancel on the side diagonally opposite the main entrance, with amphitheatre arrangement of pews on a bowled floor, the latter on what is called the isocoustic curve, falling from the front toward the pulpit in such a way as to give all rows of pews equal sight angles of pulpit. The ceiling is domed and vaulted; the chapel, at either the right or left of pulpit, opening into the audience room on special occasions fully, by automatic rolling partitions, giving the united audiences full view of the speaker; the positions of those in the chapel are as near or nearer to him even, than those in the main room, contrary to the old way of having them twice as far away.

Some examples of this arrangement from Mr. Hayes' studio at 704-5-6, Sykes Block, Minn., are Immanuel Baptist, First Congregational, First Presbyterian, Calvary Baptist, Wesley M. E., Fowler M. E., the latter under construction, in Minneapolis. In St. Paul, Central Presbyterian, across the street from the Capitol; First Presbyterian in Peoria, Elmwood and Hamilton, Ill. First Baptist, Portland, Or., the finest on the Pacific coast. First Presbyterian at Nanaimo, B. C., Christ Presbyterian, Madison, Wis., and one at Oconto; First Congregational at Menominee, Wis.; Plymouth at Oshkosh; Union Congregational at Rockville, Conn.; First Congregational at Rockland, Mass.; First M. E. of Fargo, N. D., and many others.

Some of his school buildings may be seen in the structures of Hamline University, St. Paul, and the Convent of the Good Shepherds, near the latter.

Although having made church architecture a distinct branch of his practice for over twenty-three years, Mr. Hayes does not confine himself exclusively to church and school designing, as is readily seen when such structures as the Hugh Harrison Jobbing House and the H. G. Harrison blocks on Third street, and the Thorpe Block across the way are noted, also the Sykes fire-proof, eight story block on Hennepin at Nos. 254-256; also some of the finer residences, as H. B. Frey's on Fifth street southeast; that of Mrs. H. O. Hamlin, on Hawthorn; the residence of Mr. Hobart, Superintendent of Lakewood, at the main entrance, etc.

Mr. Hayes prepared himself for his chosen profession, Architecture, at Cornell University, graduating in 1871, having taken two President White first prizes for meritorious work in this line and the natural sciences. After ten years practice in New York he opened an office in Minneapolis, (at 408 Nicollet avenue and later moving to 704 Sykes Block) in 1881, as being more central for an expanding clientage extending from the New England to the Pacific states.

With able and trained assistants and his own natural bent for his calling, added to the popularity of his invention, the above mentioned DIAGONAL, OCTAGONAL PLAN often miscalled the "corner plan" much has been accomplished in the uplifting and adaptation of modern church architecture and church edifices to the requirements of the times.

Particular attention is given to orders from a distance by mail, in giving such clients very full and clear detail drawings and specifications so that much personal supervision on the building may be dispensed with and deputized to a local superintendent.

THE FARRAND & VOTEY ORGAN CO.

The city of Detroit can boast of having within her borders not only one of the leading firms in the music trade, but a concern who have by the great improvements that they have introduced into organ building have made themselves famous throughout the world.

The Farrand & Votey Organ Co.

stands now in a most prominent position in the trade. In the course of a few years they have built up a large and extensive business, and have also manufactured instruments of such great merit that they have everywhere received the highest commendation.

The Farrand & Votey Organ Co. can trace its original foundation back to 1882, when the business was started with about 12 or 15 employes, and for a number of years only Reed organs were manufactured, but they were of the highest grade only, and their reputation spread and the business increased, until now their shipments go all over the world. In 1888 they began to build pipe organs and in 1889 bought out the Granville Wood & Sons Pipe Organ concern and employed all their men including the firm. And in 1892 bought out the famous Roosevelt Pipe Organ business of New York and employed many of their best mechanics. They have built the most famous pipe organ constructed in this country in the past few years, notably the great World's Fair organ in Festival Hall, for which the World's Fair Directors gave them a subsidy of ten thousand dollars and the organ was their property at the close of the Exposition, and has since been sold to the University of Michigan, in Ann Arbor.

They now have 250 employes on their pay-roll and have branch offices with skilled workmen, in New York, Chicago and Pittsburg. Their buildings are 550 feet long and most of them four stories and a basement.

THE MINNEAPOLIS DRY GOODS STORE

This mercantile institution, which occupied such a prominent position among the people of Minneapolis, conducts its business upon the principle of reciprocity. By making the interest of the public its constant aim, the people have responded by a patronage that has steadily promoted the business activity and interest of this great and growing store. The Minneapolis Dry Goods Store is able to supply almost every necessity of life, outside of the provision line. It is a great department store. Everything that ladies wear, from bonnets to gloves and shoes, is here in magnificent

INTERIOR VIEW OF STORE

MILLINERY DEPARTMENT

assortment. With the exception of clothing, hats and shoes, gentlemen can also be supplied, according to the latest styles. Hundreds of homes in Minneapolis have been entirely furnished out of the vast and varied stock of this People's Supply Palace.

Its trade is not confined to the city, for it has a large mail order department which is equipped for the most effective service and through which thousands of orders are sent throughout the entire Northwest.

This popular company is under the proprietorship and management of the Gordon Brothers, genial gentlemen, progressive business men and patriotic citizens. They are members, one of the Westminster Church, and the other of the congregation of the Hennepin Avenue Church.

They have, in the various departments of the store, an army of clerks, polite, wide-awake and attentive to every wish of the customer. Under such management and complete service it is not a wonder that the Minneapolis Dry Goods Store is a favorite business resort for a multitude of people.

THE PALACE CLOTHING CO.

The Palace Clothing Co. started seven years ago as the youngest clothing house of any prominence in the city, and yet it has become the largest by continually doing exactly as advertised. Every garment The Palace Clothing Co. sells bears its guarantee, and it is a rule that money will be cheerfully refunded on any unsatisfactory purchase.

It has been the custom of The Palace Clothing Co. to handle only the best grades of merchandise.

The Palace Clothing Co. employ none but the very best help. The goods are marked in plain figures, and there is no deviation from those prices except to ministers, to whom they give 10 per cent discount.

The Palace Clothing Co. never carries goods from one season to another; any styles left over are sold to wholesale jobbers throughout the country.

It is the special pleasure of The Palace Clothing Co. to meet everyone, whether they are purchasers or spectators.

Mr. Maurice L. Rothschild is manager of the store, and to him belongs the credit of the great advance this institution has made.

INTERIOR VIEW OF STORE

Among the many great manufacturing industries located in Minneapolis, none is a greater credit to the city than the factory of the Century Piano Co., where the ANDERSON piano is manufactured.

The factory is located on Grant street, corner of Nicollet avenue, and the warerooms in the five story Century building, corner of Fourth street and First avenue south.

The ANDERSON piano is the marvel of the age, and is to-day without a rival in volume and perfection of tone.

From The Musical Courier—"It is much to the credit of the new concerns who are beginning to manufacture pianos in the West, that they are setting for themselves a standard of excellence far higher than one would expect, and that they seem to have an abiding faith that fine grade goods are the ones that will in the long run meet with more encouragement than cheap trash.

"From what has been already said regarding the Anderson Piano one expects to find the instruments excellent, and they are not a disappointment. Made in a factory where nothing in the shape of machinery is wanted to aid experienced workmen, one glance shows you that they are, so far as workmanship is concerned, all that you can ask for.

"Mr. John Anderson is responsible for the scale, and in quality and power and freedom from overtones it is certainly remarkable. The company will not permit any inferior materials of any kind to enter into the construction of the Anderson piano; the best of everything is used, and in some features they have had difficulty in procuring the quality of the material desired, and some of our supply houses have been put to considerable trouble to meet the exacting demands of this new company."

In addition to manufacturing the ANDERSON piano, the Century Piano Co. is general western agent for the HENRY F. MILLER, STERLING and many other fine pianos, and the STORY & CLARK and STERLING organs.

Their warerooms in the Century building are among the largest and finest in this part of the country, and are completely stocked with everything in the music line.

T. J. ZIEGLER

Manager Browning, King & Co.

This is the Minneapolis branch of the famous firm of Messrs. Browning, King & Co., manufacturing retailers of fine clothing and furnishings, whose principal offices are located in New York City at 406-412 Browne street. They have also very extensive branches in St. Louis, Kansas City, Chicago, Milwaukee, Cincinnati, Cleveland, Philadelphia, Omaha, Lincoln, St. Paul, Harlem, N. Y., Brooklyn, N. Y., Providence, R. I, and Boston, Mass. The premises occupied in Minneapolis at 415, 417 and 419 Nicollet avenue comprise a superior three-story and basement building 44x140 feet in dimensions, fully equipped with all modern appliances, steam heat, electric light, passenger and freight elevators, etc.

The basement is devoted to the dynamos and steam heating plant, the first floor to gents' furnishings, hats, caps, ready made clothing and spring overcoats, the second to the boys' and children's departments, while the third floor is fully stocked with men's overcoats. They employ forty clerks, salesmen, etc., in Minneapolis alone, where they transact an extensive business. This is easily accounted for, when the quality of the goods is taken into consideration with the low prices at which they are offered to customers. We would observe that the clothing and furnishings manufactured by Messrs. Browning, King & Co. are absolutely unsurpassed in the United States for quality, elegance of design, finish and workmanship, and their ready made garments of the finer grades are quite equal to the best custom work in the country. Their sales amount to over $9,000.000 annually, and last year they turned out 1,367,000 garments, and paid for labor $1,500,000. They employ some thousands of hands, and are heartily in accord with all labor organizations, believing them to be of the utmost public

good, a protection against the enslavement of the poor and a guarantee of legitimate profits to the employer. The fact that this
popular firm treats its employes so justly should always commend
their stores to laboring men and women who appreciate the recognition of organized labor. The Minneapolis branch is under
the able and energetic management of Mr. T. J. Ziegler, who is
highly esteemed by the community. Mr. Ziegler was born in Car-
lisle, Penn., 1846. He engaged in the clothing business in Illinois from
1869 to 1884; Janesville, Wis., from 1884 to 1891; Minneapolis
from 1891 to 1894 as manager of Browning, King & Co., the
largest makers of fine ready-to-wear clothing in the world. The
output of this large concern for the past year was over nine million
dollars and over a million and a half of this amount was paid out for
labor. Mr. Ziegler is a thorough clothing man, having been
brought up in it from a boy. Aside from the management of
Browning, King & Co's. Minneapolis store, he owns and controls
several clothing stores of his own in the states of Iowa and Wiscon-
son which are all under his supervision and management. He is
certainly one of the most successful clothing merchants of the day.
He is very fond of Minneapolis and a firm believer in the future of
the great and phenomenal city.

C. A. SMITH

C. A. Smith was born in Vermont in 1830. His parents
were old line Baptists, always loyal to the church and intense
in their religion convictions. They lived on a farm and the subject of this sketch devoted his early years to farming. He was
early impressed with the importance of education and availed himself of the meagre opportunities of those times to acquire a common school training. This was accompained with great disadvantage, for the farm demanded most of his time and energy, and the
district school, open but a few months in the year, was scarcely
worthy the name of school, yet young Smith was alert to his opportunities and made what advancement was possible.

At the age of twenty-two he was married to Miss Elizabeth
Jefts, to whose faithfulness and good common sense much of his
subsequent means is due. He continued on the farm until he was

thirty-one years of age, when he removed to Waltham, Mass., and engaged in the bakery business for eight years. He then came to Northfield, Minn., where he engaged in carpentering for four years.

From Northfield he moved to Minneapolis, his present home. Soon after coming to Minneapolis he located at 3501 Portland avenue, where he has lived ever since. It was here, at his Port-

SMITH FLORAL DESIGN

land avenue home, that he started with one greenhouse, in the business that is now second to none in the floral line in the city.

There were few flowers grown in Minneapolis then, and the market was scarcely large enough to encourage the business. Mr. Smith is really the pioneer florist of Minneapolis, for when he began there was but one greenhouse in the city and that was more private than commercial. It was impossible to buy a dozen roses a day then. Since that time his business has increased until now his greenhouses show thirty-five thousand feet of glass. This represents five houses of roses, one house of carnations and one of violets, besides a large supply of bedding plants and bulbous flowers.

Seven men are constantly employed in the care of this immense property. Mr. Smith is an artist; he does all kinds of floral decorations and makes a specialty of furnishing churches for Easter Sunday. His business place is at 77 South Seventh street.

THE END

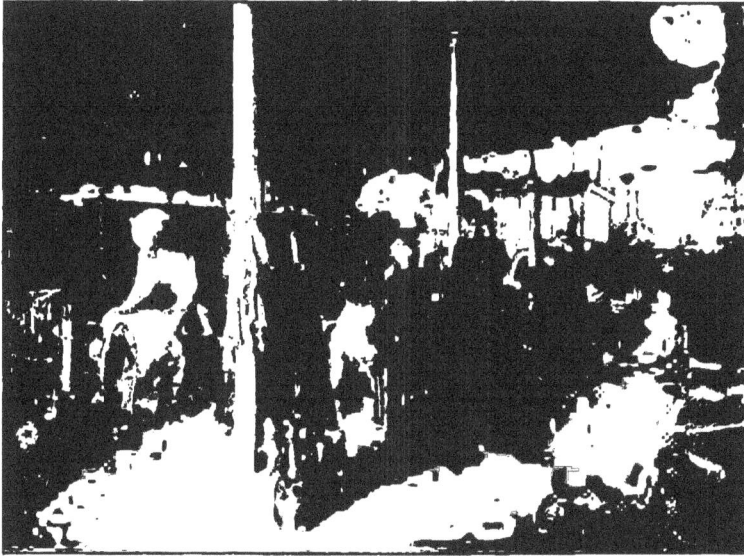

INTERIOR VIEW OF

Geo. Vetters'
Hat and Fur Store

25 and 27 South Fifth Street, Minneapolis, Minn.

MANUFACTURER OF

High Grade FURS Only

Sealskin Garments A Specialty

Sole Agents for the World Renowned

KNOX HATS

Nothing Like It

In the entire country: **Our Establishment**. We have just right to be proud of it. We are House Furnishers; we are Office Furnishers; we are Hotel Furnishers; we are Church Furnishers; we are Lodge Furnishers, but pre-eminently **House Furnishers**. It is the **Homes** of the people that interest us. We shall talk it to our dying day, that the last place for a man to economize is in his Home, and if we never make a record for anything else, we shall be remembered for everlastingly having preached and dinned into the ears of the public the word **Home! Home! Home!**

Wonder if you know what kind of an establishment the "New England" is anyway. We cover more floor space than five full sized blocks, or, to put in another way, than ten blocks the size of the Syndicate Block.

But it is not floor space than counts. It is the **stuff** we show **on** it. We defy you to mention a thing that can possibly be called a feature of House Furnishing, but what we can supply, and instantly. Our immense amount of space enables us to do what no other establishment in the country can do, viz: To carry **Complete Assortments in both Very Fine, Medium and Low Cost Goods.**

Yes, we furnish the Drawing Room, the Hall, the "Den", the Library, the Dining Room, Home Chamber, Guest Chamber, "Baby's Room" and all. Nor do we leave out the Kitchen, the Basement, or Servant's Room. We shade your Windows, drape your Walls, carpet your Floors, furnish you Chairs to sit in, Lounges to laze on, Beds to sleep in, including the choicest and daintiest Bed Linens; Tables to eat off of, and not only the Tables, but the choicest China, Glass and Cutlery.

Why, do you know that many a party comes to us, not to shop, but to select? What does this mean? That they rightly give us the credit for having the goods they need, while, as to prices, why, everyone knows that the **New England** has always set the pace in price making. So it is an every-day occurrence for Intending House Furnishers to bring their lists to us; sit down quietly; compare their ideas with ours; frankly tell us about how much money they want to put into their House Furnishings, and with our assistance, secure a most tastefully furnished home.

Nor is this all. Our Credit Plan of House Furnishing is directly in line with the goods themselves. It is utterly reliable, and simplicity itself, purposely arranged for the mutual benefit of our customers and ourselves. You leave an order with us, say for $100 worth of goods, pay for them, receive a receipted bill and cordial thanks.

On the other hand, if you prefer, instead of paying us the $100 in a lump, to pay us, say $20 down and the balance every 30 days, in payments of $8 a month, we thank you just as much, take the same care of you, and feel the same responsibility as to your perfect satisfaction with goods selected, (perhaps a little more so) as in the Cash Transaction.

The Chicago, Milwaukee & St. Paul R. R.

The General Passenger Department of the Chicago, Milwaukee & St. Paul R. R., under the head of "Hints to Travelers" gives this advice . . . .

When you start upon a railroad journey, select a road

That affords excellent and most comfortable facilities.

That traverses a delightful and picturesque portion of the country.

That has— and merits—the reputation of strength and reliability.

That enjoys popularity and is stamped with public approval.

That has a substantial roadbed and most frequent train service.

That regards, always, the comfort, ease and safety of its patrons.

That furnishes the latest private compartment cars and latest library-buffet-smoking cars.

That furnishes elegant drawing-room parlor cars, free reclining chair cars, and sumptuous dining cars.

That has exclusive use of the electric berth reading lamp.

IT is needless to say that if "above hints" are heeded, travelers will use "The Milwaukee." Its name in the Northwest is synonymous with comfort, strength, reliability and progress. It has also taken the lead in modern improvements and appliances. The people West of the Mississippi River are indebted in a large measure to The Milwaukee for the present facilities and means of comfort now greatly enjoyed. Five trains run daily; one through the Twin Cities to Chicago; one to St. Louis, and one to Kansas.

The immortal Lincoln said "Follow the people and you cannot be far from right."

The "People" use THE MILWAUKEE

IT is a sign of the growth and power of the Northwest that one finds such magnificent trains as are encountered on the Chicago, Milwaukee & St. Paul. The traveler as he occupies a place in one of these elegant flying palaces and reads by the individual and private electric light in his section or apartment feels that the great through lines in the East have nothing to make the West envious or ashamed. The great Pennsylvania road and the famous New York Central may find here models for improvment.

If one must travel, The MILWAUKEE leaves the least possible to desire. Speed, ease, elegance, safety, punctuality—what more shall I say?

Always sincerely,

C. H. FOWLER.

BROWN & HAYWOOD CO.

STAINED GLASS WORKS

COMPLETE STOCK ALWAYS CARRIED OF

Plate and Window

GLASS ..

Ribbed Skylight Glass and French Mirrors

WE MANUFACTURE

Sand Blast, Bevelled
Crystalline and
Ornamental Glass

124, 126, 128 N. Third St.   41 East Third St.
         MINNEAPOLIS   ST. PAUL

CHURCH WORK A SPECIALTY

Send for Catalogues, Designs and Estimates

373

NICKEL PLATE

The

NEW YORK
CHICAGO AND
ST. LOUIS
RY.

THROUGH TRAINS....

CHICAGO
TO ALL POINTS EAST

LEAVES Chicago 2.00 p. m. daily, arrives New York 8.00 p. m., except Sunday. The car leaving Chicago on Saturday reaches New York at 6.30 a. m. Monday.

Niagara Falls

REMEMBER that the Shortest Line to Niagara Falls, via Cleveland and Buffalo, is the NICKEL PLATE ROAD.

Passengers holding through tickets to points east of Syracuse, will be permitted to stop over at Niagara Falls on application to the Conductor of the Nickel Plate Road, or at the City Ticket Office, No. 23 Exchange Street, Buffalo, N. Y.

For reservation of sleeping car space and further information address

H. THORNE, City Ticket Agent,
TELEPHONE "MAIN 389,"
199 CLARK ST., CHICAGO.

J. Y. CALAHAN, General Agent,
TELEPHONE "MAIN 389,"
199 CLARK ST., CHICAGO.

376

M. C. KUMMERER

Practical Watch Maker

FINE WATCH WORK

. . A SPECIALTY

All work done on Short Notice

Satisfaction Guaranteed or Money Refunded

940 Guaranty Loan Building

MINNEAPOLIS, = = MINNESOTA

WATCH INSPECTOR FOR
MINN. & ST. LOUIS RY. CO.
THE NORTHERN PACIFIC RY. CO.
THE GREAT NORTHERN RY. CO.

Jewelry Repaired at Reasonable Prices

= A Good Investment

Is ever sought for by shrewd business men. Do you know of any investment that will bring your church any better returns than fitting your building throughout with modern and attractive furniture that combines elegance and comfort in the highest degree, with the beauty and harmony of interior church decorations.

Quality is the **Bid of Superiority**, cheapness the bid of inferiority. Don't experiment—buy the **best**, you will find it the cheapest.

The **Manitowoc Seating Co.**, of Manitowoc, Wis., is a Northwestern institution. Its extensive plant, recently erected and thoroughly equipped with the latest improved machinery and skilled workmen, places it in the lead for **Church Furniture** of all kinds. Their goods are sold only by specialists by sample and special drawings.

300 Churches were seated by them in 1893. A Church for every day in 1894

Their designs are unique. Their work is first-class.

Their prices are consistent with the grade of work.

If your church is in need of furniture, address,

THE MANITOWOC SEATING CO.

Manitowoc, Wis., U. S. A.

HART'S PHARMACY

A. B. HART, Phm. D. and Registered Pharmacist

A FULL LINE OF . . .

Pure Drugs

Patent Medicines

Wright's and Ricksecker's Perfumes and
Toilet Articles

Domestic and Imported Cigars

We also Claim Superior Advantages for Filling
Physician's Prescriptions

1229 Nicollet Ave., Cor. 13th Street

OPEN ALL NIGHT
TELEPHONE 1079

MINNEAPOLIS, MINN.

M. E. Smith

PLAIN and
ORNAMENTAL

 PLASTERING

2210 Eighteenth Ave. S.

Minneapolis

H. Downs & Son

GENERAL . . .

CONTRACTORS

HEAVY MASONRY A SPECIALTY

Lumber Exchange Building

Quarries: State and Essex St. E. D.

NICHOLSON BROS.

Tailors

709 NICOLLET AVE.   MINNEAPOLIS, MINN.

Have in stock a choice selection of Imported and Domestic Woolens and make a spec= ialty of English Novelties for the best trade at moderate prices . . . . .

Send your collections on all Northwestern Points

——TO——

THE SECURITY BANK OF MINNESOTA

MINNEAPOLIS, MINN.

F. A. CHAMBERLAIN, President   PERRY HARRISON, Cashier
HENRY M. KNOX, Vice-President   THOMAS F. HURLEY, Ass't Cashier
E. F. MEARKLE, Second Vice-President

THE

Security Bank of Minnesota

MINNEAPOLIS

Surplus and Undivided Profits, 500,000 }
Capital,   -   - $1,000,000 } $1,500,000

Accounts of Banks, Bankers, Corporations, Manufacturers,
and others received on the most favorable terms

Special attention given to Collections on Minneapolis, St. Paul and
throughout the Northwest

*Buy and sell Foreign Exchange and issue Travelers' Letters of Credit available in all
parts of the World*

With our list of correspondents covering all points of importance in Minnesota, Iowa, North
Dakota, South Dakota, Montana and Washington, we are enabled to
collect promptly and at lowest rates

SPECIAL RATES

With all Express Companies for shipment of Currency. Interest allowed on Daily Balances to Banks and
Bankers. Telegraphic Transfers made

All business entrusted to us will be attended to carefully and without delay

Price Bros. Printing Co.

Book and Job Printing
Embossing
Blank Book Manufacturing

Third Floor Palace Block
323 Nicollet Avenue

Telephone 171 . . . . . Minneapolis

386

CHICAGO
GREAT
WESTERN
⟶ RAILWAY

F. H. LORD
Gen'l Pass. and Ticket Agent
C. H. HOLDRIDGE
Gen'l Agent Passenger Dept.
R. W. THOMPSON
City Pass. and Ticket Agent

The Fast and Popular Line between

MINNEAPOLIS
ST. PAUL
and CHICAGO

THE SHORT AND ONLY LINE
UNDER ONE MANAGEMENT BETWEEN

MINNEAPOLIS & KANSAS CITY
⟶ THROUGH ⟶
Marshalltown, Des Moines, St. Joseph and Leavenworth

Pullman and Compartment Cars on Through Trains
Dining Cars on all Trains

For information as to rates, time of trains, etc., apply to

R. W. THOMPSON
City Passenger and Ticket Agent

No. 7 Nicollet House Block   MINNEAPOLIS

388

REFERENCES
  Security Bank
  Metropolitan Bank
  Hennepin County Bank

ESTABLISHED 1886

NOTARY PUPLIC

AGENT FOR LOWRY HILL

.

Edmund G. Walton

Homes and Fine Residences
.. Acres ..
Business and Building Lots

326 Hennepin Ave.   Minneapolis

JOHN WUNDER

Contractor and Builder.....

NO. 8 KASOTA BUILDING

Telephone 911   **Minneapolis**

GUARANTY RESTAURANT

The Guaranty Restaurant stands at the head of its department in the Northwest. It is doubtless better located, officered and equipped than any restaurant northwest of Chicago.

It is located on the top floor of the Guaranty Loan Building, from which the entire city can be seen stretching out like a panorama of beauty.

Under the proprietorship of Mr. C. B. Struble, the service is all that could be required by the most fastidious. It is elegantly furnished, both in the general and private rooms, reflecting the finest taste and the most artistic arrangement.

Its bill of fare, always laden with the products of the season, and the freshest and best in the market, is good enough for a king.

While the Guaranty Restaurant commands the best trade of the city, the prices are within easy reach of all. It is the resort of business men.

Always bright, clean, cheerful and attractive, it is at once a dining palace of which the people of Minneapolis are justly proud.

To try it once is to become a regular patron.

www.ingramcontent.com/pod-product-compliance
Lightning Source LLC
Chambersburg PA
CBHW030858270326
41929CB00008B/482